STOP ABUSING YOURSELF WITH YOUR PAST

A comprehensive guide to being human…

PLANT PEOPLE HEAL LLC.

PUBLISHING

(928) 457-6844

D.L. NELSON

Website: http://www.plantpeopleheal.com

Disclaimer: This book has been produced for educational purposes only and is not a replacement for diagnoses or treatment of any disease, ailment, or mental health issue. If you are having any symptoms that fall under the category of mental illness, seek a health professional who can provide authoritative treatment for your individual needs. The opinions, viewpoints, and beliefs within this book are offered by the writer as that only, and in no way should be misinterpreted as anything else. The data collected about other authors, authorities and professionals, influential persons, references, statistics, and citations have been collected from the internet and are free, publicly available information that does not conflict with copyright issues to any of their published works. Seek the authoritative sources provided for further study of the concepts presented within this book. This book is an original work and a compilation of practices, teachings, techniques, research, studies, and concepts from the respective sources mentioned within. The author assumes no liability for accidents happening to, or injuries sustained by, readers who engage in the activities described within this book. Readers assume full responsibility for their level of health, experience, capabilities, and risks that are associated with engaging in the practices, exercises, and methods described in this book.

Table of Contents

Introduction

How it came to be

What does it mean to be a human being? Let me begin by introducing myself. I am first and foremost just a person, a woman who has been on this planet for 40+ years. This is the only accreditation I have behind my name that qualifies me to write this book. Being autodidactic (a self-learner) has been the fuel for my personal growth, determination, and reaching the definiteness of purpose required to get this book into the world and into your hands, reader.

My mother impressed upon me, at a very early age, the importance of learning; not just when we are in school, but every single day. In every moment we have the chance to learn something new. What I didn't know at that time, was just how powerful that teaching really was to my budding child-self. Our household book was Louise L. Hay's Heal Your Body. It focuses on the emotional and mental aspects of wellness and disease and gives affirmations to help rewrite the script of negative thinking. We referred to it for everything: a scrape, a broken bone, rashes and the like. Kids get hurt in a multitude of ways, and that book seemed to have an answer for any dis-ease that came up in our lives for my sister and me.

When we are all children, the importance of such practices can pass over our understanding. It was only as an adult that I gained a deep appreciation of my mother's methods and techniques that focused on our emotional health as something paramount to a good life. "Be young as long as you can, for old you are a long, long time." She had many sayings that have stayed with me. As an adult, I maintained the practice of looking up ailments and reading or memorizing affirmations, then saying them as a mantra whenever I got sick or hurt. I don't think it was quite enough, even though I have a fundamental grasp of the "why" behind the practice of affirming. I knew happiness was important and that our emotional and mental state could heal any disease.

But Why?

That was growing up in the 1980s. The Care Bear generation, I call it. Everything was fair, and DARE was teaching us the dangers that lurked in our backyards and quiet neighborhoods. We had no cell phones, and only a few homes had a computer (we did because my dad was in the Navy) and no internet. I still think it was a fairytale era in our modern century regardless of the growing fear around kidnappings and the looming threats from overseas that took place in the early 90s. We played outside, in the sun, and were hardly supervised for most of the day. Weekends would have us swimming at T-Dock and floating on the river with no parental supervision. Could we have drowned? Maybe, but we didn't. The world is a very different place now.

Another thing I can thank my mother for, which I resented at the time, was hauling my sister and me to every church imaginable to "find our people". No one was using the term "tribe" during those days. Communities were growing suspicious of their neighbors and no matter how hard my mom searched, we never found a place we "fit into", like a peg in a hole, or a cog in a wheel. We were asked to leave more than once because my mom was "making their kids think about things". Apparently, that was a dangerous endeavor and threatening in some way.

Overall, I've lived a spiritual life and practiced methods of growing my internal resilience, and those practices have developed into an unshakeable faith that I draw on in times of great pain and turmoil. Through the ups and downs, trials, and errors, I have persisted with a deep sense that I have the ability to transcend anything that happens in my life. I've known things that no standardized education could teach me, and I've come to realize that this intuitive sense of the world and internal self has guided me in profound and unimaginable ways. Science is beginning to confirm some of the things I had an inner sense of, through standardized research and controlled studies. Innate knowledge is not something we value much in a world that wants proof, academic certification, and accreditation behind our names, so I doubted myself for a long time. My mother and I felt very alone in a world that was shifting its value structure; losing its real connection to things that matter, separating people from within, as well as manufacturing creative methods of further fragmenting us in our external world. Dividing us all with fear, political tension, negative media, and identification with all the stuff we accumulate for status and value, among others. My mom and I thought we would never figure out where we fit into a world that was so estranged from our belief structure; the idea that we are all divine, above and beyond this human experience, without a religious connotation.

We may never find our place in the wider world; of this I have grown some radical acceptance. With that, we have both gained invaluable wisdom about what we can do personally to assist the ever-expanding transitions within ourselves and the people who come into our lives. This can bring about the kind of worldly change that everyone talks about. The hundredth monkey concept rings in my mind, and it has been proven through studies that once the threshold is reached, growth on a mass scale is inevitable in any species. That gives me great hope for humanity.

Self-help was a budding concept in America in the 1970s, gaining traction throughout the 80s blossoming in the 90s, and finally becoming a fine-tuned machine by the early 2000s as it transformed into personal development and personal growth. People began to understand that they had to work on themselves before they could fully love other people, gaining concepts from influencers like Wayne Dyer, Dr, Joe Dispenza, Dr. Masaru Emoto and so many others. We started looking inside of ourselves for the answers that we had been told for our entire lives resided with a higher authority, whether that be God, or a professional; you as an individual were not smart enough to manage your own care before this evolutionary threshold. These teachers came onto the stage and told us the opposite of what we'd been taught, and it transformed the way people thought about their role in their own lives.

In 2013, after watching (yet another) episode of Oprah Winfrey who featured a researcher named Brene Brown, my internal barometer of truth was in alignment with what she was saying. She focused on shame and guilt. What was the difference and why did that matter? She offered a course with one of her books called The Gifts of Imperfection. I will refer to it often throughout this book. Three of us in my family, who were living together at the time, jumped in (feet first!) because the message spoke to our love of learning and a deep seeded unworthiness that we hadn't realized we were walking around with.

Everyone has issues, right? Parents aren't perfect and kids grow up with stigmas that develop into maladaptive coping mechanisms. They usually become aware of them once they cross the gateway into adulthood and take responsibility for their own lives for the first time. While that's true, being a mother (and doing it quite badly, I will admit) I wanted more for my kids than to have to sort out a pile of unhealthy coping mechanisms once they were ready to explore the wide world as adult people. I have failed at this of course, which is normal; we all do, and we all will.

Brene's course was laid out over twelve weeks. We got all the art supplies, dedicated ourselves to the practices and kept each other focused on what mattered so we could get the most out of what we were learning. At that time, I would not have believed anyone if they told me that I would be developing my own course to share with the world so that my lifetime of experiences, practices and studies can help others reach the kind of life they really want to have. I never would have guessed that a breakdown after losing my job in 2019, and then another in mid-2020 that shook me even further, would leave me suicidal, empty, and nearly catatonic. My children forged through this one-year roller coaster with me, and I know it left a mark on them. Being teenagers, they had developed plenty of their own views, judgments, and opinions, about me as their mother, life, and the world. Some days were connecting for us, and others were complete hell. They didn't know what to do for their mom who was supposed to be strong, infallible, and their stabilizing force. I could no longer be trusted. I will add that my trust was already on shaky ground because of a lifetime of dysfunctional behavior, poor choices in partners that they had to put up with and discovering myself while doing my darndest to raise two healthy kids.

My life partner tried to bring me back to reality when I lost control of my emotions and sank into consecutive and devastating depressive states. It stretched the fabric of our relationship to the brink. We separated for a few months in 2020, and it was the push I needed to dig as deep as I could into all the places that had been in the dark for too long. I grabbed my etheric flashlight, descended the stairs of my psyche, opened the creaky door to the basement of my mind, and tentatively took each step into the unknown parts of myself that were controlling my unconscious actions.

I revisited the course I took in 2013, sat down with myself very honestly, and began doing the work. It was so hard! It took nearly a full year to pull out of that shame spiral, creating a new sense of normal for myself that lifted me by the bootstraps and forced me to move forward, because if I didn't, the only other option was to see my demise, and oh how I thought about it! Reality kicked me a third time when a co-worker committed suicide in 2021. It was quite a loss for everyone who loved him, and a shock to me, seeing the aftermath of that choice face to face, because of all the terrible things I had been thinking of doing the year before. Over the next month, four more people committed suicide that were friends of my friends, and my daughter, who was in high school at this time, lost six of her schoolmates, in the span of her high school experience, by their own hand. I didn't know any of these people, but it rocked me to my core. I couldn't even consider leaving the world now! There was far too much to do. A purpose began to grow within me where a deep void had been. A tiny seed that was there all along, waiting to be covered over and watered with compassion so it could sprout. That seed is growing within me daily, with every challenge I face. It is weathering storms and sometimes I prop it up with sticks during a fierce wind… but I tend it conscientiously now, I love it!

I have trusted that the universe would guide my steps and my path during most of my life. The problem had been that I couldn't get out of my own way for long enough to see it working for extended periods of time. The inconsistent roller coaster that was my life was "normal", and I believed that I was so well put together - yet never quite able to reach the goals and dreams I desired most. The "stuckness" I kept experiencing was proof that I kept falling back into negative patterns of living and thinking that were not serving me and preventing me from serving others correctly. Yes, I brought a lot of good into the world, but I also, inadvertently, caused much harm as well.

Going through the highs and lows has always taught me that everything is temporary, whether that's for better or worse. I can honestly say that I was living in a quasi-delusional state of being and that self-deception was at near mastery level during certain periods. The massive difference with my new mindset was in high contrast to how I had conducted myself before my breakthrough/breakdown. I started to see the divinity in all things and refused to interact with myself or others from a lesser place. When I did, it became obvious to me of what I had been doing that went against myself and became easier to correct in the moment. One night in January of 2022, I received a download from the universe, and wrote for three hours straight during the twilight hours of dawn. Twenty-nine pages later, I was looking at the skeletal structure for the book you're about to read.

Acknowledgements

Many Influences Went into The Making of This Book

There are so many people that have made this book manifest that it's hard to order them all in one place. Sometimes it is more valuable to know where to seek knowledge, by the example of others who have come before us, than to spend a lifetime of studying one field exclusively. I have gathered the wisdom of many learned people so others may benefit from their brilliance. Many of the references I use in this book come from renowned psychologists, researchers, spiritual figures, teachers, and scientists. Their fields range from quantum physics, neuroplasticity, communication, philosophy, theology, metaphysics, a Zumba instructor, epigenetics, shame and guilt research, neuroscience and doctors, a clinical psychologist, shamanism, worldly religious studies, and inspirational authors and speakers. To top the list off, and because of this modern era we live in, I have drawn from podcasts and interviews from YouTube featuring many of the professionals I have included in this book. YouTube, in my opinion is the Alexandria's library of our age, filled with vast amounts of specialized knowledge, audiobooks in all genres, and world-renowned authorities. It is so rich in nutritional data for our ever-expanding minds, that we would be fools not to utilize this incredible resource for our benefit. I am grateful to all of them for their decades of constant pursuit that has reached my small life.

My mother Victoria Scibilia has been one of my greatest teachers, and we continue to travel this journey of life together, still seeking, still knowing what we know, and still sharing our experiences and skills with anyone open to hearing them. My mom has been the one person in the world who is my Spiritual Partner in this life. I think we came here with the agreement to keep one another real, honest, and ever progressing towards our divinity in love. It has been difficult and traumatic for both of us. I bless every challenging experience we have gone through together, because without them we would not be who we are today. Our connection remains strong and, as she transitions into her cronehood, I am dedicated to being able to care for her with the tenacity, patience, strength, and love that she gave to me as her child. As her adult-child now, I take up the torch to be her pillar as she ages. For me, it is the natural progression of life. I embrace all that we have gone through together and now have new tools to be able to share with her as she gets ever closer to reconnecting with the spirit world, and the new challenges that will bring for both of us.

My sister Jessy Nelson has taught me the value of taking a multi-faceted perspective. I would not be walking this Earth today if it were not for her non-judgmental and neutral approach as I walked hand in hand with my suicidal potential. She was always at the other end of a phone call when I was crying my soul out, crawling out of my skin and in deep despair. In short, she saved my life. I may never be able to repay to the world, in any form, her great contribution to the continuation of my existence but I endeavor to make it meaningful every single day now. Although we have gone through our own trials and tribulations throughout the course of our sisterly relationship, we remain close and strongly bonded in knowing that for the rest of our lives on this Earth we will relate to each other through our divine connection. She is the most amazing human being to me and prompted some of the practices and concepts that you will find throughout this book. It was her prompts, questions, and introspective approach that I have incorporated for you here, that saved my life. With the greatest sincerity I say this; she pulled me back into living, earning my eternal gratitude.

To my incredible partner William Elijah, who never gave up on the pursuit of healthy behaviors and lifestyle, protecting himself by respecting himself and his own mental health by leaving me, then returning to the commitment we both held dear to our hearts. He has taught me the meaning of real love, for oneself, and for a partner. He also taught me that you can love someone and leave them, and how very noble that actually is. Through our relationship I have healed a lifetime of pairing with unhealthy men who just mirrored the vibrational frequency I was at within myself, a perfect vibrational match every time. I know I am growing because the relationship I am in now is the healthiest one I've ever been in. We grow closer every day and continue to reach higher states of being together with our own individual work to share with the world. He is my forever guy, and I knew it right from the beginning.

I want to say a special thanks to Michael Turner (Mickle Bear) who has been my editor on many works over the span of eight years and watched me evolve as a person, through my writing. His loyalty to my work has taught me about believing in people and investing in those you value, as he has worked on all my writing projects for no money whatsoever. Belief in others and offering your time and skills to them can make the difference between their success and failure. I don't know that I would be here, doing this in the way that I am, if it were not for his kindness and dedication to my work. His experience, tenacity, and desire to teach has elevated my writing and my confidence to the level that made it possible for this book to exist.

I want to express my deepest gratitude for both of my children

For my daughter, who was the first to teach me that it's okay to think differently from your parents and forge a path all your own, regardless of how you grew up. Her fierce determination to dedicate herself to a cause and see it through to the end is commendable. Her sheer will and strong sense of self showed me that we come into this life already being who we are, regardless of what our parents teach us. She is a gift, and I hope to get to share in her adult life as she carves a path in the world that will make a clearing where others can blossom into their best selves. Her kindness and investments in her people have taught me the value of checking in with the ones we love. She remembers little details about her people with such deep thoughtfulness that I am sometimes blown away at the level of care she shows them. I hope that one day she can turn that inward and see herself as valuable as she perceives others to be.

To my son, he is one of the most humanitarian and forgiving teachers I've had as an adult. He's taught me the power of silence and honoring the masculine at all ages. Through his primal infancy of destroying everything in sight, I gained the gift of grace that opens a safe place for men to be men. Throughout his early childhood, being emasculated by all the women closest to him, myself included, and overcoming that, he has grown into a fine young man with deep values over boundaries. He has taught me that even though I made a lot of mistakes in his youth, I am still worth hugging. His compassionate nature shines through and touches the hearts of all who meet him, and he has been praised by strangers for his outgoing consideration of others. I thought I could never be a "boys' mom" and that I failed him repeatedly in his childhood, but he continues to show me daily that some things are worth negotiating and others are better left unsaid. What a powerful teacher.

Both of my kids have grown into amazing human beings, and I have grown personally with their influence in my life as they mirrored my youth back to me at every single age and in different ways.

WEEK 1

Getting Started, Gathering your Seeds

"There is no greater gift you can give or receive than to honor your calling. It's why you were born. And how you become most truly alive."

– Oprah Winfrey

You Are Here for a Reason

Have you ever heard the phrase "planting the seeds of thought"? You have been given an entire duffle bag of seeds throughout your life. These seeds are the foundation of your thinking and being. Do you believe that rewriting your subconscious thought patterns is possible? If it were, would you be able to live, think and behave in a way that suits you best? It doesn't matter what your background is, who you are as a person, or your status in the world. You are absolutely worthy and capable of changing unhealthy behaviors and rewriting negative thoughts and habits that do not serve your greater purpose in life. No matter what we have experienced, we have the power to change our now and our future regardless of our past.

There will be a variety of tools laid out in this book; some may be familiar; others may be new. I encourage you to work in teams, if you are able, to get the most out of these practices, with greater accountability and lasting results. Individual study is beneficial, but the power of working with others will make this a much more fulfilling experience for everyone involved, and you will make bonding connections with those on your "cultivation team". You are planting a garden in your mind by using this course. When you work as a team, you gain the benefit of other people's perspectives, ideas, and observations about one another. Sometimes other people see things in us that we don't. A team of three is the ideal size to do this course. You can make a group as large as five, but I don't recommend getting much larger than that, so everyone has time to do the journaling, the contemplation work, and the quiet inner work that accompanies the teachings and practices laid out in this course. Time with others and time for oneself must be balanced so you can manage all the areas you need to focus on.

You Are Plants - Yes, That's Plural

You are a being that requires fertile (mental) soil, (life giving) water, (physical) movement, (vitamin rich) sunshine, and harmonic (vibrational) frequency to thrive on this planet. That is why every chapter is littered with reference to plant cultivation. Some people are roses, have thorns, are a socially typical beauty and require high maintenance and rich soil. Some are dandelions that can grow from the cracks of the pavement and in adverse conditions, thriving in harsh circumstances and shining through the struggles. Some are like a Siberian elm tree, taking root in any hard surface where there is shelter and digging in deep to spread roots before the wind can blow them away. Yet others are like an oak, slow growing, taking time to reach the sky, while establishing hardy roots that will grow into a colony of trees, creating a mini forest around a central parent plant. Every plant has its strengths and weaknesses that make it unique and wonderful. Every plant has ideal conditions for thriving. This is meant to help identify what that looks like for you, so you can grow into whatever plant(s) you are meant to be, with the optimum conditions possible. As we move from chapter to chapter, week to week, you will begin to understand that you are an entire garden and not just one of the plants I mentioned above. You are many of them simultaneously and that is important because you are a multidimensional being who wears many hats at any given time.

You may have been told your entire life that you are daisy, or a clover or a mulberry tree. (Yes, it's a metaphor, work with me here.) You may be something completely different under all those social conditionings, false belief structures, and a lifetime of executing other people's ideals for you. What you may grow into, with the proper cultivation, might happily surprise you. Even the most delicate plants like an orchid carry within them inherent potential beauty that can only be seen when tended well. This is one plant I have yet to master in my care, which is why I use it as an example. It requires very special attention, and it is so fulfilling to witness them bloom. There are people that make it look easy to care for orchids. I just kill whatever poor unsuspecting orchid enters my household. Some people make things look easy to those who don’t have the same skills.

Following this metaphor, I want everyone to understand that when identifying yourself as whatever plant you are in this moment, recognize that there is also more than one dandelion, or marigold, or wisteria vine in the world. One dandelion growing in a verdant field will look and behave differently from one struggling in the crack in the concrete. The growing conditions are not the same, even though it's the SAME plant. To further elaborate on that concept, two dandelions growing out of a crack in the pavement can differ too; one might be under a drippy eave, getting watered regularly, while the other is subjected to scorching sunshine with no reprieve. Same plant, same environment, different conditioning. Be aware of what is watering and scorching you. Your environment and conditioning play a massive role in whether you thrive or just survive.

The potent medicines that come from these plants will also differ in the same ways that two people who seem the same can be quite varied in the ways they perceive life, the tools they were given as children, and what belief structures they have developed into habits. While one person thrives, the other may not be able to. They might not even know why. It is unwise to dismiss the value of another person's path or the struggles they've experienced to become who they are.

You Don't Know What You Don't Know

Valuable Questions to Get Us Started

In life I've noticed that I keep transitioning into new stages of being, attempting to reach that enlightened state we have always been told is "Christ like". This ideal state of being has been ingrained in us through our religious influences; we seek the far-reaching goal of self-mastery. I've got to say that I've discovered that it's less about the goal and more about the journey. As babies, we learn how to walk for the first time and who our immediate family members are. As a toddler it's about how to make friends, developing tactile skills and entering the world of school. As a young adult, we learn about peer pressure, fitting in and inserting ourselves, sometimes in conflicting ways, into our surroundings. We gather a perspective on life that is truly our own, outside of our parents, during our teen years. Then comes adulthood…

If we don't go to college immediately after high school, we are pretty much done with standardized education. Maybe we get a job (some high school students also work during their last years of juggling classes) and have bills and all the other things we didn't know were part of the package of growing up. We so desperately wanted this when we were kids and didn't know any better. Our adult lives become a landscape of unimaginable stresses that our (hopefully) carefree childhood could never truly prepare us for.

So how do we know what we don't know? The short answer is, we don't. Most times we blindly move through life wondering why we're here and how we fit into things on a fundamental level. This doesn't give us the kind of insights we need to live intentionally, purposefully, and with meaning. What direction creates the life we really want to have? We float down the river of life hoping not to crash into the banks or tip over a waterfall while we are clinging to our dingy with all the seeds people hand over to us in the form of ideas, values, morals, standards, and beliefs. Where's the solid ground to plant anything?

This sets up a lifestyle of survival. One that doesn't give us any time or energy to dig the hole within our own soul, where we can consciously cultivate our best selves. There's always going to be something to be afraid of. Adults are not the only ones subjected to these social fears. Teens and younger and younger children have access to aspects of our reality that they never used to have before our technological era. Some parts of life were considered “adult concepts” that were intentionally kept from children to keep them innocent for as long as possible. That innocence is leaving us at an earlier and earlier age. And all that means is that the fears of the world, whether real or imagined, are now face to face with some of the youngest members of our society.

They are more aware of financial disaster, serious health issues like diabetes and osteoporosis, gender struggles and identity, suicide within their own peer groups, multiple forms of abuses, racial and social injustices and so much more! Our youth do not have the buffer of innocence like they used to. Bottom line. It's a statistical fact in our world. Their struggles continue to compound. As parents, we can't take the load from them while we suffer silently as their strong and stable force. Sometimes we are internally falling apart because we just don't have the tools to stay strong enough for long enough, and for everyone we take care of. We are beginning to see what kinds of adults are being produced because of the loss of our youthful innocence. So, what questions need to be asked? What is it that we really don't know?

I offer questions based on my experiences because that's all I can speak to

- Why does anyone struggle in a civilized world that no longer challenges our survival?
- Why do people of all ages struggle with worthiness and feelings of not being enough?
- What are the catalysts to discover who we really are?
- Where do we find real hope?
- What leads people of any age to commit suicide?
- Do we really love every part of ourselves?
- If we don't love ourselves, why not?
- Why aren't we always happy?
- Why do we believe what we believe?
- Do our beliefs serve us or hold us back?
- Why don't we, as humanity, have a universal perspective on life and meaning after thousands of years of existence?
- What can we do to help ourselves and others be their best selves NOW?
- Why don't we have the proper systems in place to genuinely support people in a world that is so focused on mental health and social issues?

- Do we know what it really means to be human?
- What are my own patterns in life and how do I move through the world?
- Am I dancing or dragging myself kicking and screaming through life?
- How do we truly "know thyself"?

These are just a FEW questions that I have asked myself over the years and recently as well. Sometimes I feel like I've really sucked at being a human being. Sometimes I've wondered why I'm here and what I'm supposed to do with the time I have on Earth, which is a relatively short amount of time overall. I've contemplated what balance really looks like and means when living in a dualistic world, and it is a dualistic world. We have so many dichotomies and contradictions within ourselves that we often don't know what to do with it. We are the hero and the villain simultaneously. We are both powerful and weak. We are good people with bad behavior. Life and death are also integral aspects of being on this planet.

The best thing about being in 3D reality is that everything eventually dies. Now that might come across as nihilistic, but it's not! The blessing of being able to die in the cycles of life is often swept under the rug and demonized in a world that is doing everything it can to extend life and the quality of it. When we are given a time frame, and we understand how to use it, we can recognize our passing from this world as something benign. We can have a mission and purpose throughout our life with less uncertainty if we accept what it means to be human in this 3D world. It's not about getting somewhere and what we can accomplish tomorrow. It's about what we bring to the table just by being us right now. No one else can do you, like you do. Regardless of what walk of life we have gone through; we each have a unique perspective on our world. Its value is immeasurable.

Well, why?

What the heck does my life matter when I can't even get my emotions right, get my kids to their appointments on time, and have enough energy to get through the workday while still smiling even though all I want to do is cry and give up?

One Word Answer

Divinity

I'm not going all preachy on you by using this word. I mean it, in a serious, no-nonsense way. This is what spirituality teaches us, which is not religion. Spirituality is, by definition, the cultivation of your soul.

spir·it·u·al·i·ty
/ˌspiriCHo͞oˈalədē/
noun

1. the quality of being concerned with the human spirit or soul as opposed to material or physical things.
Ex. "The shift in priorities allows us to embrace our spirituality in a more profound way."

You've walked in a forest and gasped in joy at the ridiculous amount of beauty, connection, and perfection of the landscape. It's a grounding force to see such a miracle of life and just be in it. Nothing is being asked of you, you went out there to just be, not do. The forest is beautiful, and it reflects only beauty back to you.

What you don't see within all the beauty, is the dead carcasses decaying under the leaf litter. You don't see the insects boring holes in the trees, or the birds devouring bugs by the millions, ultimately murdering entire species for their survival. You aren't seeing the bear stripping berry bushes clean so they can hibernate for the winter, or what happens when the creek floods its banks and uproots all the plants around its borders. Death and recycling is everywhere, but you don't see it! You see beauty, peace, and tranquility.

So why are you so miserable in your own life? Why do you see only what is gnawing at you and the little inconveniences and "bugs" that keep picking away at your resolve? Where is the beauty, peace, and tranquility in your own life's forest? Every single person walking the Earth is an ecosystem unto themselves with 50 trillion cells. You have gut "flora", bacteria that are alive and other organisms living within your own body. You have organs and filtration systems in the same way that the Earth has streams and forests. Your entire body is a walking planet or plant… in an ecosystem of other plants in a forest of civilization. Some call it the concrete jungle. There's a reason for all the metaphors we use. They speak to us on a deeper, and often subconscious level; that's why we use them. I tend to use mixed metaphors a lot, only because I can't keep things straight in my own head, and they come out in often comical ways at which everyone is laughing and I'm the last to get the joke because I actually meant what I said.

In this book, for the duration of this course, you are a plant. It's a metaphor to help bring your awareness back to a fundamental level of connectedness to all living beings. Plants just exist in the world, they don't have jobs or other worries, they don't question their existence, and they don't struggle to find greater meaning in their existence. Granted they have their own kinds of struggles but it's vastly different from anything we experience daily. They just are. By taking the perspective of a plant, we can gain a better understanding of what it really means to be human. Sometimes we must take a step back to get the larger picture onto a viewable surface for contemplation to take over properly. If you are a plant, then the struggles you are facing right now all fall away. The stress of "doing" takes a back seat so perspective can shift into a framework that shapes reality differently. We need that! We get so caught up in doing everything right that it can be almost impossible to put the brakes on and ask ourselves if what is "right" is actually the most beneficial to our lives and the lives of everyone we encounter.

Spirituality is the cultivation of your soul. So, we are going to cultivate ourselves in some intensely conscious ways by doing practices that realign us with the divinity within all life. This is a daily practice of living with yourself in this 3D reality without escaping, or wishing it were different, better or anything other than what it is. It may suck entirely right now. You may be struggling to be good at being a human being. That's okay. I struggle with it too, that's why I wrote this book. The goal is to understand the importance of those struggles and why we need them in our lives. Without conflict we would not grow. Plants have all kinds of stresses to deal with even if they aren't the same as ours, and they still thrive. We can too, and we will, once we identify the places we need love, connection, and acceptance. It's our responsibility to give those things to ourselves. When every single person can take their own power of thriving back into their hands, the world miraculously changes in the blink of an eye. Magic is real and it begins with the lenses we view the world through. Put your plant glasses on now. Green is the color of the heart chakra because it is in perfect balance within the energy field of the body. It sits right in the middle between the cool and warm energies (positive and negative); it is in neutral alignment. We are going to paint our world green for a little while and get back into neutral alignment with our very soul. It's a starting point that has no pitfalls because it's centered in peace.

It is valuable to note here that divinity as a practice, belief structure and tenable element of our very existence has been part of every single religious, spiritual and pagan practice I have come across in my research of thirty years. Yes, at 10 years of age I was already collecting data on this concept. It's also found in at least, and not limited to, over twenty separate secular, orthodox and non-religious groups throughout history. The commonest to be sure, but also those that are not as widely recognized, some even lost to time now. Divinity, being the link between this world and the next, has sometimes been referred to as "soul" or "consciousness" in our modern times as quantum physics reaches farther into the understanding of human existence. Which is why I say that science and spirituality have coalesced in their understanding of this fundamental aspect of our shared humanity. It can be further stated that divinity is the weighable part of our being that leaves us upon death. I have included this, although it is not supported by the scientific community (MacDougall, 1907):

> *"THE 21 GRAMS EXPERIMENT REFERS TO A SCIENTIFIC STUDY PUBLISHED IN 1907 BY DUNCAN MACDOUGALL, A PHYSICIAN FROM HAVERHILL, MASSACHUSETTS. MACDOUGALL HYPOTHESIZED THAT SOULS HAVE PHYSICAL WEIGHT, AND ATTEMPTED TO MEASURE THE MASS LOST BY A HUMAN WHEN THE SOUL DEPARTED THE BODY. MACDOUGALL ATTEMPTED TO MEASURE THE MASS CHANGE OF SIX PATIENTS AT THE MOMENT OF DEATH. ONE OF THE SIX SUBJECTS LOST THREE-QUARTERS OF AN OUNCE (21.3 GRAMS).*

I just wanted to outline for you an idea of how very important it is to consider the wide range of beliefs regarding divinity and its practical implementation in our lives. When we become aware of it as a presence, we can focus our attention upon the unifying aspect that encompasses us within the collective parameters of "humanity".

Personal Story

I will just lay this out there in the first line. I was suicidal in 2020. How the heck did I even get there? I had a great childhood (navy family, all my needs were met, lots of religious and spiritual influences, etc...). I was a perfectionist though, because of the values that I was taught. I learned that I had to produce and perform to be valuable to the larger world. My mom did counter this misperception when I would come home from school after a day of harsh bullying (from everything under the sun like my socks, my clothes, my attitude, my everything) and she could tell me, "If they don't like you just the way you are, then there's something wrong with them, not you." and it helped to stabilize my short-term emotional state.

I was such an overwhelmed child that I used confidence to mask my sense of inadequacies. If I put a strong front forward, then no one would knock me down, again. I wasn't being honest though, not with myself or the world. I understood the spiritual lining of life and that we are all connected on a deep and fundamental level, but it wasn't enough to keep me stable in my daily lived experience so that I could show up in a way that expressed my true self. I felt the need to hide and "mask up" to function as a kid. I could break down at home with my mom, who really saw me (and even then, there was a lot she didn't know at the time). I wasn't vulnerable as a kid. I used humor and silliness as my mask so that I was dynamic in any situation, with any person. This is what I call the "chameleon" who can engage in any scenario and "fit in". I didn't fit in, it just looked like I did. I was able to take on the characteristics of anything I was around, and I used it as a cover just so that I felt I belonged and could connect with the outside world in any kind of meaningful way. Connection and belonging are paramount to feeling meaning in our lives. Regardless of my spiritual background, I wasn't finding that connection and belonging within myself, so I sought it out in any interaction I could find to validate that I was meant to be here.

I experienced depression and high levels of anxiety throughout my childhood that were never diagnosed because I hid it well. My sister and I went to counseling and spoke with therapists. We even did hypnotherapy at one time, but it wasn't helping me learn how to value myself from a divine point of view so that I could move through the world with real confidence. My authentic self could only shine through in moments. I couldn't be vulnerable in many places because I got run over repeatedly by my peers and shoved aside by the adults around me, and that led me to spend a lot of solitude with plants and animals because they were non-judgmental of my innate and strange way of being that others couldn't accept. I was accepted by nature, so I sought out natural settings to be myself, rather than find that in social settings. I didn't understand plants at that time like I do now, but this connection helped me develop my place in the world on a fundamental level. I related to trees and saw the process of growing things as a beautiful and perfect incarnation and often meditated with them, imagining myself as one of them. I couldn't relate to people in the same way.

This is what would later develop into my love for shamanism, witchcraft, and spirituality, and seeking the divine in all things. It was a blessing and curse simultaneously. At the time it was a curse because I always felt like an outsider looking in. It has become a blessing as I flourished into an adult, because I could use that connection to stabilize myself in the world of people, which I didn't understand. I now know that this kind of childhood has prepared me to become the person I am today, who was able to write this book and do the work that is in alignment with my life's purpose. I couldn't have changed a thing, regardless of how painful, how disconnected, how traumatic it felt at the time. I had to experience all of it, so that I could share this message with the world. I had an entire garden in my own head that was growing everything I would become. It was laid out by others, but through my own determination, curiosity and will, I would transform that garden into my own paradise, one that would produce the fruits I needed to do the work I came here for.

The First Step: Plotting Your Garden

Spend some time this week to assemble your "cultivation team" if you choose to take this journey as a group. The benefits are vast! It can be profoundly insightful to have 2 other people with you on this long road. 12 weeks is a long time to dedicate yourself to anything. Having others with you, who you dearly trust and also want to do this kind of work can create lasting bonds, self-mastery and a well needed sounding board for some of the difficult work to come.

You will need to get some art supplies. I will list some ideas here, so you have a good starting point.

- **(REQUIRED)** An art book, any size, high quality, thick paper. Blank pages preferably so you can create art in it.
- **(REQUIRED)** A spiral bound notebook for some of your lengthy writing exercises. It's nice to have lined paper for writing.
- Glue of any kind. I'm an Elmer's fan myself.
- Old magazines, or printed images. You will be doing some collage work so having a stack of old magazines that you can cut words, shapes, colors, and other images out of will be an invaluable resource. You can usually snag a few from the doctor's office or ask a friend if they have any they are tossing out, sometimes even thrift stores have some going cheap if you can't procure some for free. There are plenty of magazines in the world. Arizona Highways, Better Homes and Gardens and PHOENIX are some of my favorites.
- Pens, markers, crayons, paint, and anything else you like to use to express yourself with creatively.
- Stickers! Stickers are so much fun and add the extra little flair to your art that you can't get with any other medium. You can find them anywhere so keep on the lookout for some fun stickers you can use during this course.

PRACTICE: Take a picture of yourself right now. Not your best selfie with all your makeup or a perfectly trimmed beard (if you have a stunningly perfect beard) but just in an ordinary moment of your day. You can print it on your computer or at a kiosk, but you must print it so you can paste it into your journal. Say two things about the person you see. One positive, what you absolutely love about this person, and one negative, something you either hate or would change about this individual. Make it a work of art! Make it fantastic and colorful and use lots of creative energy to get this into your book. Take some extra time to do this step because you will look back at this image and the thoughts you put on paper about your preconceived ideas you had at the beginning of this course. It will matter in the long run, and you will see yourself differently, without question, by the end of this twelve-week practice.

You don't have to believe me. That's okay. You're here, and showing up for the work, and that is enough right now. You are plotting your garden and we are sorting through your seed packs at the moment. You must know what you are already working with to even begin the process. Because how do you know what you don't know? You don't.

- ❖ Art it! Write It: On the page facing your personal portrait, draw a plant. It can be a fictional one, created out of your own imagination or a likeness of one of your favorites. Draw something that inspires you and use a lot of green! Play with different shades of green too. It doesn't have to be one color. The spectrum of color we have at our disposal is impressive. You can even use several mediums to pull off a multilayered effect. Crayons and markers, colored pencils, and paint, even magazine images! Make this a fun thing for you to do. You don't have to be an artist and don't even try to make it perfect. It should be messy and wild looking! This is a peek into your soul, it should be a little bit wild, just like your true self.
- ❖ **SOC Writing:** I want you to think about why you decided to take this course. What were your motivations? Where are you RIGHT NOW that led you to make this decision? Now, with that in your conscious mind, take as many pages as you need to, but get it out of your head, and don't think about how coherent it sounds at the moment. You are going to do some stream of consciousness writing (SOC).
- ❖ Below is a sample of something I have written to myself, just to clear my head. I wrote in stream of consciousness method (SOC), and I urge you to do the same for this exercise, because a lot of subconscious, deep level issues surface when you are not taking

your time and thinking about each part of your writing. When you don't know what to write, write that!

Example

"I am doing this exercise and have no idea why. I can't think properly. I'm tired. I feel stuck in my life, and I just want to die. I know I need to be strong for my kids and sometimes I am really good at it, but right now, I just don't have any energy left and I don't know where to get it. I try to eat good, but donuts. Damn I love donuts. I don't like how I feel when I eat them but I just crave them sometimes and don't know why. I could eat donuts everyday. I want to change how I eat. I look in the mirror and I hate the person I see. I have big bulgy bubble fat that sticks out over my yoga pants and even when I suck in my breath, it doesn't go away. I know I should exercise, but when?! I can't even lift my eyes in the morning. I want to spend more time with my kids, with myself. I need a break. Like a week or two maybe. Just need to stop thinking so much. This is really stupid. No one is going to ever read this thank god. Its just so stupid to write anything that comes to mind. I don't know why I'm doing this. It's really dumb and I keep writing, because that's what I'm supposed to be doing and I'm told its supposed to help, but right now I want to stab the paper with the pen and make a big hole. A big hole would be a satisfying thing to see on this paper. All the words just rolling into a void right in the middle, getting bigger. I could just draw it until the paper rips. What would that help? I have to make sure I remember to take Alex to the dentist. I hate appointments. I'm just not very good at being an adult. I'm failing as a parent. They can see it and they hate me for it. My kids hate me, I'm sure of it. I can't be their friend, I have to just make sure they grow up right. I don't even have a handle on me, how the hell am I going to raise two kids?"

This was written in 2015 when I was at one of the lowest points with my health, battling a mold problem in our home, adrenal fatigue, thyroid issues, and candida. So, there's one of my trainwreck journal entries. The point is… it DOESN'T MATTER what you write! Please understand this. This is a brain drain exercise. Stream of consciousness writing is a way to derail your conscious mind from its automations (that tell you all the things you want to hear). It can reveal things that you might not want to admit. It may take half a page to get there, it might take four pages. When you are thinking hard of what you need to say and how to write it in a politically correct way, you miss some key elements of the intuitive part of yourself that is desperately wanting a voice. It wants to be heard and valued, and you've got to get out of your own way long enough so it can come through and offer you some hard truths. Eventually, your brain can't keep up with how fast your pen is moving. You just have to keep making words on paper. The coherency will reveal itself later in this course. DO NOT REREAD IT NOW! This is important. I urge you to simply turn the page and allow it to marinate and MOVE ON to the next part. You will be glad you did! One of the things to remember about our intuition, when it doesn't get heard, it raises the volume. Choose not to listen again and it gets even louder. It if reaches the point where it is screaming at you and you still aren't able to pay attention to it, some serious health issues can occur as a result.

Take a few deep breaths, clear your mind, and put the pen to the paper. Don't lift your pen! Write an entire pageful if you can manage to stick with it for that long. A minimum of 5 minutes of stream of consciousness writing can do wonders for your overthinking brain.

❖ Journal Practice: Make an art page of your perceived goals and ideas you are consciously thinking about RIGHT NOW. Ask important questions even if you don't have the answers yet. Make a numbered list of your questions, as many or as few as you want to. It's okay if you only have two, but since you drained your brain with the first exercise, I bet you are thinking a bit clearer now. Like the example questions I listed earlier. What do you ask yourself about life, you, and the world? Get it out there.

We will need this list for later review so make it legible and precise.

Art journaling is a way of engaging your creative and intuitive mind. It ties your analytical thinking brain to a creative process, utilizing both parts of your psyche. The parts of our inner world that feel a connectedness to every living being reside in the creative part of our minds. When you use both sides of your brain interchangeably, you employ your analytical, thinking brain, your intuitive, creative brain, and your innate spiritual knowing. You begin unlocking doors within your psyche that will create new grooves and neural pathways for long lasting changes in patterns, habits and old belief structures that haven't been the pillars holding you up, but the ruins of a false foundational system crushing the life out of you from the inside out.

I know this feels like a lot, but it's our foundation and we want it to be strong, so we aren't cutting any corners with these first chapters. The upcoming exercises will be easier, I promise, and less intense. We've got to develop a powerful starting point. Remember, you have an entire week to do these practices, so don't get overwhelmed. There is always time.

WEEK 2

(DAAT)

Just Keep Digging…

"Mental pain is less dramatic than physical pain, but it is more common and also more hard to bear. The frequent attempt to conceal mental pain increases the burden: it is easier to say, 'My tooth is aching' than to say, 'My heart is broken.' — C.S. Lewis, The Problem of Pain

"Some friends don't understand this. They don't understand how desperate I am to have someone say, I love you and I support you just the way you are because you're wonderful just the way you are. They don't understand that I can't remember anyone ever saying that to me. I am so demanding and difficult for my friends because I want to crumble and fall apart before them so that they will love me even though I am no fun, lying in bed, crying all the time, not moving. Depression is all about If you loved me you would." — Elizabeth Wurtzel, Prozac Nation

Is Depression Really That Big of an Issue?

What is DAAT? Depression, Anxiety/Abuse and Trauma. Why do we struggle in a world that no longer challenges our survival? It's important to open this topic by immediately highlighting some important statistics and numbers that have to do with the state of mental health in our world. I promise I'm not a sadist, torturing you with facts and stats. Mental health has been in the spotlight of social justice groups for at least ten years. The study of mental health goes back much further, but with science to back its findings now, and with all the data collected, we have a crystal-clear view into the causes, age ranges, effects, symptoms and even some methods for healing. With all this data and study, why is it still on the rise? We think of mental health under the term "mental illness" and misguidedly paint a picture of this as a minority issue. We must approach this as a human issue by understanding without a doubt that this is something every single human being "has" all the time. It's up to us to decide if we are mentally "healthy" or mentally "ill". The difference lies in how we execute our daily lives. Are our minds the cause of our suffering or the cause of our thriving? The data below was gathered directly from Google, anyone can access it, so why don't we know it and what do we do about it?

> *The percentage of adults in the USA who experienced any symptoms of depression was highest among those aged 18–29 (21.0%), followed by those aged 45–64 (18.4%) and 65 and over (18.4%), and lastly, by those aged 30–44 (16.8%). Women were more likely than men to experience mild, moderate, or severe symptoms of depression. (Maria A. Villarroel, 2020)*

> *"Ever having been diagnosed with either anxiety or depression" among children aged 6–17 years*

increased from 5.4% in 2003 to 8% in 2007 and to 8.4% in 2011–2012.

"Ever having been diagnosed with anxiety" increased from 5.5% in 2007 to 6.4% in 2011–2012.

"Ever having been diagnosed with depression" did not change between 2007 (4.7%) and 2011-2012 (4.9%). - (CDC, 2022)

"Depression is a common illness worldwide, with an estimated 3.8% of the population affected, including 5.0% among adults and 5.7% among adults older than 60 years. Approximately 280 million people in the world have depression." - (WHO, 2021)

According to the University of Michigan Healthy Minds Study:

"Last fall, college students reported their highest levels of depression and anxiety of any prior semester, according to the University of Michigan Healthy Minds Study, an annual web-based survey looking at mental health and service utilization among undergraduate and graduate college students. Among the respondents, 47% screened positive for clinically significant symptoms of depression and/or anxiety—up from 44% last year and the highest since the survey was started in 2007. The study included data from 32,754 students from 36 colleges and universities (response rate 14%).

The Healthy Minds Study began in 2007 to look into how to invest most effectively in the mental health and well being of college students. The study collects population-level descriptive data to understand the prevalence of mental health challenges on campus—

things like depression, anxiety and eating disorders—and uses that data to help design and evaluate programs and interventions. The program then evaluates these interventions so universities and colleges can direct their resources most effectively to improve the health of their students." said Justin Heinze, one of the principal investigators of the report. (Bickel, 2021)

What causes depression?

I bring this up right at the beginning of this chapter because I want to illustrate just how big of a problem this has become. Regardless of the technological era we are living in, and all the advances we've made with our modern technology, these numbers are increasing rather than decreasing. If it is so easy for me to pull this information off the internet with little effort, then I wonder why mental health problems are still plaguing our society while steadily increasing. Things should be getting better, not worse, right? At least that is my logical mind speaking here and my innate curiosity.

My personal experience has told me that depression is a symptom of not living our calling. It is linked to the people pleasing perfectionism that infects our rational thinking. It is in the inauthentic interactions we have with the world when we think we've got to be "something" for "somebody" rather than being who we really are. It's the soul sucking void that makes the world feel less interesting, less joyful, and less real. It can be crippling, and the longer it lingers, the harder it is to convince ourselves that there is anything other than the graying landscape visible through lenses we didn't even know we had on. It's also a trauma response.

Five major causes of depression are:

"Different causes can often combine to trigger depression. For example, you may feel low after being ill and then experience a traumatic event,

such as a bereavement, which brings on depression." (NHS, 2019)

1. Family history

Depression does not have a clear pattern of inheritance in families. It has been documented that people who have family members who have suffered from depression stand a greater chance of experiencing it in their own lives. However, many people who develop depression do not have a family history of the disorder, and many people with an affected relative never develop the disorder. So, this is a small factor that may play a part, but epigenetics sheds some light on environmental factors that have an even greater impact on how we move through the world regarding our mental awareness.

2. Illness and health issues

Physical illnesses or injuries can have a significant impact on your mental health. Chronic health issues, long-term health issues, or physical health issues that drastically change your lifestyle can cause depression. This kind of significant life event can trigger an overwhelming emotional response. Many doctors understand this and some even offer mental health treatment as a part of your overall care. Issues connected to your brain, hormones, menstrual cycle or menopause, low blood sugar, or sleep problems can be very impactful. When your life goes through sudden and unexpected changes, it may take some time for the mind to catch up to what is happening. The period before acceptance can lead a person into a depressive state, especially when the illness or health issue was caused by a trauma.

3. Medication, drugs, and alcohol

Many different medications, some of which are quite common, are known to have side effects like depression. It is always important when you are starting a new medication, to track your symptoms and communicate with your doctor if you notice a change in your mood, behaviors, or thoughts. Recreational drugs and alcohol use can also cause or worsen depression. While you would think this would be obvious, recreational and social activities like drinking alcohol can greatly affect your mood. While they may initially feel like they help symptoms of depression, they can, over time, make you feel worse.

4. Personality

Current evidence suggests that depression is linked to traits such as neuroticism/negative emotionality, extraversion/positive emotionality, and conscientiousness. It has been seen that people who have habits of worry, high stress lifestyles, low self-esteem, and are perfectionists are naturally more likely to be depressed. Those who are emotionally sensitive are at a higher risk of developing a depressive state because they tend to focus on negative life events and memories more than those of other personality types.

5. Life Events

It has been found through research that life events can increase your chances of being depressed. Examples of events like this include:

- Losing your job
- Being in a dysfunctional relationship
- Stress at work
- Isolation
- Going through a breakup or divorce
- Being diagnosed with an illness
- Being unemployed for a long time
- Grieving a loved one

While negative life events can cause depression, it's not always the case. Often, it is more about how you deal with these difficult situations rather than just experiencing them. Many of us have gone through this entire list in our lifetime with little to no adverse reactions, while others have a devastating, life changing, increase in negative moods.

Chemicals in the Brain

Brain chemistry is a vastly complex and developing field of medical study. There is much that is still being researched while new information comes out daily as scientific breakthroughs develop. In addition, there are so many other factors besides simple brain chemistry that can lead to depression. Therefore, depression is not merely caused by a lack of certain chemicals. However, there are specific processes between nerve cells that can contribute to depression. People with clinical depression often have increased levels of monoamine oxidase A (MAO-A), an enzyme that breaks down key neurotransmitters, resulting in very low levels of serotonin, dopamine, and norepinephrine (nor-ep-in-efrin). Serotonin plays a role in sleep and in depression, but this inhibitory chemical also plays a major role in many of your body's essential functions, including appetite, arousal, and mood. Brain chemistry is complex, and we all have a unique distribution of these chemicals based on our life experiences and current circumstances. Even though our brains all make the same chemicals, as individuals we make different amounts of these chemicals in different combinations. We are all walking, talking, chemical cocktails. When we understand how our own body/brain chemistry works, we can harness the way the brain releases these chemicals for our benefit rather than our detriment. I'm no scientist, so I won't go into depth on this subject. A recent finding just revealed that serotonin does not play as large a role in depression as they once thought. As science learns more, so do we.

Treatments for depression

Many of the medications used to treat depression target the brain's messaging system. Some stimulate serotonin (which is now being questioned radically) or noradrenaline (*nor-adren-alin*) production or prolong their activity. Some treatments like transcranial magnetic stimulation (TMS) or electroconvulsive therapy (ECT) are used to treat depression because they also target the brain's messaging processes. However, these types of treatments should only be used when therapy, lifestyle changes, social change, and medication have not helped. Most depression can be treated without medication if it has not reached an unmanageable level. Therapy and counseling can help identify the cause of a depressive state and offer some positive feedback and practices to reestablish different thought patterns, habits, and behaviors. Lifestyle changes are often the most useful, producing long lasting habit changes. These create new neural pathways that remain in place long after the depression has passed.

Personal Story

Depression doesn't always rear its ugly head in obvious ways. It can be slow to develop and even slower to identify. I left my daughter's father when I was six months pregnant, in 2003. Something about being pregnant with her gave me an intuitive sense of what would be best for our lives moving forward. Having said that, I need to make a note here that he was a mean drunk. Regardless of how much he professed to love me and the child we were making, he would say cruel things to me that left an impact on my sense of worthiness. I wanted to believe that I loved him too, but at that time I believed that I wouldn't be able love him and stay sane and left the relationship. I knew that leaving was the only way my daughter would blossom into who she was meant to be, so I packed up what I could in my little truck, (with the help of my mother and some mutual friends) and moved us out of Northern New Mexico and back to Northern Arizona to live on our forty-acre family homestead.

I knew it was the right choice, so why did I feel so bad about it? I cried almost every day. The last several months of my pregnancy with her were so emotionally trying that some days I didn't get out of bed at all. In highly lucid moments, I would find projects and focus on the future, but I was hardly present in reality. What I hadn't understood at the time was that the thought of leaving my child's father felt like a failure on my part. I had let down an ideal I held firmly in my mind; a belief structure given to me during childhood from a mother who stayed in a 15-year marriage that wasn't supporting either of them. I was taught through her example that you stayed no matter what, no matter how bad, till death do you part. So, by leaving him, I was breaking one generational trauma, and creating a new one at the same time.

When my daughter was born, it should have been a happy time, a moment to celebrate a victory in our lives together. When I look back at pictures now, I can see the blank expression on my face that I tried to hide from those around me. Masking it with false confidence, like I'd learned to do as a child and pretending my way through life. I journaled nearly every day and many of those entries revealed the negative thoughts that my brain was using to establish a "normal" I was comfortable with. It took a year and half for me to see those negative and disempowering patterns and begin unraveling them. By then, a lot of damage had been done that I wouldn't be able to see until my daughter reached the age of four. Those early bonding moments when I could have been truly present manifested themselves later in her childhood when I experienced another wave of depression, and she had reached an age to experience it differently. She grew angry with me for my flaws and took it upon herself to micro-manage her baby brother because her mom couldn't be trusted.

If I had known just how impactful those very first impressions had been for her, I would have never allowed myself to sink so deeply into my own suffering. It reared its ugly head again when she turned seven, her brother was four, and I was just trying to do the best I could with them with the few resources I had. I withdrew and drank too much, which left them teaming up to find stability in one another when they couldn't count on me for it.

It pains me to admit that. But it happened. I can't take anything back, but I can change our future and I can change every moment we have now so that I'm present when we do spend time together for the remainder of our time here.

Our behavior affects everyone around us, especially our children. We can't always see the ways that others are impacted by our deep suffering, so it's difficult to understand how to act differently, how to correct it when it's happening, and how to fix it. If I had reached out in any of those moments, enrolled in counseling, confided in a friend, dropped the unhealthy coping mechanisms, I may have been able to write a better story for that chapter of our lives together.

Trauma and your Brain

Trauma can happen in a variety of ways, and we all feel the severity at different volumes. Experiences that are traumatic for some affect others mildly. Abuse is one of the predominant factors for trauma. PTSD is a long-term physical injury of the brain from experiencing something traumatic. Soldiers who come home from war are more likely to have PTSD due to the traumatic situations of life and death in the environments they experienced. When the environment changes, and they return home to safe surroundings, their brains still relive the trauma as though it were happening in the present moment. Other traumas can include a sudden health decline, an accident, or the death of a loved one. Trauma on smaller scales can be seen from bullying, peer pressure, stress, break ups in relationships, or abuse, long or short term.

The brain won't always move beyond the traumatic experience and will keep triggering you to see it repeatedly in related situations. As a result, this can bring on symptoms like severe anxiety, withdrawal, anti-social behavior, contentious communication, bouts of unwarranted or unjustified rage, and even paranoia or projection. When we don't learn the lesson the first time, life will keep cranking up the volume dial until it gets loud enough for us to hear it. We can attune ourselves to hear these messages when they are but a whisper in our ear. We need to tune up our awareness so that the volume doesn't have to keep being adjusted higher for us to get the message; we have become deaf to this kind of internal language. This is what we are going to learn to do in this lesson, tune up our awareness so we can keep the volume at a reasonable level. Our intuition is a powerful tool in our bag of goodies for living. It is underused and often dismissed because we value things of substance, proof, and action over less tangible sources of information. We rarely follow through with those intuitional indicator lights on our dashboard, even though afterwards we often ask the question, "Why didn't I listen to that voice?", when we end up with validation from an external source that it was right all along. We go deaf to our own internal dialog and rely on others for the external validation that we could have easily given to ourselves had we trusted ourselves enough to just listen the first time. Trauma has a way of making us believe that we are not trustworthy with our own choices. We doubt ourselves and often wonder why we feel so alone and afraid of the world, and find it hard to develop meaningful relationships with friends, family, and lovers. When we don't trust ourselves, how can we trust anyone else? How can we rely on any source of information about the world, ourselves, and reality when we have gotten so fearful of doing something wrong, badly, or inadequately?

When I talk about "digging the hole into your psyche", I am specifically bringing into awareness the act of consciously re-writing your subconscious drives and motivations. It starts with a hole. Taking that etheric shovel in your hand and breaking into the soil of your own mind is the only way to get to the place where all your buried stuff lives. It's buried for a reason. You put it all in there and you're the only one who can take the time and energy to find the detrimental habits and the responses/reactions that you've normalized to cope with them. We will talk more about automations as we go through these chapters, but they deserve an honorable mention here. If you aren't consciously working on something, you have relegated it to automation. It's your default method of dealing. Very much like when you drive your car and take the exact same route to work every day. You hardly even look at the road because it's become so ingrained and familiar, like breathing… unless you're stoned, then breathing can be something you actually have to think about. But I digress; automations are subconscious processes that originally needed conscious use of accuracy and skill.

Plants and Trauma

Plants do experience trauma. Have you ever walked in a forest and noticed an entire stand of pines all bent in exactly the same place on their trunks? Whatever event occurred in their environment that damaged them, the ones that lived through the trauma ALL grew the same way as they recovered from it. This speaks to large scale events that have taken place in our history. We know about what happened at Auschwitz… enough said. That kind of trauma leaves a mark on people. Plants experience environmental and circumstantial trauma in the same ways we do. We can see the damage when we walk through that forest. We can't always see the damage on people though. It shows up in their behaviors, personality quirks and habits. Someone who lived through war might, for example, save every piece of string and newspaper because it could be useful later. Entire groups of soldiers who experience a traumatic event during wartime will come home and exhibit similar behaviors when the war is over and have bonded in the life threatening situations they endured. Infestations of bugs can take out entire crops. Fungal issues can stunt the growth of a plant. Fungus can be so tenacious that it emits spores into the soil that can adversely affect the next year's seeds as well. It's working on the parent plant… and the next generation. Plants and people are not so different after all. Any grown-up child of a wartime survivor will be able to identify the kind of behaviors I'm referring to here. It leaves a residue that can affect the generations afterwards, and potentially stunt their growth without them even knowing it.

Dig the Hole: Your Plants Need Proper Depth and Drainage

- **Journal Practice:** Using color and images ONLY, (no words this time!) fill a blank page with everything that represents YOU at your lowest point, your darkest moments, your deepest struggles. What would it look like if others could see how you feel on the inside when you are hurting? What colors, images and shapes come to mind that represent your internal mess? No words for this one. Just feelings. If other people could see it, what would it look like?

- **Write down**, in a list form, what your triggers are for overwhelming and difficult emotions that lead to painful experiences, and next to that, your reaction to them.

My Triggers...	...And Reactions:
Talking to my son's dad	Cry, shake and doubt my worth
Forgetting appointments	Brutally scold myself internally
When my to-do list gets too big	Eat half a loaf of shepherd's bread and do nothing
Mistakes made at work	In my head, recite the conversation I will have with my boss
Forgetting an important event	Self-blame and criticism for my shortcoming
Letting the laundry or dishes pile up	Either "toxic clean" the entire house or do nothing at all, paralysis.

- Like the example above, next to your trigger list, write what you have done in the past to negatively react to those triggers, your reactions. I wrote mine down to give you an example of some of the ways that I have dealt with these triggers badly. Nowadays, I no longer have an adverse reaction to talking to my son's father. That was a huge one for me, because the trauma of that experience would creep up in random moments when it shouldn't have reared its ugly head. Since my worthiness regarding that is no longer an issue for me, I don't have the trigger response and I continue to heal others as they surface.

It all takes time. This practice is important because right now you aren't sure yet what exactly you're dealing with inside. What you list might be surface issues that will lead to a greater revelation later of something that was so deeply buried, even years of counseling couldn't identify it. DAAT takes on many faces to camouflage itself from us because we need that protection in order to function daily. Revealing a deep trauma can turn our lives upside down. I know that sounds scary, but you are supported, and we won't move any faster than you're ready to. It's okay to be afraid, and it's okay to cry. Digging holes gets easier with practice. It's dark down there… we are taught that scary things are in the dark, but the scariest thing, and the one to keep remembering is that if it continues to go unidentified, unburied, unnoticed, it will wreak havoc in your life in any way it can to get your attention.

WEEK 3

Planting the Seed, On Top of Mt. Mindfulness

"If while washing dishes, we think only of the cup of tea that awaits us, thus hurrying to get the dishes out of the way as if they were a nuisance, then we are not "washing the dishes to wash the dishes." What's more, we are not alive during the time we are washing the dishes. In fact we are completely incapable of realizing the miracle of life while standing at the sink. If we can't wash the dishes, the chances are we won't be able to drink our tea either. While drinking the cup of tea, we will only be thinking of other things, barely aware of the cup in our hands. Thus we are sucked away into the future -and we are incapable of actually living one minute of life."

-Thich Nhat Hanh

Mindful Management & Your Automations

What do you think about when you are engaged in daily activities? Do you know where your mind is going while you are involved in an automatic task? Mindful living has been talked about in several ways, employing a wide range of techniques to help bring awareness into our lives, creating a presence practice. Oftentimes we don't keep up with these practices because they aren't sustainable, aren't meaningful, or we don't recognize the value they are bringing into our lives. I feel confident in saying that we have all made a new year's resolution that we commit to and then fall short when it comes to following through with it. Mindfulness can be a form of meditation, yoga, breathing exercises, walking once a day and other small micro-rituals that center our thoughts and get us back on track with the present moment.

mind·ful·ness
/ˈmīn(d)f(ə)lnəs/
noun

1. the quality or state of being conscious or aware of something.
Ex. "their mindfulness of the wider cinematic tradition"
2. a mental state achieved by focusing one's awareness on the present moment, while calmly acknowledging and accepting one's feelings, thoughts, and bodily sensations, used as a therapeutic technique.

Neuroplasticity and the Present Moment

I want to talk about neuroplasticity now because I believe that it contributes to mindfulness. Have you heard of neuroplasticity? I hadn't until early 2021. As this was a new concept to me, I delved deeply into it and listened to some authorities on the matter so I could better understand just what this means for all of us, in layman's terms.

Basically, our brains are plastic. No, I'm kidding of course. Our brains are mutable, which is great news for us.

neu·ro·plas·tic·i·ty
/ˌn(y)ooroˉˌplaˈstisədē/
noun
1. the ability of the brain to form and reorganize synaptic connections, especially in response to learning or experience or following injury.
Ex. "Neuroplasticity offers real hope to everyone from stroke victims to dyslexics"

All people experience life and process those experiences in an individual and personal way. There are commonalities of course, we are all human beings and can't say with definite conviction that we are SO vastly different that there aren't universal truths to us all. It is our common collective suffering that we can all relate to in some way that spans throughout the course of our human experience. We all have the potential to rewrite the neural pathways in our brain by reorganizing synaptic connections. We can do that through movement and mindfulness practices that matter. Granted, it's much easier to utilize the plasticity in our brains from birth to seven years old, but that doesn't mean that your learning window has shut itself forever (or fogged over because you haven't cleaned the window recently, or lenses). During that early stage of development, we can learn any language, or any instrument and hardwire ourselves for learning anything we set our minds to. It's a golden age for our brains, a critical period of learning. When we don't capitalize on that stage of development, it can become more difficult to set up new grooves or "train tracks" which makes some of the changes we face later in life much harder for us. Fear not though! We are incredibly resilient creatures.

The brain requires stability (certainty) as well as plasticity (uncertainty) because that balance is where your social structure lives, what language you predominantly speak, what your values and morals are, motor skills, and sensory and spatial awareness. The stable aspects of the brain are just as vital as being able to learn new things once we get older. You really can teach an old dog new tricks, it's just easier to teach a puppy. There is also a "use it or lose it" system within our brains that requires consistency to maintain connections in the places that we determine are of high importance. The brain will tend to prune anything not being used on a regular basis. This is quite good for us because if there were no pruning taking place, we would be bogged down with a bunch of habitual processes and memories and tidbits of information that have no real practical use in our lives. The brain must determine which synapses are being used regularly and which ones can safely be pruned away. Our brains are so amazing. Because of the way pruning works, clinical neurologists have discovered that there are ways to prolong the critical window of learning and how neural plasticity benefits the ways we can learn, even much later in life. There's a magic number that neuroscience has figured out quite accurately. That number is 52. 52 hours of movement over the span of 6 months for maximum cognitive function retention (Sandoiu, 2018). That boils down to (roughly) 18 minutes a day of meaningful movement. That's so minimal in the long scheme of things.

Routine engagement with associated emotional regulation has been proven to slow the onset of the degrading cognition that can come with Alzheimer's and dementia. Habit forming is natural for the brain. Habit is deeply ingrained in us, it's just a matter of using conscious cognitive training to get us to a place where we can begin learning how to cultivate the habits that are worth repeating. If you could give yourself 18 minutes of movement a day, as "brain medicine", to retain the maximum amount of your cognitive function, would you? Why wouldn't you? Oh, but you don't because it's not impacting your life right now. Yeah, we will address that form of self-sabotage later.

Now, I have intentionally not covered addiction in this chapter so far. It is a huge aspect of this conversation. Because we can correct imbalances in habit and automated mental functions, I have seen through the research that even the most stubborn forms of addiction have been overcome by repetitive, empowering actions associated with movement and reward systems. So, I will leave addiction there for now and we will revisit it again in a later chapter on gremlins.

Extreme examples of over-plasticity can be seen in people like savants and individuals on the autistic spectrum. They learn immediately and excessively because pruning is not taking place at the rate that science has determined is “normal” for a regular and balanced brain. The synapses are firing in specific areas at a higher rate of activity, while other areas are almost shut off entirely. This allows the autistic individual to pay closer attention to certain things and unable to focus on others. It goes much deeper than this, we are just barely scratching the surface of this topic. For a more in-depth explanation of why it is important to have many different kinds of brains in our society, please take the time to either read or watch Temple Grandin. She is quite a useful resource for learning about autism (Mary Temple Grandin, Current) and its value in our society. In short, it’s the balance we are aiming for within our own lives and with our own habits. Autism is, after all, a spectrum that runs from very high functioning to disrupting a healthy lifestyle and interpersonal relationships. So, our “normal” brains need to be balanced so we can address all the areas of our lives that hold the most value and meaning to us. Movement is a key component to making this balance possible.

Another piece of the puzzle within this model has to do with early childhood adversity. It's proven that emotional dysregulation that shows up later in life is often directly linked to early childhood dysfunctions, abuses/anxiety and traumas (DAAT), as well as the environments they are growing up in. So, when the brain has a greater plasticity within high adversity environments, those neural pathways are creating grooves of normalcy and stability that are directly linked to suffering, difficult emotions and challenging situations. So, early childhood development is a key factor in why we, as adults, function the way we do. Negative thought patterns, self-criticism, feelings of unworthiness and many other symptoms are associated with our childhood environmental stresses. So, we cannot deny the fact that the majority of our current behaviors are molded by what kind of environment we grew up in, as well as what kind of stimuli our brains were getting as children that our neural pathways set up as “normal” for each of us.

Many other mammalian species have a relatively short period of immaturity. They learn how to be an adult animal in weeks or months, but the human being takes years to develop itself during the most formative time in our lifecycle. There must be an evolutionary reason for this lengthy timeframe that we are given to develop as functional creatures. I am going to say something that might be perceived as inflammatory, so I urge you to just think about this concept. *Parents know that it's a huge resource drain to raise a child into a functioning adult.* No joke. It takes a lot of the nutrients that mothers have in their own bodies to create a brand new being that has to gestate in a womb. Science tells us this is so. There are also the emotional and physical challenges of rearing and raising children that can age us dramatically as well. The depletion of resources in the brain, used up in creating the neural pathways needed for learning patience, understanding and grace, is vital in raising children. We also come to realize that parenting demands that we interact with our difficult emotions, past childhood traumas, and all the internal conditioning we were given that are now face to face with us as our own children. The payoffs are, of course, beyond measure, and I'll go so far as to say that it is the most difficult and rewarding "job" on the planet. Parenting is a necessary part of nature, it furthers our species, and we wouldn't be here without our parents, grandparents and so on down the line of our ancestral lineage.

Climbing the mountain of belief

Belief and culture play a major role in how we shape our social structures, family tribes and community engagement. Our beliefs are the framework within which we gather evidence from our experiences to determine what it is that we value, how resilient we are, and how our mindset on the world is structured. Belief is a powerful driving force, and it can be misguided if we have suffered dysfunction, abuse and/or trauma (another facet of DAAT) early on in our childhood developmental stage. Our degree of mindful practice is directly linked to our belief systems. People who grew up in households where hope was a core value have a higher resilience in times of adversity. Conversely those growing up in an environment where they were told they were stupid or unlovable, or suffered from extreme traumatic situations, especially at the hands of a parent or close relative, scientific studies tell us, have a much more difficult time overcoming adverse situations, are prone to addictive behaviors, and develop maladaptive coping mechanisms and antisocial behavior, among other negative outcomes.

For a much deeper glimpse into the world of trauma and how we adjust physiologically to this kind of external input, I urge you to read "The Body Keeps the Score" (Kolk, 2015), because he really gives the reader a peek into the medical profession, psychology and medication from his many years of involvement and his personal journey through understanding how to help his own patients by listening to their stories, learning new methods and unravelling the way the body tells us everything we need to know.

The beliefs we carry within us become our self-talk, self-care methods (or lack thereof), criticisms and judgements, to what degree we take offense, and how quickly we recover from adverse situations. Belief is incredibly powerful and lives both within the conscious and subconscious parts of our brains. These beliefs form the automations you've created as well as how you consciously interact with the world. That's huge! It infiltrates every part of your life. The conscious way we use belief was explained earlier: gathering evidence. If you have ever experienced a failure, small or large and then it's repeated in some other way, your brain will gather evidence that suggests that you fail at everything. Eventually, you might stop trying altogether. If you don't have the resilience to recognize that failure as a part of learning, then it becomes defeat. Oftentimes people get defeated right before they succeed at something because of patterns of repeated failures that tell them to stop right before the finish line.

When we dissect belief into parts and pieces that can be easily identified, it helps us realize which beliefs were given to us and which ones we developed out of personal experience. The ones given to us are those we get from teachers, parents, peers, the media, and the external sources that validate our learning to be true about either ourselves or the world. Repetition is a core function of the brain, and it is predictive. It wants to make connections, even between dots that aren't supposed to match up. Associations tell us a lot about ourselves and how we judge what we see, experience, and do. Our judgments can be helpful, but they can also be detrimental and divisive. We make snap judgements about everyone we see. Whether it's their clothes, hair, smile, children, or accessories that we notice, we are judging people, sometimes brutally. We also turn this judgment inward and say terrible things about ourselves that are essentially untrue. We must be very mindful about what we think, because even when we aren't speaking out loud, we are creating reality through the conversations we have internally with the one person who matters most - ourselves. Discernment is our ability to "judge well". When we become discerning, rather than just judging, it is a sign that we are growing and addressing the areas where belief has shaped our perspectives. Rewriting certain beliefs is paramount so we can trust what we are experiencing. Discernment is us trusting ourselves to make correct choices that are good for us and taking right action in places that will be beneficial for our highest selves.

"If you are still here, then you have a 100% success rate for surviving the worst experiences you have ever been through." -Facebook Meme

Take that quote to heart. You are stronger than you might think.

Purpose VS Purposelessness

In the late 90's (before I had kids) I went to a Feng Shui class and we all got to pick a packet from the pile randomly. The sticker at the top of my packet said *PURPOSE* in bold letters. It took years for me to unpack the meaning of that moment. It was a good class, but I think I gained more from seeing that sticker on my packet than the rest of the teachings I learned there.

I spent the next ten years considering the meaning of purpose and how it applied to me and my life.

pur·pose
/ˈpərpəs/
Noun
1. the reason for which something is done or created or for which something exists.
Ex. "the purpose of the meeting is to appoint a trustee"
2. have as one's intention or objective.
Ex. "God has allowed suffering, even purposed it"

That's all great and wonderful, but what does it *mean*? I realized that I had to define it for myself. After reading a book by Napoleon Hill, called Think and Grow Rich, (Hill N. , Think and Grow Rich, 1937) I began to understand purpose in a more personal way. Purpose is tied to meaning. It is also tied to our value system. Let me explain. The definition above talks about the reason something is done or created. Well, we are created, so this touches quite existentially on our reason for being alive, for existing. Our values are what we learn in childhood that give us morals and principles, rules to live by. When you wrap them all up together, because life does not exist in a vacuum and everything is connected, it makes a more realistic painting of what purpose actually means.

My new definition of purpose is this:

> *"The thing we cannot live without, the driving force in our lives that moves us ever closer to our form of service." -Dannielle Nelson*

This new definition ties in value and meaning. The values you have developed, (which we will discuss) and the meaning you derive from living and being, help you discover your true purpose. When you work hard to reach a certain goal and you really aim for it, it's the reason for your motivation and when you grab on to it, you feel satisfaction.

Purpose can guide your life decisions, influence behavior, shape goals, offer a sense of direction, and create deeper meaning. For some people, purpose is connected to vocation—meaningful, satisfying work. Many people feel most purposeful when they are in service. That's why it's easier to feel meaning when we have a driven goal, or a job that helps others.

Your purpose is like a personal mission statement, and we will return to this theme later. It's how you plan to make your mark in this world. It will drive your decisions, strengthen your relationships, and steer you towards greater happiness and success. We all want greater happiness and success in our lives but many of us have no idea where to begin. That's one big reason that depression is running loose in our society like a rabid lion. What purpose do we have in an unstable world?

What is my purpose?

Purpose is where we find meaning—what we want to do and contribute. Purpose certainly can be linked to your job or career, but many people don't find their purpose in their work. And even if it is linked, the purpose is broader than just a job. We must be mindful of how we are showing up and interacting with the world. If we just lollygag through life without ever being truly present, then how will we be able to bring value to anything we attempt to do?

What are the FIVE purposes illustrated in the Purpose Driven Life?

In the book, "The Purpose Driven Life", Pastor Rick Warren reveals the meaning of life from a Christian perspective—five purposes that you were created by God to fulfill: worship, unselfish fellowship, spiritual maturity, your ministry, and your mission. This is obviously religious, and I am NOT religious in any particular way. I include it here as an example for you to see how this individual has defined a purpose for themself. We must all define purpose for ourselves, so we know how we are going to move through life in an intentional, mindful and meaningful way.

What are the types of purpose?

The eleven different types of purpose are the following:

to express

to explore/learn

to inform

to argue

to evaluate

to mediate

to describe

to entertain

to explain

to persuade

to problem solve

Your purpose is directly tied to who you are. How do we ever really discover who we truly are in a society that shapes us in ways that are aimed at keeping itself running, rather than keeping the individual empowered? You have a purpose in each act you commit to, whether it's a conversation with a friend and you are trying to get a point across, or you want to learn something, or find a solution to a problem. The purposes listed above can be expressed in so many of our daily experiences. When we interact with others our purpose can sometimes be clearer than when we are interacting with ourselves. Our unconscious self-interactions that don't seem to fulfill a purpose can have incredibly detrimental effects on our wellbeing. Are we trying to persuade ourselves to do something? Are we arguing with ourselves? Are we evaluating, describing, or finding a solution? Are we just running programs that have become so automated we don't even realize how they are affecting us?

"You're a bad employee and a worse boss," says Jordan (Peterson, Jordan Peterson Homepage, n.d.) about the way we tend to sabotage our successes by focusing on failures, on a podcast with Tom Bilyeu. The micro-victories deserve as much attention as the big wins. I can further add that the micro-victories, when repeated, set up a winning perspective in the brain that releases dopamine, the reward center activator. This reinforces our willingness to do things that are a bit harder and more challenging.

Purposeful self-talk is the key to our inner world. When we consciously and mindfully unlock that secret inner place and stop the disempowering patterns we've developed in the quiet space between our ears, the kingdom of US opens wide and a wonderful new way of viewing the world emerges. I'm sure you've heard someone ask, "would you talk to your friend or a child the way you talk to yourself?" Of course not! No one can hear how judgmental we are with ourselves, the terrible things we say, even in jest, when we've done something we don't like.

- "YOU IDIOT."
- "WHAT WERE YOU THINKING?"
- "I AM SO STUPID."
- "IF I WEREN'T SO FAT, OR DUMB OR LAZY…"
- "IF I WERE PRETTIER, SMARTER AND MOTIVATED…"

Every single one of our "*I am*s" shapes us profoundly. Our "*what if*s" as well as the "*If I*" mantras can all become automations if we use them enough. Again, to our benefit or detriment. "*I am*" is a form of self-talk we use often. There are many affirmations that help rewrite the "*I am*s" in a more empowering direction. These alone aren't enough to change years of bad behavior and learned negativity though. It's only part of the process.

Divinity, You're Halfway up the Mountain

Without sounding overly religious, I want to introduce everyone to the word divine.

di·vine
/dəˈvīn/
adjective

1. of, from, or like God or a god.
Ex. "heroes with divine powers"
excellent; delightful.
Ex. "he had the most divine smile"

The words divine and divinity have declined in use in our language dramatically over the past one hundred years. Their uses are mainly religious in context, so their popularity has dwindled as New Age practices and atheism are on the rise. Overall, our population is less religious now than at any other time in our history. I know how it is possible for people to get the wrong impressions about why I bring this up, so I will gladly explain.

Side note… and some explanation of my purpose

Again, I am NOT a religious person. I identify with a long lineage spanning from both of my parents' ancestors from Sicily as well as Scandinavia, as a Witch. This is quite outside the realm of orthodox religions, so I felt it necessary for the purposes of this section to let you know where my own beliefs and practices are rooted. There was a time I would have been burned at the stake, tortured, and subjected to other atrocities for having such beliefs, practices, and lifestyle. We live in an age of allowing. We allow others to identify with anything, and yet we are highly offended by much. Judgmental and often inflammatory reactions when someone expresses themselves in a way that branches out of mainstream thinking have become so commonplace that we rarely question them anymore. Common definitions of "Witch" (Webster, 2022) are quite arbitrary in my opinion and speak to the biases that we have collectively adopted about the meaning behind it. Look it up… I was disturbed. I have no disempowering associations attached to calling myself a Witch because for me, it defines quite clearly my connection to all life and the path of service I have chosen for the benefit of humanity. There is nothing in the official definition that implies anything of the kind; however, other words do not reflect this meaning either and I rather like "Witch" over some of my other options. W(oman) I(n) T(otal) C(ontrol) of H(erself) (Cole, 2022). So, there you have it, definitions are quite important, and we have to be mindful in understanding how people have defined themselves. When they say a word, we think we know what they are saying. This could not be more complicated than it is in our current era. This is the age of allowing, as I mentioned before, which makes it tricky to interact with one another on a solid foundation of understanding. I am giving you the opportunity here to understand yourself first, so that you can understand others to a deeper and more realistic degree. Be mindful of the words you use and choose to repeat. They are shaping your beliefs, your personality, your perspective of the world and everyone you meet.

Now Back to Divinity

The concept of divinity is directly connected to God and the divine. There's no disconnecting that even if we want to define it differently. It can also be used to describe a behavior, which is what I would like to focus on for this section. Divine behavior, as illustrated in the definition I included above, is how we treat other people. Our service to others and to ourselves is how we express our divinity. People who follow some religions believe that it is their mission to spread God's word on Earth. That is their divine purpose. What if we just interacted with every single person we meet as if they were absolutely divine just as they are? How would that change our perception of them? Would we genuinely be kinder, more compassionate and understanding of their struggles? Hm. I would say yes, we definitely would. It is a core part of our humanity to see the light in others. Our own divine purpose in the world can ground us to see what is good in life and how to cultivate a practice of recognizing ourselves in every other person we encounter.

(Disclaimer: I am not saying that you must tolerate abuse in any form, stay in situations that are traumatic, or put up with manipulation or disrespect from any source.)

Respecting ourselves and others is a core value and it's not just important, it's tied to our integrity. The book, “The Four Agreements” by Don Miguel Ruiz (Ruiz, 1997) covers the subject of integrity at length and lays out some core practices people can use in their lives to gain greater peace of mind in an ever-turbulent world.

What we've got to keep in mind is that the world happening around us is a direct reflection of what we are going through internally and how we perceive everything. When we correct internal imbalances the stresses, fears, and anxiety related to certain situations decrease. Our internal world is the first and last place where existence lives. It is so easy to get caught up in situations and circumstances that are outside of our control. The only thing we have true control over is what goes on inside of ourselves. That's why we began by plotting our garden and digging the hole. Soon we can plant the seeds we've been hauling around in that duffle bag I mentioned earlier. Our minds are a fertile place, so it's vital to our overall health that we scrutinize what takes place beyond the realm of what others can see and touch. External validation has become a crutch that we use to help us move through the world because we were taught not to trust ourselves. When you look at it honestly, the question arises, "why should I trust myself? I've experienced years of failures and suffering at my own hand."

Everything that happened in your life so far has built you, just as you are right now. You may not be able to see the value of that yet, just as it's difficult to imagine a tiny seed growing into a mighty, 100ft tall tree. But you will, as we continue investigating your motivations, subconscious drives and deliberate actions that keep sabotaging your successes. (Stop abusing yourself with your past.)

An Experiment In Consciousness

(TEDxBermuda, 2020) One thing that neural scientist Dr. Kelly Lambert discovered in her work with rats is that movement and reward are connected to meaning and learning new things. They had two groups of rats in controlled environments where one group had to work for their reward (fruit loops) and the other group didn't have to do anything for theirs. They called the groups the "country rats" and the "city rats". The country rats would be given fruit loops that they had to dig up, climb over objects or solve puzzles to earn. The city rats were offered their fruit loops laying on the ground where they could indulge in instant gratification. What they discovered is that the country rats learned much quicker, were happier overall, and their adaptability to change was much higher than the city rats. The country rats even went on to learn how to drive cars made specially for their physiology, and what surprised the scientists the most was that they were self-correcting while driving! This means that they could avoid obstacles like walls and objects in their paths, suggesting that their neural connections were sharper and more adaptive than their city rat companions. The city rats never proceeded so far in the study because they could not learn how to operate the vehicle at all.

What does this mean for you? You aren't a rat obviously. In short, when you have to do a little work to earn the reward you are seeking, you are much healthier mentally, more resilient in times of adversity, and your brain is much more receptive to learning new things because reward is tied to movement and action. Mindfulness is the art of tying your rewards to meaningful tasks. I mentioned earlier that there are many ways to practice mindfulness. Now, these aren’t plants, but rats are a good model to work with in understanding ourselves better too. I will use a wide variety of metaphors, examples and parallels to illustrate some of our unconscious behaviors, how we relate to the world, what similarities exist, and how we can extract valuable information from these examples. We just need to take a moment to step out of our known “humanness” by putting on different lenses through which to view life.

If you really want to dig a bit deeper into the brain and some of the incredible ways in which it operates, Dr. Joe Dispenza wrote a book called “Evolve Your Brain” (Dispenza J. , 2008) . This is a lengthy and worthwhile activity for your developing consciousness as it provides a clinical observation of the power of the brain. I began listening to the audiobook partway through writing this course. My curiosity and love for learning were greatly satisfied by this mental buffet. I was able to plug in the headphones and put my body to work. How deeply meaningful for me to learn at the same time I am physically active! One of my favorite methods.

This chapter has covered a wide range of topics that all circle back to mindfulness at their core. It may be difficult to fully integrate all the information that you just absorbed here, so don't try. We will revisit all of these concepts in the weeks to come. This has been a preliminary foundation for perspective building. You are learning how to look at life in different ways, so I gave many different examples for you to chew on. We will come back to this chapter at the end of the book with new lenses, and a fresh perspective. Breathe. You just ate a huge meal of input while climbing a mountain. Good job, I'm proud of you. Those seeds are heavy and you carried them all.

Personal Story

My mom found a place called the Positive Mind Bookstore during my childhood that offered classes. She took my sister and I there often. I remember playing games with some of the mentors like imagining a color and trying to guess it. We would pair off into groups of two and see if we could guess shapes, colors, and numbers that our partner was thinking of. These "games" were teaching us the basics of telepathy and honing our intuitive senses. I didn't know that at the time. I enjoyed playing, all kids do! Developing our intuitive selves at a young age gave my sister and I amazing tools, but we didn't really understand the value of it all while we were going through it. However there came a point in our lives when my sister, my mom and I could anticipate one another's moods and needs. We would hand one another an object that the person was thinking of asking for. We could determine when one of us was angry or sad without being told. We became highly in tune with each other on a non-physical level. Our mindfulness of each other's needs had become well developed. We had set up automations of conscientiousness relating to one another. We paid attention to the cues that were just under the surface of conscious awareness. By playing these games, we were establishing a mindfulness practice that taught us how to intuit what other people needed without voicing those needs.

In 2019, I took a weekend long course on dowsing. I had never heard of dowsing before, so I was intrigued by it. By the end of the course, I realized that all the tools that were shown - pendulums, dowsing rods, charts and diagrams - were things I hadn't needed in my early teachings from the bookstore but were essentially the same practice I had been taught. I had been practicing an internal form of dowsing that required no external tools… since childhood! It solidified my understanding of the divine, the energetic interconnectedness of all life, and the innate knowledge we have within us as human beings. It gave me the perspective I needed to be able to "do what I do" without relying on external validation. I wasn't aware that I had been given these tools, and I didn't know that I was using them automatically. When I began intentionally applying the practices I already knew, coupled with what I had just learned at the class, it set me up perfectly to do my work with confidence and grace. I now have a sense of value for these innate abilities that I was taught when the learning window of my childhood was wide open. What I understand now is that childhood learning is something that remains with us regardless of whether we use it, value it, or understand it, and it lies dormant for a trigger to bring it to the forefront of our awareness. It's been there all along, waiting for the right circumstances, situations, or synchronicities to line up in just the right ways to reveal itself to us. Some of the tools you were given as a child are superpowers, you just don't know it yet.

Planting the Seed of Mindfulness: Adding Movement to your Day

- **MOVE IT!** Begin with 5 minutes of movement a day. Eventually, it will be good to work up to a minimum of 18 minutes to reach the goal of optimum cognitive retention. Retrain your thoughts while moving your body. Be aware of what you are thinking about when you are doing your movement exercises. If daily movement does not come naturally to you, you may notice some interesting thoughts arise. Let them come but be mindful of them. Be aware of what they are saying to you, this may be years of unconscious programming rising to the surface.

- **Journaling Practice:** How do I feel doing this? Silly, strong, awkward. Write it! Art it! Commit to this every single day even if you don't feel like doing it. Motivation is a myth. You MAKE your own determination by doing! By writing down all the things that come to mind when you begin moving, will begin to develop a pattern emerging on paper. It's easy to dismiss our thoughts as fleeting, unimportant processes that pass through us as we are engaged in an activity. We pay them no attention most of the time. We've got to pay attention to them! They offer us important information about our beliefs and the internal structure of our mental world. Whether they are positive or negative thoughts, be sure to journal them once you've finished your mindfulness movement. Do this every day this week and continue it throughout the entire course if you are inclined to. We've got to start somewhere, and we are going to begin by reconnecting our body and mind as one so we can touch our divinity in a way we may not have thought about before. This sets us up to be more purposeful in how we interact with the ALL. (More about the ALL later… Keep reading, wink)
- **Journal Work:** Snap judgements are a part of life. Keep a small notebook with you or give yourself an allocation of 5 minutes each night to write out the snap judgements you made that day. Did you see a woman entering the grocery store with a purse that stood out to you? Did you notice someone's shoes? Did a thought arise when you looked at them? Did you do something and then chastise yourself for it mentally, in the safe space between your ears when no one else could hear you? What did you think to yourself? Be honest, you're the only one in there anyway.

WEEK 4

Introduction to Gratitude As a Practice

"Once we believe in ourselves, we can risk curiosity, wonder, spontaneous delight, or any experience that reveals the human spirit."

I Am Grateful For... Establishing The "I AM's"

Gratitude is almost a buzzword nowadays, but what does it mean? I ask that a lot huh? I like to know what things mean. Have you ever done a gratitude practice? What does gratitude mean to YOU? The first thing to say about this subject is that it's not a new age concept, and it's not religious. Whew, now that we have that out of the way, I can start to delve into all the things it is. Loving what you have right now… regardless of how miserable it may seem, is the core of gratitude. Did you know that some of the poorest countries on Earth house the most grateful people? Why? This has to do with challenges, struggles and the process of living. These people know what it takes to keep their lives going daily.

Do you know what it takes to keep you moving forward every day? No, I'm not referring to that first cup of coffee in the morning, or the first three even. I'm talking about the process it takes for you to maintain your daily life. What steps do you have to take to get and prepare food? What process do you have to do, to have clean, fresh water to drink? What do you need to do to clothe yourself and have shelter over your head? Some people have got to pay close attention to these aspects of life that most of us (in America in particular) take for granted. We have created so many automations around our daily lived experience that we don't think about these things on a conscious level, or in any meaningful way. We have supermarkets where our food comes out of pretty boxes and packages, and water on tap. Easy, done, we can get on with our lives being busy, right?

But we can't, because we are SO busy filling our time with schedules, routines, appointments, work, and emergencies that arise, that we've filled up every gap of usable space we have in our heads. Gratitude is not only a mindset, but it's also an attitude. It's a lifestyle choice, and not just a word or a little thing you can tell people you do to virtue signal that you are "doing good" in your life. Gratitude is also a practice, like everything else in this book. We engage in these daily practices consciously, to shift our minds out of autopilot and move into a creative/conscious mindset. This can dramatically alter the direction of our projected futures and the greater world around us. When we live in a gratitude attitude the world around us does change. We no longer focus on the negative media influences that drag our thinking into limited patterns. We expand our consciousness into the realm of potentials and possibilities that are always available to us, waiting for us to get out of our own way long enough to see it. Take those particular lenses off (just for a moment, you'll put them back on automatically anyway) so you can view the world with new eyes and a fresh perspective. You might just see how quickly it begins to work as the world subtly shifts to adjust to your new attitude. Whatever tragedies and dramas are taking place around you might have less of an effect on your wellbeing and peace of mind. Even your ideas and thoughts about yourself can shift in a way that gives you permission to do things you had previously considered unacceptable by social standards. Authenticity and gratitude go hand in hand. You see, when you are grateful for all of the ordinary things you have in life, you begin to behave in a different way. Gratitude is the call to action that your soul requires for thriving, by feeding you at the roots. I will offer an example so you can see just how powerful and influential this is in your everyday life.

Imagine this: *Your children are wild, playing like animals and making lots of noise. This can be a stressful scenario when you have a million other things to focus on. It can feel distracting when you've got to pay the bills and do uncomfortable things. Instead of lashing out with a stress response, go inward and express to your mind how very grateful you feel to hear them laughing and playing instead of being ill or having some other calamity that would silence their voices. Be grateful for their healthy bodies, that they can move freely and enjoy being children instead of being crippled and bedridden. You can take a few deep breaths and listen deeply to the sounds of their play and remember a time in your own childhood when you were just as vital and strong and new to the world. Sit with that memory for a moment, allow it to imbue you with all the positive sensations that you* *experienced at the time, and be grateful for that too. Then breathe in deeply, open your eyes (if you had shut them, which is an automatic response to remembering) and look at the scene before you without the lenses of stress and discomfort. Remind yourself how very precious these children are to you, and focus only on what you have, right now. It will melt the anger and frustration of whatever it is you are trying to accomplish amid what you just perceived as noise, rather than the beautiful ballet of innocence. It is now all in alignment once again, and life is peaceful. You are blessed, truly blessed to be a parent, and have these wild, playful children being authentically themselves.*

Now you can approach this situation with love. Perhaps you ask your kids to play quietly so you can work with ease, maybe you offer them a quieter game, or maybe the noise of their play is no longer an issue or distraction, but a background song to accompany your work with greater purpose.

People who practice gratitude naturally, researchers show, have a higher amount of oxytocin in their system, suggesting that it can be an inherited trait. As we know, oxytocin has positive benefits on our health overall and is called the "love hormone" for a reason. Another helpful scientific discovery, connecting gratitude intervention with patients diagnosed with depression, shows that it is beneficial in retraining the mind to overcome negative influences that a depressive state can bring on.

It is much easier to practice gratitude when someone has done a service for us or given us a gift. The amount of gratitude felt by the receiver is directly proportional to the effort we believe is exerted by the giver. However, what do you do when nothing perceptible is given? How do we turn that gratitude inwards to ourselves? Afterall, we are an ecosystem within. We are a living, walking, breathing planet filled with organs, cells, bacteria, and multitudes of other lifeforms that are dependent on us as living organisms to sustain their lives. Have you ever been grateful for all those trillions of cells? Have you ever been grateful for your feet? Those suckers carry your entire body around all day long and do not ask you for a thing in return. What about your liver, have you ever been grateful for the organ that filters all the grease and medication you take and alcohol you may consume? We have so much to be grateful for inside of our own bodies that we could spend an entire day (or longer) listing every piece and part individually. Gratitude is a practice, not just a word. Writing down your gratitude has been the proven method that researchers tell us lasts the longest. This does not have to be done daily, but weekly. The practice of writing out our gratitude once a week can have powerful effects on our thinking. Resilience is a benefit that we gain without even trying to attain it. We spoke on resilience earlier and why it's important. Understanding that situations and circumstances are fleeting experiences is the core benefit of a gratitude practice. When we focus on aspects of our lives that we are grateful for, it leaves less room to focus on thoughts that can have a detrimental impact on our worldview, beliefs, and habits. When gratitude is practiced consistently, it replaces old patterns and creates new, positive habits: empowerment through doing. We want reasonable thinking to replace negative and neutral thinking that can keep us locked into habits and routines known to have damaging symptoms in ways we don't even realize.

grat·i·tude
/ˈgradəˌt(y)o͞od/
Noun

1. the quality of being thankful; readiness to show appreciation for and to return kindness.
Ex. "she expressed her gratitude to the committee for their support"

ouch, that hurts - do it again

Do we actively return kindnesses to ourselves like we do for other people in our lives? Not usually. We are too busy criticizing ourselves for all our perceived faults. Mental degradation takes place far more than you may realize and can be just as dangerous as physical abuse if we allow it to continue. The worst part is that we are our own abusers. No one can see what we are doing, so no one can make us accountable for the bad behavior we are unleashing on our precious selves. This is frightening when you frame it in such a way. We aren't taught about the kinds of abuse that take place from within because it is nearly unrecognizable and harder to prove. There are no perceivable victims because even though people see us struggling, they don't know why or how to help. Our friends and family may be able to soothe us in a moment of struggle, but how do they really help us when *we* are the core of the problem? I have done research since 2013 about shame, gratitude, resilience, hope, spirituality, abuse, behaviors, disrespect, many facets of mental health, brain researchers in several fields, neuroplasticity, and the list goes on.

Abuse in any form should not be tolerated, yet we are trained at an early age to self-shame, criticize and degrade ourselves, create guilt and put ourselves down. When are we taught about accountability? You don't believe that could be true? Did you ever have a moment in your childhood when you did something, anything, and instantly began shaming yourself for it mentally. How about as an adult? You wanted that donut so badly, but then had nothing but negative things to say to yourself when you decided to eat it.

"I'm going to get fat if I keep doing this." "I know it's not good for me, but it tastes so good that I don't care." Or how about this one, "I can't believe I'm so stupid!" That last one hits home for me. Why do we keep reiterating how stupid how we are, even though we are not? Its trained behavior based on a series of beliefs we adopted as children. Our childhood has a far greater impact on us than any other generation before us could ever have known. We are learning so much about how those formative years shape our adult selves and solidify concrete blocks in our thinking that can drown us if we don't take the chisel out and do some forceful chipping at the edges. You know that they are drowning you when a flood comes and you are so rooted in misguided thinking that you sink, rather than float. Sinking, as it implies, is the feeling we get when we "just can't" anymore. We just have nothing stable to keep us going safely along and we "lose it". Bear in mind too that some of those concrete blocks in your head are your foundation materials and must be examined to see if they are still in good shape!

Are they cracked? Do they need to be replaced or repaired? Is there a leak in your foundation that requires mending. Concrete blocks have utility because they have shaped you. What shape are you? More importantly, what shape are you in?

There are 3 stages of gratitude (Law, 2020)

RECOGNITION

Feeling grateful is the first step, even if it's difficult to learn how to begin. Cultivating feelings of deep gratefulness can start with the smallest recognition. Like I pointed out, how often are you grateful to your body for the miraculous wonders it performs for you every second of every day? Thankfulness is defined as being "pleased or relieved" and to be grateful is "showing an appreciation of kindness". These are not the same but connected by linking feeling to action.

ACKNOWLEDGEMENT

Expressing gratitude comes in many forms. A mindfulness practice to realign yourself to what is truly important in life is a vital step in seeing the goodness all around you. There are many people, things and moments that make our lives better. Paying heed to these aspects and influences by acknowledging their presence goes miles for our mental wellbeing. We change our optics by choosing what to focus on and allow ourselves to adjust to a new mindset that highlights everything wonderful around us. New lenses, new view.

APPRECIATION

Changing our habitual behaviors by consciously paying attention to our blessings sends ripples out to the entire world of our dedication to feeling good. We are not going to feel good about everything going on all the time, and we wouldn't want to. But this new mindset and behavioral pattern can help us through those challenging times with the resilience we need to move through "it" with a powerful inner strength. Religions speak about the power of prayer. Affirming your appreciation outwardly and inwardly can indeed be a form of prayer for some; but even without religious connotations we can reap the benefits of a more appreciative mental attitude by paying the proper amount of attention.

SIX Gratitude Examples that you can Practice

Be Grateful for Things You Hate

This seems highly contradictory, but how many lessons have you learned in life due to something you hated? I bet, more than a few. There are valuable lessons to be gained from experiences, people and situations that make us angry and hateful. Those emotions are there to keep you on track, uphold boundaries and look hard at uncomfortable parts of ourselves. They can even challenge our belief structures, which is not as bad as it seems. Some of our most difficult emotions come out of challenging situations. Contemplate that for a while.

Start a Gratitude Journal

I mentioned this earlier. A once-a-week gratitude practice, in a journal, helps you track your progression as you rewrite your brain and the beliefs that exist within you. Make it a fun challenge by finding different gratitude "triggers" each time you write, rather than repeating yourself every week with the same lines. A "trigger" can be something that makes you feel lighter rather than heavier, expansive as opposed to contractive.

Count Your Blessings

Ah, back to the noisy children again! Are the losses you have perceived actually blessings in disguise? Are the hardships you've faced traumas, or character-building experiences? We face many challenges in life and yet we continue to wake up every single day and survive everything we go through, no matter how tragic and painful it might feel in the moment. Your survival rate is 100% so far; that's a huge blessing in my mind, and worth a timely reminder.

Say More Thank Yous

This might feel like a redundant or useless practice at first, but it really helps you pinpoint some of the services that are being offered to you in places you have not recognized until now. The worker in a store stocking shelves; randomly thank them for their effort. They are working for you! Your legs. Yes, you read that right! Thank your legs for moving you forward and the muscles it takes to do that, the ligaments that make your knees bend and the bones that hold the whole structure of YOU together. Thank your legs, they work hard for you, and you would miss them if they were to suddenly disappear or be rendered useless.

Watch & Read Things That Motivate You

In our technological age, we have motivation on tap, at our fingertips, anywhere, anytime. You can get audiobooks, motivational speeches, documentaries, even TED talks and other lectures on a topic you are currently interested in. What are you doing to stimulate new processes in your brain? Don't watch something familiar just because you know about it. Actively search out new information. This practice will keep your brain young and engaged, and might just lead you down a rabbit hole of potential that was buried deep in your subconscious, just screaming to get out! Motivation and momentum are NOT the same thing. Motivation is what gets us fired up about something, momentum is what keeps us there. You need both.

Express Gratitude in Challenging Moments

Have you had to have a difficult conversation with your partner because they had to bring up something that bothered them? Did it trigger a negative reaction in you? Or maybe your boss said something that made you angry and you stewed over it for hours? You can silently express your gratitude towards a person you're interacting with, while they're talking. Remember to pay attention to what they're saying too, but in your mind, you can begin to say things like "I love the way (insert person's name here) lips move when they speak." "I am so grateful they feel comfortable talking to me, even about hard things" "(Person's name) is really a great listener, I am so grateful for that." By offering this silent gratitude practice towards another person in what might have been a difficult emotional moment for both of you, you are activating the hydroelectric properties within us all. Water, and electricity course through our veins and thoughts are a wavelength.

This dynamic makes it possible for us to think things about people in ways that they feel our grateful thoughts within themselves. They may become uncomfortable and get quiet. They might begin fidgeting. They will perhaps visibly calm down. The reaction is based on their purpose for speaking with you, like we mentioned earlier. Are they trying to persuade you, create a solution, perhaps they just want to argue? Try it, the results may just surprise you.

Gratitude practice helps people acknowledge the goodness in their lives. People can feel higher levels of positive emotions overall, find more joy in ordinary experiences, improve health on a broad scale spectrum, deal with adverse situations with greater resilience, and build strong relationships.

What Does a Lack of Gratitude Look Like?

The Cambridge Dictionary defines gratitude as "a strong feeling of appreciation to someone or something for what the person has done to help you". (Dictionary, n.d.) Without a gratitude attitude we limit ourselves to the amount of love we are willing to receive and give. Everyone wants to feel loved, and gratitude is the fertilizer that makes our leaves a bit greener, our roots grow stronger and deeper, and helps us reach for the sun and praise all the wonders around us.

Plants do not necessarily "feel or express" gratitude for existing. They too have ecosystems living within themselves, just like we do. Endophytes are tiny plants and fungi that live inside of other plants. They have their own chemical needs and can influence the plants or change their makeup to get what they need to survive.

Why do I bring this up? What could that have to do with us as people? You have living organisms inside of you that are driven by chemical processes. You are a thermodynamic being. When you feed a feeling by expressing it, a craving by eating, and develop habits, you are feeding something inside of you. One group of organisms are cheering for your vitality and success by encouraging you through a series of chemical processes that elicit feelings of calm, strength, health, and vitality. Another group of organisms feed a cycle of decomposition, taking for themselves what they need to survive while leaving you feeling depleted, uncomfortable, unsatisfied, and unhealthy.

You know the parable of the two wolves living inside of you right? Whichever one you feed is the one who will grow stronger. You've got to be mindful of which one you are feeding, because if you are making a choice unconsciously, chances are the decomposition team of organisms are in control. Your health may deteriorate dramatically, and often it is not a quick descent, but a long hard road of health issues, mental gymnastics, discordant relationships, and all forms of chaos inside and outside of your body. Lacking gratitude feeds the decomposition organisms and stimulates chemical distribution centers in the brain that elicit feelings of stress, worry, fear, anxiety, and many other negatively associated feelings.

Expressing gratitude feeds the organisms that help you thrive. The act of feeling grateful floods your body with oxytocin, which science has proven helps us feel calmer, happier and in a loving space. Your body responds by having more energy and carries you through the world with a sense of order in your daily lived experience. Even if you are going through immense pain, oxytocin reduces the pain response, giving you a higher tolerance for adversity. The cooperative organisms in your body, AKA the regeneration organisms, go to work repairing all the places we have stopped paying attention to. What happens if they can't do their jobs? They begin to rot and so do you. I know that sounds gross, but that's all aging is anyway, a natural process of decomposition. We can prolong and extend this cycle of course. It's obviously not just gratitude that will get you back into this cycle of repair, there are many factors and aspects of life that need to be addressed. I am saying that gratitude practice can get the process started in a powerful way, leading to many other practices and opportunities to help your body function at an optimum level. It can build the momentum you need so you can get through something painful, recover quicker and feel at ease while it runs its course.

It Sounds Like Science Fiction but it's Really Just Science

Let's get back to plants. Have you noticed how some house plants in the winter will look dull, a bit droopy and pale in color? I have a lot of them that I pay close attention to, so I notice these subtle changes in their appearance as the seasons change. I give them more fertilizer during the winter months because they need the pick-me-up. A nearly fluorescent glow begins to emanate from them, and they perk up with incredible vitality. Gratitude is fertilizer for people. You won't need it all the time once you learn how to use it. When you are happy and in an environment that supports you, you will naturally thrive. When times are harder, you may need a boost to get you through until the next sunny times. The trick is in knowing when those moments are, by paying attention to your rhythms and cycles and understanding at which times are harder or more stressful for you, when you'll need a dose of gratitude fertilizer to ride out a storm in grace.

Personal Story

In 2021, as I was learning about gratitude on a whole new level and how to use my language in better ways, I discovered (by accident) that I could tap into gratitude during the most complicated moments of my life. Instead of speaking, which has always been my default mode when something isn't working, I sat silently with myself. My partner and I were fighting for about 2 days and not coming to any logical solutions that would move us both forward. During the middle of the second day, we were both emotionally spent, and our minds were racing. I wanted to say more, get to the bottom of the issue, talk it out. I was taught as a kid that we need to talk until the solution or closure was found. This wasn't working anymore.

We couldn't connect with one another in a meaningful way, so I went inward. We were sitting together on our bed, both in our heads over the entire mess we were in. I decided to try out a gratitude practice that I hadn't fully conceptualized yet. I laid back on the bed, took several deep breaths and began thinking of all the reasons I loved my partner. I visualized his smile, his toes, his leathery hands, and with each visualization, I made sure to say "I am so grateful for…" before each item I noted. This was my lead in… The gratitude evolved into a deeper language. "I am grateful that I can appreciate the little aspects of my partner." "I am grateful that we met." "I am so very grateful for this current challenge we are going through." "…that our souls have aligned in this moment to shed light on all the places I still resist my highest self." "…that the light within each of us knows the way forward." "…that our highest selves will not come down to the petty level we have chosen to engage in." "…that our love resides as the foundation of everything we do, which radiates through this current struggle." And so on.

As this gratitude began to develop, he placed a hand on my leg. He hadn't touched me in over a day and could hardly look in my direction. This was not a coincidence. We never finished the conversation that created that argument. I laid there on our bed for one and half hours silently chanting my gratitude into the Universal Vibration, allowing it to imbue every inch of my being. We didn't need to discuss it further; it didn't matter what the problem had been. I had vibrationally interrupted the frequency that was keeping us locked into a low level function where conflict lives. After that meditation, I sat up and kissed his cheek. He did not immediately come out of the haze that our argument created but was receptive to my cue of affection and for the rest of the day, we spoke kindly to one another, and sparsely. We were no longer emotionally volatile, and we slowly came back to the divine love that our relationship is built on. Energy transference took place and he physically felt all the gratitude that I was silently sending into our energy field.

I spent another hour and a half later that evening doing this practice again. By that point we were lying together, my head on his chest, quietly being with ourselves. I lifted my awareness to focusing on the divine aspects that were connecting us, as though we were one being, as though I was breathing with his lungs, feeling the sensations on his skin, and our flesh was singular. When I delved into this deep mediation that melded us together, he squeezed me a little bit and sighed.

I must point out here that he was unaware that I was doing this, and I didn't tell him that I had done this meditation until many months later. I have used this method to realign our collective energies when we have a disagreement. It doesn't stop us from talking to one another. What it does for me is to let me respond in ways that elicit a love reaction rather than that of fear. It also flooded his energy field with love, rather than distress. It interrupted the dis-ease we were both feeling so we could remember what was important. It helps me communicate better too because I can focus on the real energy underlying the experience. Even though it can still be uncomfortable, the pain is lessened by using this practice, and our dialog is truer to the love that we both want to express. From a scientific standpoint I can see that I was flooding my body with oxytocin by focusing on the love. This lessened the pain I was experiencing which made it possible for my rational and logical thinking to come through so that whatever conversation was necessary to have, was done in grace, rather than reactivity.

Fertilization: Introduction to Gratitude as a Practice

- **Gratitude journal practice begins:** List 5 things every single day this week. We are setting the groundwork for a practice of gratitude that you will be able to continue once a week as it becomes a new habit. This daily practice will get you into the mindset of when you will need to use it in the future. So be sure to make this practice a priority. You can do it in the morning or at night, whichever fits into your schedule best. Art it! Make this practice your own by adding pictures if you have them. You don't have to just list your gratitude; you can make it however colorful and creative you want to. Perhaps you find a lot of fun images that represent a meaningful part of your life. Paste them in and then label them with gratitude tags.

- **Creating** a micro-ritual with 5 minutes of gratitude thinking every morning when you first wake up and every night before bed by just thinking to yourself about anything you are grateful for. This can help begin and end your day with fertilizer for your mind. This practice is easy to do because it's all internal and requires no tools, journaling, or other external devices. Continue this practice every day so your mind can learn how to focus on all the things going well in your life. This practice aligns your head and heart to the intuitive thoughts that reside in the unseen and is worthy of your attention.

- **OPTIONAL:** Make a reminder poster if you feel inspired to do so; some people are more artistic and have more time than others. This poster should be simple but gives you a visual cue to keep you on track with your new habit building practices. It could be a reminder for a once-a-week moment of gratitude, your movement exercise, your stream of consciousness writing, anything that you need help remembering so you prioritize it daily.

WEEK 5

You are Enough.

"With NO Prerequisites"

"The only thing that's keeping you from getting what you want is the story you keep telling yourself."

– Tony Robbins

MENTAL HEALTH: IT'S MINE, YOURS AND EVERYONE ELSE'S TOO

We have talked quite extensively about belief systems already. One of the negative core beliefs we can develop as children is a sense of unworthiness. This can manifest itself in a number of ways, through perfectionism, doubting ourselves, cutting off our connection to others, and the feeling of being unlovable regardless of what we do, who we are, and how we show up for the world.

The truth is that this sense of unworthiness can prevent us from showing up. It locks us into a spiral of shame that infiltrates our lives and lines every experience we have. When we believe we are unlovable as a core belief, our mental chatter and the "critic" in our heads becomes the predominant voice that fuels our subconscious drives. The subconscious is where much of our creative power is rooted. Therefore, when you aren't managing your life on a conscious level, your subconscious is at the steering wheel, driving you to all the experiences that have become the core of who you are on a fundamental level. The greatest danger of wearing a subconscious badge of being unlovable/unworthy is that our brains will lead us to anything *it* understands that will validate that belief.

This has its pitfalls. We have all experienced varying degrees of this kind of manifestation within our lives. Whether it's the pattern of coupling with people that do not value us, getting right up against our goals and falling short, consistently finding ourselves in situations where we feel stuck, trapped, or paralyzed by our circumstances, working very hard and never achieving the big goals we set for ourselves, having difficulty forming stable relationships with friends and family, and so many more. The list of symptoms for this negative core belief structure is lengthy, but the ones above are the most common across all walks of life.

I have addressed the idea that we are whole beings regardless of what we have been taught by our experiences and interactions with people, our culture, and media input. The truth is, many of us don't really believe that we are whole, which is why we keep "finding ourselves" in undesirable life events that keep affirming that we will never be "enough" regardless of what we accomplish, who we become, and how we live our lives. So why try? It can become defeating, resulting in depressive states, high anxiety, social dysphoria, despair, and other mental health issues that are usually treated with medication by most official agencies set up in our society. This is a symptom though, and not the core of the issue. I question here whether, if they got to the root of the cause, would medication be necessary? Would it become a therapy of the past once we begin treating people on a fundamental level of belief, by teaching mental exercises that rewrite these adopted beliefs? I believe that this book is a big step in that direction. If we decided that there was nothing wrong with us to begin with, we wouldn't need medication (perhaps), because we are in fact, not ill. We are just thinking incorrectly, and not because we want to! We would never intentionally generate abusive situations or beat ourselves up by affirming our unworthiness repeatedly, like a mantra. We would never, never, I repeat, never, if we knew this beyond the shadow of a doubt, pass onto our children debilitating belief systems that would staunch their potential and dim their shine. We do though. We have shameful ways of speaking to one another, we affirm repeatedly how limited we are, we pass on all the generational belief systems that have kept us so mentally stuck that we have developed entire organizations around mental illness/health and medicine.

I am proposing that most people would not even need these "services", and I put it in quotes because I use this term loosely when referring to the resources we have available for this particular area of our everyday lives. I am proposing here that, regardless of what you have been told throughout your entire life and which you subconsciously repeat to yourself, you are 100% worthy, capable and so very lovable that you can achieve anything, have the love you desire, and feel so completely satisfied your life, that you need nothing outside of yourself to keep the dopamine and oxytocin hormonal balance at peak performance.

Why dopamine and oxytocin?

We humans are designed to seek pleasure. Satisfaction in life is one of the core driving functions that keep everyone moving, every single day. Dopamine is our chemical rewards system, as well as the chemical responsible for craving, motivation, and drive. Historically, this has kept us alive by associating survival habits with high reward. When we harvested berries, conquered an enemy, or engaged with our tribe in meaningful ways, we would get a shot of dopamine that would make some of the challenging aspects of life worthwhile. Addiction is a process that has hijacked our dopamine receptors to provide more pleasure when engaging with substances or situations that can be detrimental to our health by dumping large quantities of dopamine on us all at once. The problem with this is that once we balance back out, our baseline is lower than before, and lower, and so on each time we indulge. This backwards method of satiating our dopamine requirements has led to many unsatisfying habits we develop in life. The kicker here is that it is all executed on a subconscious level, so you aren't even aware you are being hijacked. You feel high, and you are satisfied, temporarily. We can and are addicted to everything under the sun, even seemingly benign things. Whether it's a person, a particular type of interaction, a substance, food or even the act of shopping, and that phone in your hand. We have addictions that activate our dopamine chemical systems to keep us feeling pleasure and satisfaction by engaging with external stimuli that will provide the desired feeling we end up chasing and/or craving. Andrew Huberman (Huberman, 2022) talks about how dopamine plays a major role in our lives, and he speaks on this subject in far greater detail than I could. If you are interested in learning more about how dopamine works, he has additional resources that you might find useful.

Now that we have gazed upon the maze of dopamine and the role it plays in our subconscious programming daily habitual practices, we can begin to understand why we do what we do. That leads us to oxytocin, which we did just mention, but there is more to say about this amazing chemical that is naturally occurring in our miraculous brains. Oxytocin is most recognized with the process of giving birth. It's vital in getting a baby into the body by creating that over-the-top love feeling we get when we are engaged with another. Therefore, we call it "falling in love" because it's like a fall over the edge of a cliff and oxytocin is what gives you wings. (OK, Red Bull gives you wings too, but those are jet powered. Just saying.) Oxytocin is a major component in regulating the pain of childbirth. You have to understand that we need incentives to do hard things, especially painful ones, and childbirth has been scientifically proven to be one of the most painful experiences a human can endure. Is the reward great? Of course, you get another human being out of the deal. Oxytocin floods your entire body to counteract the pain you experience during childbirth. I bring this to your attention because we often don't associate oxytocin with other, less eventful, aspects of our lives and don't understand how it works in our personal lived experience. I am going to lay a truth bomb here that will hopefully get you thinking about this in a very real way.

Oxytocin regulates emotional response

Read that again and let it sink in for a moment. *Oxytocin regulates emotional response.* This is vital in understanding why you react the way you do to everything you encounter. Emotional regulation is a core function that every single human being needs to survive in this world. Regardless of the era, the culture, the programming, the job, the relationship, the power structure of your nation, it is about how YOU interact with the world. It is about how YOU respond to it, and that, my friends, is worth more than its weight in gold. Remember what I told you about unworthiness? How many people walk around with a belief that they are not enough? Well, well, well, we are getting somewhere with that now, aren't we? Our unworthiness stems from dysregulation of oxytocin. Hm. That's a powerful statement. How can we ever feel unworthy if our love chemical response system is working properly for us? How can we ever feel unlovable if we have a chemical in our brains that keeps pumping us with the cocktail we need to feel and know that we are lovable?

Our emotional regulation is so out of control that we have lost touch with one of the most significant processes our bodies have to keep us feeling well. I am not referring to that temporary feeling that addiction provides, but an ongoing, long lasting, on-drip, tap of a wellspring of empowering chemical Kool-Aid that we have access to, 24/7. How then can we possibly EVER feel anything but incredibly blessed and grateful? We do, and it's absolutely normal. We need conflict too, but more on that later. By the way, gratitude releases oxytocin. (Kader, 2015) quotes Dr. Susan Ferguson this in an article from Seattle Children's Hospital about how oxytocin and gratitude are connected.

We covered the fact that childhood trauma sets us up for adulthood in some concrete ways. Did you ever know, as a child, that you had this internal chemical regulator within your own body? Did anyone ever tell you that you can tap that chemical wellspring to regulate some of the more complicated emotions you were going through? Of course not. Because we never knew. But science does know this now. So why isn't it being taught to everyone? You are born with all the medication you need to regulate your physical body perfectly.

(Disclaimer: There are of course, certain individuals who are born with, or acquire by accident or disease, abnormalities in the brain that can affect the way their chemical and emotional regulation works for them. This is not a one size fits all generalization and there will always be exceptions to anything I present in this book.)

Take a deep breath. I know, you're still reading… so don't close your eyes. But stop for a moment and think about the pharmacopeia inside of you. A little alchemy shop in your head stocked with bottles and vials of glowing, electric liquid that a quirky shopkeeper wants to sell to you.

If you didn't know about this before, think of the devastation you have caused by rampaging into this shop, toppling shelves, and drinking anything you thought might help you in a moment of dire need. The scene is disturbing to say the least. No well-meaning person would ever do this in real life, and yet, this is exactly what we do when we are not in control of our chemical, emotional regulation faculties that were given to us at birth. Let's take a detour on this for a moment to discuss something else.

Serotonin and Adrenaline - the quiet effectors

Serotonin is a chemical that many people are quite familiar with because it primarily regulates sleep and mood. We understand this on a common level. It also plays a huge part in our entertainment, happiness, appetite, and even sexual arousal. Serotonin has gotten the spotlight on our world stage as a vital part of what makes our lives exciting, calm, and fun. Fun is a huge component to what makes you feel balanced and whole. Well, feeling whole is what we strive for, on a base functioning level. There are so many aspects of living that use serotonin regulation that we saturate ourselves or inhibit ourselves from its release based on what we think will make us feel "good". This can get confusing, really fast, because some of what we were taught makes us "feel good" is actually harming us.

Appetite is a good place to start because we eat, right? That one is blatantly obvious because it's so ingrained in our survival mechanisms that we often don't consciously pay much attention to it. We want food that tastes "good". The problem here is that the food in our modern age is not "created" to taste good AND be healthy for us. Sugar is a great example here because it boosts the serotonin in our brains, alleviating anxiety and improving our mood. Of course, we want more of that! So, every time we eat sugar to elicit this response, it's essentially like going into our mental store and downing a bottle of serotonin liquid. We say, "ahhhh, that was satisfying! Effervescent even." However, while we are feeling calm and chill, our pancreas is contemplating its existence as it slowly atrophies because it's no longer able to do its job while we keep shoveling sugar into our bodies in increasing increments. I'll call myself out right now, I eat more sugar than most people consider "healthy". Diet is something personal and new age hype tells us a lot of "truths" that don't mesh with everyone universally. So beware.

Stay with me, folks. I'm about to drop another truth bomb that no one wants to hear. You get the same serotonin release by exercise, sunlight, massage and… wait for it…. remembering happy events. This means that you can intentionally regulate your serotonin levels without reaching for a donut. This is especially helpful for me because I really like donuts! However, I don't always feel so good when I eat them, even though I think they taste wonderful and they "make me happy".

If remembering happy events can boost our serotonin release response, then why do we walk around telling everyone about all the horrible things taking place in our lives as a default? I know you've done it, particularly when stressed out, and I sure have too. And I know that it's sometimes easier to lie to people and say, "I'm fine", instead of unloading all our horrible experiences onto an innocent party who asked a seemingly simple question. What matters aside from all of that is that you THOUGHT about those horrible things even though you may not have voiced them in that moment. By thinking about them, you keep them alive and thriving in your conscious creative positioning.

Moving on

Adrenaline is a valuable component of our health when it's used properly. It is a hormone secreted by the adrenal glands. Everyone agrees on that, and its function is to increase our blood circulation, metabolize carbohydrates and prepare muscles for exertion, and not to mention breathing. These are all important and vital functions for health and wellbeing. Great, we should be feeling amazing right? Not always. Adrenaline is called the stress hormone for a reason. I know it's not a chemical made by the brain like the others

I've mentioned here, but it works for us, or against us, in the same ways and we need to understand this to fully take responsibility for our emotional regulation. Cortisol has gotten a bad rap as well because we use it incorrectly. Cortisol is the chemical that gets you up and moving. It can work perfectly for us in the morning when we need to be up, take action, and plan the day. It works against us when we are in a stressful environment, and it ramps up production telling us in no uncertain terms, "you are in danger and need to run. NOW." You can't argue with it. It's a primal response to danger and has its function. All our emotional regulation faculties work for or against us depending on how we are employing them.

"Overproduction of adrenaline is very common. Most people are exposed to stressful situations on occasion and so most of us are familiar with the typical symptoms of adrenaline release, such as: rapid heartbeat, high blood pressure, anxiety, weight loss, excessive sweating, and palpitations."
I believe this article (You and Your Hormones, 2021) gives us a simple enough explanation of what can happen when we overuse and misuse this valuable resource. Anxiety can result from being overstressed. This lowers your immune response, can affect your cortisol levels, and leaves you feeling tired and overworked, even if you haven't done anything to warrant it. Why am I bringing this up in a chapter about worthiness? I will take you back to one of our first chapters when I was discussing childhood trauma. The fight or flight reaction we get in stressful situations is the activation of the sympathetic nervous system which signals the release of adrenaline.

The correlation between the memories you make, and the chemical responses evoked by those memories will affect how you experience life as an adult. We are alchemical beings, as well as being electrical in nature.

There are many more chemicals we haven't covered, simply to avoid the scientific jargon required to discuss them usefully. One reason it's important to be aware of these chemicals is that even plants use chemical signatures and messengers so they too can survive in their environments.

The Chemical World of Plants

Plants have evolved many secondary metabolites that they use to defend themselves. These toxic chemicals can deter natural predators by emitting a strong odor, or with stinging cells and trichomes that inject histamines to irritate a hungry animal trying to eat them. They also have chemical safeguards built in that kill insects, fungi, and bacteria.

Plants have made all kinds of evolutionary adaptations to survive within an environment. In desert regions where there is little water, lots of wind and blazing sunshine, plants will grow deeper roots that can store water and may have smaller leaves. We also adapt to our environments; this is called epigenetics. Scientists have discovered that we can change our cellular health by changing the environment we are in. So, even though we may have adapted to an unhealthy environment that is not suitable for our highest growth, the good news is that we can adjust some key elements within our lives and literally rewrite cellular structure, neuronal pathways in the brain, physical health, and our emotional regulation systems.

The reason we must have this level of awareness of our own body's functioning is explained above; we are all individual cocktails of chemicals that have evolved to our personal environments, just like plants. Have you developed your chemical makeup to repel other people with your toxic traits? Have you become people pleasing as a form of camouflage so you can blend into your surroundings and don't get eaten? Have you set up internal modes of thinking that have become a detriment to yourself just so you can survive an abusive situation?

These are normal! I can't stress that enough. There is absolutely nothing wrong with you. You have evolved to survive within the environment you have been living in. The reason this is so vital for everyone to understand is that you have the power and ability to change it at any time.

Again, with plants you will notice that a dandelion growing in a crack of cement is not as lush and vibrant as one growing in a verdant field. Similarly, a rose bush in the shade may not produce as many blossoms as one grown in a sunnier spot. The amount of water, light, and protection from wind and pests, will all determine the way a plant will react and respond to its environment. Each of these plants have endophytes living inside of them that dictate how the plant will respond to certain situations, as well as other bacterial, fungal and parasitic organisms that also dictate certain characteristics the plant will display.

What does any of this have to do with worthiness?

The definition of worthiness speaks directly to this. The feeling of being good enough. We often don't feel good enough to move through life with confidence, make positive choices for ourselves or feel like we deserve attention or respect. It is more than just saying something is "good enough" as is, it must be felt and accepted before any kind of change can take place.

wor·thi·ness
/wur-thee-nis/
noun

1. the quality of being good enough; suitability.
ex: "he demonstrates his worthiness to rule"

2. the quality of deserving attention or respect.
Ex: "an argument about the moral worthiness of the nation's founders"

Changing our mental state around worthiness can dramatically influence the way we view ourselves within the world, and how we move through it (I know, I'm repeating myself. Repetition is a mantra. You become what you repeat). Worthiness provides the nutrients our brains need to maintain empowering thought forms and keep our neuro pathways flowing like a school of fish in the sea rather than a barren desert landscape devoid of life.

On a podcast with Lewis Howes on Youtube, clinical Psychologist Nicole LePera points out that presence practices can be more uncomfortable for people who do not feel safe in their own bodies. Tolerating discomfort helps develop awareness, which is the foundation of being able to pay attention. What we pay attention to is what we will experience. When we are processing trauma, we create physical health issues because we disconnect from the body. It is important to reconnect to the body through conscious and meditative practices. (LePera, 2021)

"A lot of us are blocked creatively because of our relationship to ourselves." LePera told Lewis Howes. She also went on to say that when we don't feel safe in our bodies, we have become so dysregulated on a core level that we can't even tap into our creativity at all.

Dr Rahul Jandial, a neurosurgeon, describes our brain as a global environment. *"There aren't regions in the brain. There is no spot for something. It can be in harmony. Irrigate the garden (of the brain) by keeping the arteries open. Exercise while thinking is one of the greatest electro-chemical regulators for the brain."* (Jandial, 2022)

It would not be right to write a chapter on worthiness and leave out Marissa Peer and Brene Brown. Marissa Peer is a world-renowned speaker, Rapid Transformational Therapy trainer and best-selling author, and has developed a practice for people that consists of writing "I am enough" on your mirror and reading it every morning. (Peer, n.d.)

Brene Brown is known for her research on shame, vulnerability, and leadership. She defines worthiness as *"the conviction that you are good enough as you are, flaws and all, and that you deserve to be loved. In simpler terms, we might conceive it as having high self-esteem."* (Brown, 2010)

Both influential authors and speakers point out that we must be accepting of who we are right now, flaws and all. That is our foundation for changing our mindset, awareness and attention that will help us love ourselves. We can overwrite the disempowering beliefs that have been inserted, so it becomes possible to live a healthier life. We must love ourselves first before we can love anything outside of us. It always feels easier to love external people, places, or things. When we turn that love inward, when we shower ourselves with all the love we have been pouring into everything "out there", the life changing effects are dramatic.

Resistance to this is also normal so don't think you are incapable of achieving this just because you feel resistant to the practice of self-love. It does not make you a narcissist to love yourself wholly, and it is not selfish. It is a requirement to live your full potential and step into a life that supports you. You must support yourself by loving everything about you, right now, as is. This can be especially challenging for anyone who has experienced situations or people that have knocked them down every time they begin to feel good about themselves. It is much more common than we would ever want to think. Pursuit towards a goal for self-development is valuable, yes. I will say this though, when we take the time to stabilize ourselves in the fact that we are okay as we are, then can we begin to move forward through personal pursuits of changing our reality.

Personal Story

I have never been "enough" regardless of how many tools I was given. Having said that, I will explain why this has plagued me. When I was a kid, I was a straight A student, on honor roll, and involved in extracurricular activities and events throughout the years. Anything under a B grade was devastating for me. In fourth grade I got a C. I remember my mom going into the classroom and asking the teacher why I got such a low grade. She was so proactive during our school years, mostly because she hated that we had to go and pulled us out whenever it suited her, which I must say was an absolute blessing. Nowadays she would probably be arrested for the amount of school time my sister and I missed. Anyway, she talked to my teacher, Mr. Pontias (we called him Mr. Pontiac, like the car) and he told her that the C was given so that I would have something to strive for because I seemed to do well in anything I applied myself to, and he was concerned that I would lose my "drive" if I got high grades in all places. Hm. I was so pissed. My mom was also pissed. The C became a B+ because I did deserve the higher grade. The experience taught me that my efforts were being graded by arbitrary forces and were not necessarily reflective of my proficiency. This was really bad for my "drive".

Let's go back to kindergarten. I was 5, so that's pretty early on. I had already been taught at home how to use a pen, write my name, read some basic things, and use scissors. So, does that give me an edge? I figured everyone in my class knew the same things I did, so I didn't question it. We all liked to eat the rice from the giant barrels anyway, so we were the same right? Well, not according to my teacher. Whoever this woman thought she was, I'm not so sure she should have been teaching children of any age. I don't even remember her name, but I bet my mother does. She called my mom to a meeting one time because (and this is exactly what she said) "Your daughter is alienating the other students because she cuts so much better than them with her scissors." Hm. Can you guess what happened next? I bet you can't, because it's so outrageous that I developed a fixation for scissors that I still have at 40. The teacher took my scissors away and had me tear all my work. At age 5, I was forced to tear my paper because I could use scissors with some skill. Yep. I am just not worthy… I fail at everything. All the adults in authoritative positions keep telling me so. I got so good at tearing paper that you couldn't tell it was torn. I was a fiercely stubborn child so if you told me I couldn't, I would somehow find a way. She let me have my scissors back eventually, but I hated her for the rest of the year.

Last one. Just to solidify the first two examples for you in case you didn't quite get the picture yet. I think I was in second grade (you'll have to confirm with my mom, she remembers that better than I do) and I was getting super interested in calligraphy. My mother has gorgeous handwriting. We had calligraphy books at home, so my mom let me "play" with them. She was cool like that. What is the best place to practice any new skill? At school of course! The place of learning, where the teacher can give you feedback and encourage you. NO. That's not true. I just said that to test you. When my spelling lists started coming back marked down, my mom again had to come to the school. My spelling was fine. I was good at it. It was my handwriting that was getting marks against it. I would write my spelling lists in calligraphy. She didn't like that. My words were all spirally and frilly and had whisps shooting off them in places. This was unacceptable, even though it was quite legible. So, I had to stop doing that. We were mad again, but I practiced at home instead and kept school separate from the other skills I was learning outside of the establishment. Yep. This child is doomed… How I ever managed to become an adult despite my schooling experiences (and the stories go far beyond what I've shared here), I'll never know. Reinforcing my unworthiness is the key lesson I got in school, and it didn't seem to matter what I did, I just failed at everything.

Chemically Upgrading our DNA with: "I am Always Enough"

- **Write** "I am Enough" on your mirror or in a journal every single day. If you feel resistance to it, do it anyway but add your own language to it. Make it your own by adding words that resonate with you. As I mentioned above, Marissa Peers is the source of this practice so I highly recommend looking into her further for more great wisdom from this incredible researcher because she can go deeper into why this works.

- ❖ Mine was *"I am always enough, with NO prerequisites."* I had to add the last part because my worthiness has always been attached to what I could give, produce and be for OTHERS. But I am worthy without first doing anything to warrant it. It helped to solidify the new thought pattern quicker when I attached something relevant to my personal situation. When I started out with "I am enough" only, there was nothing in that statement I really believed at the time. We must believe it to benefit from this affirming practice.

- ❖ **What keeps you from believing it?** Why do I believe I am unlovable/unworthy? You don't even have to answer it right away, just the action of writing it down is going to get your brain moving in the direction of the answer. When it does come to you, write down everything that shows up. There may be many "reasons" that are rooted in false beliefs about yourself. By identifying these false beliefs, you can rewrite them, like we did in the previous chapter by listing them on one side of a page and writing out the truth across it on the other.

- ❖ **Journal Practice:** Art page of hearts! Write compassionate statements about yourself. This can be fun and hard at the same time. Cut out hearts of various sizes and colors if you have colored paper. Basic copy paper works fine too. Write out statements like "I am beautiful", "I am smart and funny", I love my smile", "my feet are wonderful!", "I see myself as a good friend", "this is a valuable person" on your hearts.

- ❖ **ART IT!** Please take the time to print out a minimum of 3 small pictures of yourself. You may notice things about this person later in the course as your awareness develops. It's always helpful to have a visual representation that you can look back on. Don't pick your best pics… just the ones that feel right at the time. This is not a requirement, but when you visually surround yourself with love, it has a greater impact on you every time you go back and review this page. Put your pictures in the center of the page and surround yourself with all the affirming compassion you added to your pile of hearts. It becomes a beautiful piece of art that will fill you with joy when you look at it. And for me, whenever I was in the throes of a devastating shame spiral, I would open to this page, cry and read everything I had written about myself. It didn't always help pull me out of it, but it blunted the blow of my emotional turmoil and got that oxytocin flowing again because I remembered making it, and I remembered feeling GOOD when I had.

WEEK 6

The Gremlins in the Closet, "Finding Balance"

"I must also have a dark side if I am to be whole" - Carl Jung

WHAT IS A GREMLIN IN PSYCHOLOGY?

You know that nagging, gnawing voice in your head that has nothing but terrible things to say about you? What the heck is that? Why do we have such a critical, nasty voice that only we can hear? How does that help us? A gremlin is an internal habit or feeling that often speaks to us in a voice that sounds like our own. It can stop us from taking action on or completing a goal. It can sabotage us by insisting that something is dangerous, risky, or scary. It picks fault with the things you do, comes up with excuses that sound perfectly logical, and has all kinds of disparaging comments about you that can hold you back from doing something beneficial for yourself. Some have called this voice, "The Critic". It is well named because it is very good at finding all sorts of critical things to say. According to Freud, the critic is a product of the superego, which is the part of the psyche that is responsible for our sense of right and wrong and our moral standards. The superego is often in conflict with the id, which is the part of the psyche that represents our primal desires and drives.

Freud believed that the critic helped to mediate this conflict by exerting control over the id's impulses and helping the individual to behave in a way that is socially acceptable. However, he also believed that the critic could become overbearing and overly strict, leading to feelings of guilt and anxiety in the individual. (Freud)

The Mental Landscape

We are going to engage in the practice of "weeding our gardens" by pulling out the disempowering thought forms of The Critic that will gladly tell us we are not enough, and that we are stupid for attempting to achieve our dreams and goals. Your mind is a glorious garden, filled with so many beautiful flowering plants that feed your consciousness. However, weeds grow there too, and if not maintained, can infiltrate and take over even the sunniest patches that you have carefully tended. Weeds have deep roots, so waiting to snag hold of them until they have grown into monstrosities will make them more difficult to remove. When they are small and tender, we can pluck them out without a second thought and won't have to come back the next year to get the pieces of roots, or even the seedlings that took hold when we let that weed go to flower and it reseeded itself while we weren't paying attention. Keeping our awareness fixed on all the undesirable plants in our Mind Garden and removing them at the first signs of life is the only way to rid ourselves of their devastating effects, and guarantee that the next year's crop of flourishing plant life will not be overrun by these potentially harmful influences.

The difficulty in figuring out which is a weed, and which is a plant you want growing in your garden depends on what you are trying to achieve mentally. We use this analogy here, only in reference to the way that weeds choke out healthy plants and replace entire landscapes with their offspring. The mind weeds are those which keep you away from healthy practices, ignite emotional disturbances, ramp up your reaction rates and bog down your thinking with harmful and often abusive self-talk. All of these are characteristics of weeds, regardless of how pretty the plant in the garden might appear. That rose bush you love so much, and have grown so attached to, might be the very thing you need to dig out. Is it cutting you every time you walk by? It is in an undesirable location that has crowded out the primary focal point of your Mind Garden? Has it grown so old that it no longer grows roses but has oversized thorns? It could be a flourishing bush that you have tended to for years that takes up a large part of your Mind Garden. Perhaps you hadn't noticed that the bush you were tending is prone to bugs, stifles the growth of other plants that you would like to see thriving, and robs water from nearby plants that are much better suited for your mental health. You may not have realized this was taking place because this one plant, which has become so "healthy looking", has been a huge focus for so long that it took your attention away from the others that were easy to dismiss. You said to yourself, "look at what a great gardener I am! This one plant is doing so well. I am really proud of myself for keeping it alive." However, look at the rest of your Mind Garden (which is what we have begun to do in the previous chapters) with unbiased vision, scrutiny, and honesty. Do you see any incongruencies in your earlier planning (planting) that are only visible now that it has had time to become well established? I bet you will. That's why we pulled out a shovel in our first chapter. Digging up fully grown plants is hard work, and you might think at first that it isn't worth your time or energy to "start over" in certain areas. But I assure you, it will be the most rewarding practice you can do for yourself when you get intentional about what is growing and where, and whether it is contributing to your health or not.

When I brought this practice to my sister, she said to me *"A shovel? Why a shovel? I took out my shotgun and blew that plant and the gremlins crawling all over it to pieces. It was so satisfying! You've got to try it"* I have even used a bulldozer, with me sitting at the wheel, feeling the thud of uneven earth beneath the tread while I ripped out an entire forest. It needed to go, and a shovel would have taken me years. I needed immediate results, and a bulldozer was my brain's solution for it. We are highly imaginative creatures. If you want to use a shotgun, a tractor or even some etheric magic powder that dissolves the plant instantly, do it. You are only limited by what you can imagine. Make it fun. This is a challenging process, and any way you can help yourself make it easier, I am all for it.

To reiterate, even though that gorgeous rose bush, the one that represents the narcissistic relationship with your mother, is thriving, it might not be in your best interest to keep it. If it's taking over a space, and you aren't feeling like your best self, that is not a valuable plant in the garden of your mind. It may be flourishing, but at what cost to you? Redesigning your garden space can seem like a daunting task, but I assure you, once those invasive weeds are removed and the plot land is wide open for new life, the results will come quickly and powerfully as you plant with intentional purpose and only allow what is serving you to take root, get watered and be deserving of your attention.

The Art of Weeding Well

In an earlier chapter we had you digging holes. Digging deeply into the soil of your mind and looking at your garden plot with new and fresh eyes. You have A LOT of seeds that we are going to make

room for now! Each plant in your garden is representative of different aspects of your life. You have many ways of interacting with the world and they all need to be tended with careful consideration. These are the plants you tend daily. This is the focal point of your Mind Garden.
I am going to list the most common parts of life that all people, men, and women interact with universally:

- Personal relationship to self
- Familial relationships (your parents, siblings, relatives and children)
- Work relationships
- Romantic relationships
- Social relationships (friends)
- Sexual relationships
- Acquaintances
- Sitationships (a casual, undefined, commitment-free relationship)

These are the common types of interactions that we all have with the people in our lives. They vary in the amount of energy required to maintain them, and your level of commitment to each is dependent on the amount of time, resources, and value you have placed on them, and the purpose they serve in your life. These relationships are also maintained based on whatever childhood values you were given in your youth. Belief structures are at the core of every relationship we engage in. When you sort out what meaning they have for you, weeding out what no longer serves you becomes much easier. Weeding, as we described earlier, is the process of removing anything that is not serving your highest growth. It is getting rid of all sources of abuse and disempowering habits that are encroaching on all your dreams and goals. These are waiting to be fulfilled but can't thrive in an environment that is being taken over by all the distractions you keep entertaining.

Your "weeds" are also the critical thinking regarding all these relationships you maintain. The Critic judges us and other people in our lives and is often voicing well disguised lies to keep us locked into beliefs and habits that hinder the path of healing. Critical thoughts can be crippling, paralyzing, demeaning, and really do a lot of damage to our interactions with others and ourselves because of the emotional toll it takes on our wellbeing. The gremlins hang on our shoulders and whisper into our ear with a voice that sounds like our own. Don't be fooled though, they do not have your best interests at heart, and that voice can say all sorts of nasty things about you that are not true.

Have you ever gone into work and one of your co-workers didn't say hello to you one day, and you instantly thought they didn't like you? Have you been sitting with your partner in silence, watching TV, and then a thought came into your mind that they might be angry with you over something, and you have no idea why. Then you felt the need to ask them about it only to be met with a puzzled reply of, "no, why?". How about when you are spending time with one of your parents and you say something to them, they made a face but didn't speak right away, and you instantly thought they were judging you for it? They may have just been thinking about what you said before they could reply. How about sending a text to someone who did not get right back to you? Did you come up with a million reasons why they didn't respond, and were 90% of those thoughts a worst-case scenario? Have you been hanging out with your friends, and you said something in the group, and the conversation goes silent? What are they thinking? Oh heck, what did I just do? I just committed social suicide; I'm doomed! All of these are examples of how The Critic/gremlins can derail your thinking and take you off track of what really matters. These internal judges can justify all the nasty things they say. Some of which are.

- "YOU'RE UGLY"
- "YOU'RE NOT SMART ENOUGH"
- "NO ONE REALLY LOVES YOU"
- "YOU JUST FAIL AT EVERYTHING"
- "YOU'RE SUCH A LOSER!"
- "THEY HATE YOU"

And on and on it goes, like a broken merry-go-round that you wanted to get off about 20 revolutions ago. You are so sick from the ride, and it has no off switch, that the only energy you have left is used in holding on for dear life. When you have no energy to consciously counter this inner attacker, the voice gets louder, crisper and is more difficult to shrug off. This can become our internal self-talk over time. The voice of The Critic becomes indistinguishable because it has cleverly supplanted itself as our own "inner voice".

It is also important to recognize what influences in our lives (especially our early lives as children) have contributed to creating this landslide of detrimental thinking. We pick up on everything as children! If someone once told us that our new favorite pair of shoes looked like "nurse shoes" and that set up a negative self-image that we present to the world, we may never buy those shoes again or wear them regardless of how much we loved them, and how comfortable they were when we initially made the purchase. This is mental programming, and it happens on a deeply subconscious level. We take in all the criticisms offered to us by external sources, and our brains are excellent at cataloging them right under the conscious layer of intentional thinking. Subconscious programs run our lives, and we have no clue most of the time that they are the motivations behind our decision making. As children, we cannot distinguish and intellectually analyze this input because we have no experience to reference rational and reasonable thinking that adults develop later in life. Children will generally feel that there is something wrong with them (shame) or that they have done something wrong (guilt). Children usually have not developed enough resilience to be able to sort out this external input in a way that upholds their pure self-image. In many healthy environments kids do have the tools to overcome these critical influences and uphold their sense of healthy self. They can shrug off the words, beliefs and outright lies because they have been taught how to. This is becoming rarer in a society reliant on technology for connection rather than family cohesion.

Belief structures are shaped in our early youth. Your Mind Garden is plotted out subconsciously by all the external stimuli you take in, that's just how the brain works. It makes connections to everything and it's the reason we all have such a unique perspective of the world. Perspective is relative to the personal experiences that shape us. Let me give you an example.

Personal Story

I went through a rough time in my early thirties when I felt like I failed at everything (because school taught me that!). It seemed to me that everything I touched just ended up in ruin. Regardless of whether this was actually true, which isn't even important. I believed it so strongly at the time that my journal entries reflected the belief, and I was living under the assumption that it was true. This led me to come to the realization that I felt unworthy of love. How are the two connected? Well now, this is where it's tricky to sort out thoughts and feelings. As a child, my worth was tied directly to my productivity through the disease of perfectionism. It was a belief that my parents probably weren't even aware that I was developing. I was an overachieving student, outwardly confident, and inwardly overwhelmed much of the time. I thought that I had to constantly be doing, and doing better than others, always making sure everyone was happy around me, and that it was my job to "fix" whatever was wrong in my surroundings. I was in my thirties when I was ready to tackle this issue, because it had surfaced repeatedly throughout my life and I was unable to get to the core of it. It surfaced again through a series of perceived failures. These "failures" put my value as a human being into question. If I was not producing anything of value, then I was not valuable. Therefore, I was not worthy. I had gotten so good at tending plants that were destroying my mental space, that I couldn't see the forest for the trees.

This is highly oversimplified, but I'm sharing it with you to illustrate the concept. You will have your own to discover. This was not serving me. This was a longstanding gremlin that I did not have the tools to identify, trace and get to the "plant" that had been seeding my garden perennially since childhood. It had seeded itself so thoroughly that it took several more years, and a couple more relationships to get all the sprouts that had planted themselves in my Mind Garden while I had been paying attention to other things. I would pull out a patch, thinking I had gotten them all, but a year later I found those same thoughts returning. "But I dealt with this already!" I angrily told myself. I went back to that patch of my Mind Garden and realized that once again, more sprouts had grown while I wasn't looking. Upon closer inspection, I noticed that the sprouts were growing around a single devastating thought (the main plant that kept reseeding) and I went to work digging it up until I had uprooted it completely (or so I thought). That was the summer of 2020. I carried this around with me for nearly forty years before

I finally had the tools, experience and understanding to properly eradicate it. I tracked the thoughts down, connected the feelings that kept coming up every time I encountered my unworthiness, and finally felt a sense of peace and unstoppable pursuit in my own happiness that I had not ever previously been able to reach. And yet this one still gets to me from time to time. It has not gone away, but its severity has lessened greatly! This prolific "seeder" continues to sprout from time to time. As soon as I recognize them popping up in undesirable places, I can now tug gently at the tender shoots, uprooting them before they go to flower. There are fewer and fewer as I continue this process and I am confident that one day… there will be no more to look out for.

The main way I managed to do this was by speaking of the shame that surfaced to my partner. I wrote it in a journal titled "LIES, trauma triggers" at the top of the page and listed it out. Then I took some time to reality check myself with some of the achievements I had been making recently to counter the Gremlins voices. Shame must be spoken, the forest of unworthiness I have continued to dig up, bulldoze down and even shoot to bits, is STILL there. I don't want anyone to be fooled into thinking that I have gotten rid of this. I respond to it now. I give it it's due process and I MOVE ON with oxytocin producing gratitude and remembering happy moments. I know what to do now, and I catch it immediately.

Thoughts are like Bees, and we like Bees

Thoughts are tricky because they can be fleeting. Like a bee that just flits through the yard, past your face, then vanishes in the distance. They're there one moment and then our brains move on to the next thing. Now, I want to make it clear here. We WANT bees pollinating our garden, so don't think of bees as a metaphor for what you are trying to identify as the problem. The bees will lead us to the plants that are taking over. Ah! There's gold here. Follow that bee! They know where the healthiest plants are growing, and which ones are thriving. They are the key to discovering the parts of your garden plot that are doing well. By doing well, I mean to say, the plants that have grown to maturity, not necessarily the ones you want. Bees, the fleeting thoughts that whiz by, are the harbingers of a growth mindset. Fleeting thoughts can come in the form of daydreams too and have positive effects on us as well. Just keep in mind how they make you feel in the moment. Feelings, as we mentioned above, are chemical signatures that are being released in your body, usually related to a memory or experience we had in early childhood. So thought-feelings are the chemical release that happens when we are using our minds and attaching an emotional marker on what is being thought/experienced.

Following me so far? Thought-feelings are the mind-body connection that concretes belief, behavioral patterns, habits and runs our automations. We need to walk our Mind Gardens and reassess how we feel about what we have created there. Weeds grow by default. Some are obviously good because they hold in soil, prevent erosion and are beneficial to our pollinators. (Hold in soil = stabilize your mental landscape. Prevent erosion = maintain resilience in the face of adversity. Beneficial to your pollinators = leading you to the flowering plants that require your attention.) All these metaphors are easy to understand for anyone who has worked a garden, large or small. You know that foxtail grass, once it goes to seed, will take over the landscape the following year, and it is so prickly! If you've ever gotten one stuck in your shoe or sock, then you know that they are not a friend in your garden. How about goat heads, aka Tribulus? Nasty little buggers. However, let's say flax has come up. Their beautiful blue flowers and lacelike leaf tendrils, growing in ditches on roadsides, are a welcome friend in the mind. The beauty of driving past them is enough to calm the soul and help you enjoy the journey. This is what I mean about beneficial weeds in your garden. Some add beauty while others are a hindrance. The wind blows (daily activity of a busy life) seeding your verdant mental soil, (your thought landscape) and will plant your garden for you if you aren't diligent in taking a few moments every day to intentionally walk the rows, wild places and perimeter, and pull out the weeds that no longer serve you so the wind can blow in something beautiful rather than something invasive!

Whew, I love plants. Perhaps that's become quite clear by now. I hope you understand how this metaphor can help you visualize exactly what your brain is doing while you are running around interacting with the world. The "secret garden" within you is such a transformative place that is brimming with life. Some plants grow whether we tend to them or not, while other plants require specific care. Are we good gardeners? Have we been tending to the more delicate plants or simply letting them die, replanting and letting them die, over and over again? I mentioned that I do not grow orchids well. They come to my home to perish, even though they bring so much beauty to my home. I have not developed the awareness of their personal needs to keep them alive. We all have areas that are our strengths and weaknesses. Identifying them, honing our skills, and educating ourselves in the right ways can help us become good gardeners. Now, I may never be able to grow an orchid, but I know how to turn a patch of gravelly, hard earth into a wildflower oasis! It doesn't happen in one season and requires a lot of care and attention. That is a strength I have. Orchids are my weakness. Instead of buying more orchids fruitlessly, wasting time, money, and energy, I am focusing on my strengths and devoting my attention where I can do my best and FEEL good doing it. I feel terrible when I kill an orchid! Can you relate to any of this?

The Mind Garden is the landscape you live in on a subconscious level. I used to have conversations with my mother about "rewriting my subconscious programs" well before I ever heard the names Joe Dispenza and Bruce Lipton. She would say to me "How can we do that and why do we need to?"

I think I have illustrated the answer to that question in the above paragraphs so I will move on. I named this chapter "gremlins" because just like the movie from the 80's, these creatures that mess up our thinking are crafty, stealthy and root deeply into our subconscious, then multiply exponentially. The brain is a multiplier, it proliferates anything we put into it. It doesn't know how to subtract, which is why Rhonda Byrne, the author of "The Secret" (Byrne, 2006) was able to convey the Law of Attraction so artfully. It has changed the way we look at our internal world, giving people many tools to get to the causes of their ills and make radical differences in their own lives that support the desires and goals deep within themselves. Gremlins destroy our resolve. They are the precursors of depression and anxiety.

Gremlins ARE the weeds in your garden, but they are also more than that. They are nasty creatures that purposely destroy the beneficial plants you have laboriously tended. This is incredibly dangerous. The bees of fleeting thoughts are our friends. The gremlins would be their counterparts. Like an elusive shadow figure, scaring you half to death by stealing your joy, clouding your sunshine, and eating away at your sane reasoning. Gremlins are the enemy. I rarely use that example, because I feel like everything has benefits, but I am firm on the fact that has been well established by psychologists, that gremlins have never done anyone any good.

Slaying VS Satiating

How do we know when we are slaying or satiating these nasty little creatures? What would the indicator be that they are gone for good or at least for a season, because we have taken the right action to root them out, or that they have been "fed" and are lying dormant until the next attack?

We satiate our feelings with food, addictions, people, technology, and anything else under the sun that distracts us from our mission and purpose in life. Our feelings, even (or especially) the uncomfortable ones, are the key indicators of what we have been focusing on, what we need to focus on, and where our dreams live. It's easy to just wander around life without considering what our feelings are offering us, but it's harder to attain our dreams and goals if we are giving power to feelings that continually derail us from what we hope to accomplish. Feelings, any of them, are alarm systems that we don't pay enough attention to. Instead, it can become a habit of ours to stuff them down deep inside without voicing them. Or sometimes we cover them with food just to get a temporary jolt of joy (and dopamine I must say!). We are masterful at distracting ourselves from them by engaging in social events where we find no pleasure, or scroll our phones looking for instant gratification with likes. Or we mask them with rage and projection by barfing all of our hurt onto other people so that we don't feel so bad. Hopefully we aren't getting violent with others because we refuse to look inward. It's hard to admit, but it happens. Feelings can tell us a lot if we take the time to just allow them to be what they are, in the moment, and follow the "thought bees" to the flowering plants that are begging for our attention.

Satiating our gremlins is a practice. Slaying them is a process. One becomes an unconscious habit that can become automatic. The other is an intentional and conscious act that requires our time, devotion, and commitment. You know you are satiating your gremlins if you are seeking immediate relief from a feeling and dismiss whatever thoughts are connected to it. You know you are slaying them when you allow yourself to experience the discomfort without judgment and you are taking a deliberate action to "chase down" the thoughts associated with it.

CHASE THE BEES – THEY WILL SHOW YOU THE WAY, EVERY SINGLE TIME

We all know what we do in times of stress to get ourselves feeling immediate relief. We know how we sabotage ourselves. We also usually know what we need to do to feel good without needing to distract ourselves from where we are at the moment, but we often replace useful action with dismissal because it's easier. We are going to take a walk into the garden now and meander through the process of "Weeding" and "Chasing the Bees" so we can get to the "Plants" that are taking up too much space without providing fruit, flowers, or beauty in our Mind Gardens.

Weeding our Mind Garden: Let the Bees lead you to the Gremlins

- **Journal Work:** Become aware of The Mind-Body connection by pairing feelings and thoughts. On a page in your journal, I want you to identify just one place where you sabotage yourself. This can be anything in your life. Mine is unworthiness (the gremlin keeping me stuck). It is such a gigantic sabotage and an unconscious behavior that was crippling me for much of my life. Separate your page in half with a divider line or use two pages that face one another if you are feeling ambitious. Write it down, just one thing. It could be a small or large sabotage; it just has to have an emotional impact when you think about it holding you hostage. Illustrate it with art and make it really vivid so you can see how it might be holding you back. Do you know why you feel this way? What feelings are they? Write them all down!

- **Write It!** What do you use to satiate this gremlin? I used bread and what I call "Toxic cleaning". It was a distraction. I would buy a loaf of bread at the store and eat it in my car until I felt better, sometimes consuming the entire loaf before I made it home. Sometimes I would sweep through the house like a tornado, thinking all kinds of disempowering thoughts about myself and my life as I violently scrubbed dishes, counters and yes, baseboards and walls. Using the other half of the page, or the facing one, write down your "coping mechanism(s)", at least one way that you use some external source of pleasure distraction or dismissal to feed/satiate the gremlins so they retreat back to the depths temporarily. You may notice that there are several. Find a good image that represents your "thing" and paste it clearly. What thoughts come up for you? Write them down. These unhealthy coping mechanisms are some of the "little bees" that will lead you to the larger issue: the gremlin.

- **Art It!** Now, on a separate page, I want you to collage, draw or write down, in any combination that works best for you, who you could be, what you could accomplish and how you would FEEL, if you did not have this gremlin showing up and gnawing at you, and did not need the substance you use to satiate it. How would your life be different? You slay the gremlins when you practice the habit of doing the opposite of satiating. You slay them when you can finally believe the opposite of what they have been telling you. For me, instead of buying that loaf of bread, it became a healthy smoothie that I savored. Instead of cleaning in rage mode, I would practice internal gratitude meditation while I washed the dishes, wiped down the counters and purposefully ignored the baseboards.
- **Write it:** Gremlins sound like self-talk, and they tell lies. Speaking their nasty little words out loud, in a journal and to a friend disempower THEM by bringing it to light. Shame can't exist once spoken. Write out all the hurtful things they say to you and if you can, write the truth next to it. These practices of comparison help us reality check ourselves. We need to know the truth, and we've been lied to for a long time, so it's important to reestablish a trusting relationship with our inner world.

These tools are offered as methods for getting to the root of a problem. The pages you create now will be a reminder of the process, and a road map to the life you have been dreaming of, where you aren't held back by limiting/detrimental beliefs. Gremlins have no power when they aren't being fed. They cannot keep lying to you when you create a visual representation of them. You uncover their hidey-holes, and they turn to dust in the sunshine. Voicing and naming it is just as powerful, that is one reason why I urge you to work in groups of two or three people. When you have a small group of people you trust to move through this process with, it accelerates your healing journey. I did this work on my own and it took many years. If I had been presented with a book like this before 2013, and a group of people I trusted, I know beyond the shadow of a doubt that I would have gone through this issue with so much more grace and ease.

WEEK 7

Forgiveness is the Path To Your High Heart

"Forgive yourself for all of the unkind, unloving, unsupportive things you have thought about yourself. Forgive yourself for the things you have done to yourself, that support the things you believe about yourself that are not true. Forgive yourself for being so hard on yourself."

-Iyanla Vanzant

How Can We Forgive the Horrors of the World?

If you could forgive yourself for anything in your past, what would it be and how would it change your life? It is not always easy to forgive ourselves for egregious acts we have committed, either against ourselves or others. It is not as simple as saying "I'm sorry" or apologizing and calling it good enough. We can't just make amends and atone for our mistakes when we are the cause. The art of self-forgiveness is much deeper; taking on an attitude of acceptance for the mistakes we've made, or the mistakes of others. Acceptance, and an even better descriptor is radical acceptance (I heard first by Lisa Bilyeu), of the wrongdoings of the past, is the shiny key to a fulfilling future and a much more satisfying present. The act of forgiving is never for the other person, it is always for our own benefit. Forgiving ourselves has a twofold reward because we are both giver and receiver. This is what makes it harder, in my opinion, because instead of accepting what someone else has done "to us" we must accept that we were absolutely where we needed to be and had all the tools at the time to handle it in the best possible way, even if that means we did it badly. We may not believe that though. So how do we get to a point where we believe we are forgivable and worthy of receiving it from ourselves?

You are your best friend & worst enemy

You've got your back in hard times. You probably also degrade yourselves in joyful times. Not always, so don't be too hard on yourself! What does it look like when you are at your best? Have you ever been at your best, and for how long were you able to sustain it?

We are equally the villain and the hero in anyone's story. We are certainly both in our own story as well. Forgiveness is usually a practice we use for other people when someone has wronged us. What I illustrate in this chapter is that we can learn the art of forgiving ourselves. Why is forgiving ourselves important? Research is revealing that forgiveness is attached to feelings of safety and conversely revenge. So, I propose that you are your own hero when you can make yourself feel safe and you play the villain when you seek revenge. This is specifically referring to the ways in which we interact with and treat ourselves.

Our Personal Hero (Internalized)

The need to feel safe is vital to our sense of place in the world. We threaten our own safety in a variety of ways but often aren't aware of when or how we make ourselves feel unsafe. So, we seek out external sources of validation from others to reaffirm for us, rather than going within and fortifying our inner world. Projection is a common way we gather evidence to support our belief that we are in danger. Our constructs of reality can be detrimental by the way we dramatize our experiences. This can threaten our safety even in moments when we are not in real danger. We tend to want others to change around us to better suit our version of the story that keeps us in a state of internal unrest. Projection on others for something that we have the capacity to change within ourselves is a typical response when we haven't fully grieved a traumatic experience that has stayed with us, sometimes for years. There is nothing wrong with the other person (most of the time). It's just that we have used this coping mechanism of projecting our distress onto someone else to deflect from the fact that we are still wounded.

If you can talk about your life without raising your own blood pressure, then you know you have forgiven. When you can share your story from a space of true calm then it has no power over you anymore. Anything that gets you in a reactive state leading to vengeful or conversely miserable thoughts is an area where you have not yet forgiven. Calm is an indication that forgiveness is present. Calm is the Hero, scooping you up in their powerful arms and carrying you to a place where you are truly safe. Your Hero is always rooting for you and standing stoically in the background of your mental landscape until they're needed. We can call upon our Hero at any time if we know how to communicate in the language they understand. Everything is language. We have forgotten the language of plants, the language of the wind, the language of our internal inhabitants. We communicate with the external world based on our social and cultural upbringing. This language is sometimes not translated in a way that our internal landscape can comprehend. It is not always the same language! I need you to understand this. We use the same words, but we have to develop the syntax and dialect that speaks directly to our Hero within to get the most effective response. If you went to another country and tried to converse with the locals, there would be a language barrier that can limit what you gain from the experience. Your personal Hero needs to be spoken to in a particular way so you can convey what needs to be done. This takes practice. Your Hero is aligned with the Alchemist that distributes chemical cocktails to you through emotional regulation. The Hero is part of your resilience, your hope, your faith, empathy, and is the protector of self-love. The Hero is also where our accountability lives, and we must be extremely honest to get their attention. They are truly virtuous, and want to be helpful, so we've got to take an observer's stance and speak directly to our part in the folly so our Hero can do their work. They help you water the Mind Garden by calling forth rains of peace that gently fall upon the landscape. This shows up as grief. We will talk more about grief later and how useful it can be. They ARE calm, remember… peace and calm and tranquility are the benefits of our Hero understanding our needs when we communicate them properly.

The Anti-Hero (Externalized)

Externalizing the Hero has severe consequences that can harm our relationship with our environment and the people we interact with. We externalize our Hero any time we seek safety from sources outside of ourselves or we engage in acts of "rescuing" others from their perfectly imperfect lives. The externalized Hero can become a villain in the blink of an eye when we use it to deflect from our own internal growth and focus too directly on the suffering of others. Altruism is indeed a virtue. It is important to be a beneficial salve to other people's wounds, but ONLY, and I stress, only when we are coming from a place of correct thinking. There can be no judgment involved, no need to "fix" and absolutely no gain from the act. The Hero will work against you if any of these elements are involved and can cause catastrophic failures in your interpersonal relationships. You think you are being helpful… but are you really just meddling as a means of avoiding your own personal work? This is a hard question to have to ask, but our motivations and drivers that orchestrate our actions are so important to consider when we feel the need to rescue others. We can never use our Hero in this way because it is not truly helpful to us, or the others involved. This distinction can help us understand when we need to turn the Hero inward and apply salve to our own wounds, give comfort to ourselves and let go of judgment, of ourselves and others.

Remember, the Hero belongs to you and is not a crusader for the outside world. Get clear on why you are invested in a cause, because you might have things to work on inside so you can be fully present and give your very best to the cause you are supporting.

The Controversial Villain (Internalized)

When I say that we are our own worst enemy, I am bringing attention to the fact that we have some detrimental behaviors that wound us from within. This insidious aggression against ourselves goes unnoticed by the external world, that's why we are allowed to get away with it. I was shocked to discover that we go much farther than simply not loving ourselves. We reject certain aspects of who we are on a fundamental level, we condemn ourselves. The Villain is not like The Critic/gremlins. The Villain is exactly as it sounds. It is our worst enemy but not in the way you might think. We have concepts of good and evil which have polarized many aspects of the world we interact within. When I say "villain" you instantly think "bad guy". This is because of the conditioning we have been given by society. The Villain is an essential part of each and every one of us. We are made quite perfectly, and this inner aggressor can serve us well when we understand its role in how we function.

Gremlins could be considered its minions. They are a tool of the Villian to bring awareness to all the places you blame, shame and project your grievances into the world. They are the symptom of having a Villain within us. I want to normalize this for everyone, so you don't feel alone in this. Everyone has a Villain. If you don't know you do, then they operate the puppet strings of your life, sabotaging everything you try to accomplish and the relationships you engage in, and can destroy your internal landscape systematically, transforming your garden from a glorious, green sunny refuge to a wasteland of toxic plant life that strangles the color from the world. The Villain can be poisonous. It gains power every time you listen to the gremlins. Every time you ignore or dismiss a "weed" that is not beneficial, every time you engage in addictive behavior, you are helping the Villain destroy you from within. This internal aggressor has no regard for your Mind Garden because its proper place is at the borderlands of your garden's edge. The internal self-harming language that you use gets the Villain's attention away from the external things it should be focusing on, and turns it inward, to your beautiful landscape. Internalizing the Villain is dangerous because this aspect is meant to interact with your external world only and needs to remain focused on its task. We distract the Villain from its duty when we turn up the volume knob on our suffering and allowing the gremlins to have their way. It wreaks havoc, and then we feel worse, creating a perpetual cycle that our Hero has a very hard time cleaning up.

How can something like this exist within us?

The Villain is the primal part of our brains that keeps us hyper aware of dangers. The reptilian part of the brain assesses what is threatening and can turn us into monsters to move through the world under an illusion of safety seeking. This aspect of our internal world has its role to play. It would be accurate to say that the Villain is a key component in conflict resolution as well as emotional regulation. The internalized Villain can wreak havoc on your inner world because it is always looking for evidence to support our beliefs, so it will find it in any interaction we have. Inwardly, this aspect of ourselves can make us just uncomfortable enough to identify what is not working in our lives. It sabotages us, repeatedly, to get our attention, that's why the gremlins are so effective at what they do. If we refuse to listen, that discomfort quickly transforms to tragedy, accidents, or other calamities that are set up to get our attention NOW. We create it, we ask for it and this is the mechanism within us that sets it all in motion for our benefit. It can feel like an attack, and it should. These wake-up calls take place all the time. Our gut instinct (aka intuition) is part of this mechanism that operates when the Villain is involved. The Villain is perceived as the "bad guy", so it is easy to disregard it. We might think of it as the "ugly" parts of ourselves. This couldn't be further from the truth.

The Villain Savior (Externalized)

You read that right. The Villain, when called upon in the appropriate places and with the correct dialog between the two of you, is the character you rely on to create boundaries. As dangerous as the internalized villain is TO you, it is as powerful as the externalized villain is FOR you. This is the part of us that knows beyond the shadow of a doubt how to keep you safe in the outside world. They suck at managing your internal world, that's the Hero's job anyway. The Hero has no business butting its nose in your external world, leave that to the Villain! The Villain isn't afraid of pissing anyone off to protect you. Your Hero won't do that for you. Your Hero knows only what you need to feel safe internally. These two forces within us work in specific ways, and we often misuse them, thinking we are using our tools correctly and end up disappointed, unsupported, and feeling alone and scared. If we use our tools badly it's no one's fault but our own. The Villain, with all its dark connotations, persistence in goal seeking, danger awareness and aggressive attitude, has its rightful place in pointing out what needs to be avoided, addressed, and attacked. The sheer ferocity of the Villain is what makes it so beneficial. We cannot go around people pleasing our way through life. We must assert ourselves when necessary and we must create strong boundaries in situations that can be abusive, disrespectful, and disempowering. Do not demonize the Villain. There is no bad guy, and the dragons they slay can clear the path when you are goal seeking, determined, and focused on maintaining the balance between your giving and receiving. The Villain protects the borders of your Mind Garden, not allowing outside forces to "plant" anything that might disturb the balance you are creating there. The Villain will not allow intruders when you are using it properly, so that no one can ravage your peaceful space.

The descriptions above will help you determine how you are using these forces within you. If you are fearful, then the Hero is externalized, and the Villain is internalized. If you are operating from love, then the Hero is internalized, and the Villain is externalized. Keep them in their proper roles and the path to healing, growth and our highest purpose will be protected by our right and left-hand helpers. These are not the caricatures of "angel" and "demon" on the shoulders. That's your conscience and has its place as well. With everything in the proper perspective, we will see that the abundance of useful tools and mechanisms we've got to work with are infinite and the characters that live within us are some of our best friends and garden helpers. Are we operating out of love or fear? The utility of these two forces within, once properly implemented, helps us create our best selves. Let's clarify something right now because I have used the term "best selves" more than once so far. Our "best", is not the most virtuous, positive, happy, and amiable that we can be. Our "best" is a collection of seasons that we honor as we move through them in GRACE. We embody love and light just as much as the dangerous protector and the pain. You are ALL of it simultaneously and must embrace all aspects of your entire being to be whole.

Scooby Doo Taught Me That The Real Monsters Are Usually Human

Humanity has undergone a series of historic rises and falls throughout our time inhabiting this planet and interacting with one another. We have concrete examples of how truly dangerous we can become. There need not be very much provocation to elicit the kinds of despicable actions that can level a nation, genocide entire peoples and torture another person brutally, sometimes to their ultimate death. I have kept much of this book in light-hearted spirit, focusing on the empowering aspects of behavior that we can employ to live well, make better choices, develop understanding of our own nature and move through this reality with slightly less suffering.

This book would not be complete however if I were to negate or dismiss the power within all of us to become savage and nearly inexplicable monsters. Human beings have the incredible potential to do great damage to the world around us. We must maintain a proper awareness of this force within us, which I have lovingly referred to as the Villain in this chapter. For all the powers of "good" we possess and utilize to make the world wonderful, we can equally create hellish conditions by our own hand. It is up to the individual to balance these forces within, and I have gone to great lengths in the above descriptions to help you, dear reader, in understanding that we cannot toss aside any aspect of our humanity to save another. It is in the embracing of our whole selves that self-mastery can be possible for each of us. We have all had murderous thoughts, although no one else may be privy to them. We have all cursed one another for some action they did. We have all entertained dark fantasies that would never see the light of day outside of our own heads, but they exist. To deny that they exist is to deny a core part of what makes us human. To balance these forces is what makes up enlightened consciousness. The peaceful man is not the weak man, but the man who can be dangerous when necessary. This is a concept brought forth by Jordan Peterson and is worth considering. We must ask ourselves this question though: when is it necessary? When do we summon that part of our being that would kill, sacrifice and murder, and in what situations would this be needed? This is a moral question that spans time and circumstances as history has taught us. Morals depend heavily on the culture and social structure of a group, rather than a single individual, as well as the situation and our perception of it. These are the aspects of humanity that come under the highest scrutiny. Forgiveness takes on a much deeper meaning when we take this into personal reflection.

What is “Letting Go” Really?

The practice of forgiving is the act of letting go of anything that is out of our control. It is the action of taking our power back so we can let go of anger, blame, guilt, shame, projection, and fear. In a word, it is a form of acceptance. It is the antidote to highly inflammatory emotional responses to situations, circumstances, and challenges that we have experienced. Our past is full of mistakes. There is no way to go back and change anything we’ve gone through, and sometimes we don’t have access to the people who committed injustices against us, but that doesn’t mean we are imprisoned by the past. We can choose to use forgiveness as a way of liberating ourselves from an experience around which we have created a story. Oh, the stories we write! The truth is, we have no idea about what was going through anyone else's head during a difficult interaction. Our assumptions are the stories that we write to create the narrative that explains our reasons for feeling dis-ease. Your memories cannot be relied upon to tell you the truth of something that happened to you. Memories are constantly rewriting themselves and they change based on our biases, evidence gathering and our need to be right. Read that again.

We make so many assumptions about events that took place in our personal histories, especially ones that left us feeling less than ourselves or wronged in some way. These assumptions are not necessarily reality. They can be an educated guess at best, and a gross misrepresentation at worst.

In times when we have committed atrocities against others, we’ve got to take full responsibility for our role, and then accept that we cannot go back and make amends for it in the past. We can only go forward by changing the behavior that created the situation, so that we never repeat it again. That is the only way to truly forgive ourselves in situations where we have hurt another. It happens! Remember, you are part Villain, and there will be times when you behave in undesirable ways, disempower other people with your words, and take actions that can have lasting traumatic effects on others. Forgiveness is the sheath to a double-edged sword that we have wielded in the past, harming both ourselves and other people. Sheath the sword. Put it away. Stop cutting yourself repeatedly, well after the incident occurred. Time to get some bandages and salve. Finally let yourself heal by practicing forgiveness and acceptance. Forgiveness does not absolve you from what happened. The act of repairing your own behavior does. "Actions speak louder than words" is another phrase my mother drilled into her children. Your actions are where your true intentions are. You can have the most virtuous intentions and still do terrible things with it. "The road to hell is paved in good intentions" is another familiar saying that some people don't fully understand. Intention, backed by right action (on your part) through taking full responsibility for your deeds is the only way we can be truly accountable for ourselves. Accountability is key in changing behaviors, tapping into forgiveness, and letting go on a deep level.

We will talk more about your stories later as well, but I want to share something important here. Some of your stories are only meant to be shared with SOME people. Have you ever shared a story with someone, and they betrayed you by telling another person, even when you asked them not to? Your stories are where your power of self lives. The power of self-identification is what shapes who you are. What stories are you telling and to whom? Do they deserve to hear them? I have many stories, as do we all. I have selected a few for the purposes of this book to share with you, reader, because I feel they are appropriate for YOUR healing journey. I have stories that I will not share with you, and that is perfectly fine. Discernment is vital to living, and the reason I suggested that you assemble a "cultivation team" for this course. You MUST have two people to share your stories with. Some of these stories will be difficult to express and contain traumatic feeling experiences that still need to be recovered. That is why you must choose wisely. It is not beneficial to anyone when we barf our stories all over any listening ear. It's messy and hard to clean up. It also leaves lasting impressions, so practice discernment please.

Personal Story

In June of 2019 I was fired from my job. After four and a half years of dedicated employment, I knew that the owner wanted to sell the company. I wanted to buy it. I didn't have the resources or knowledge to take on something so huge, but that didn't stop me from entering a preliminary negotiation that lasted for three weeks. Instead of buying the company, I was fired for revealing some unintegral comments that the owner had made to me about my coworkers. This revealed more comments that had been made about me to several of them. The owner, who was also our boss, had a way of gossiping about us to one another as though the words would never pass between us as a group. We worked every day with each other and had become quite a close team of women. The bookkeeper quit immediately without notice and it was "my fault" for which I didn't mind taking the blame. Although it was not my fault directly, it is my responsibility to be accountable for my own part in her decision to quit because I spoke up to something that I felt she needed to hear. There's more to the story of course, but this outlines enough for the sake of how it relates to this chapter.

I was angry right afterwards, which lit a fire of determination in me for about a month, to work from home. I was already part of an online company that had advancement options for turning it into a business for myself (MLM). So, I buckled down, got to work, and contacted the people closest to me in the organization. I went for about 2 months working as hard as I could while getting some well needed writing and web design done for myself. During that time my relationship began to suffer, my emotions were a full-blown roller-coaster ride, and I wasn't getting anywhere with the online business and in-home parties that we hosted to get new memberships. I felt like I was failing at everything. My determination to succeed at something meaningful switched on the perfectionist bent that had been with me since childhood. This led to a series of emotional breakdowns and the most detrimental overwhelm I have ever experienced in my life. I knew that I could choose which kind of mental and emotional state I wanted to create for myself, but I had become so obsessed with the idea that I could work from home, create structure within a chaotic environment, and prove that I had it in me to succeed, that I wasn't recognizing what was holding me back from actually accomplishing my goals. I went back to the drawing board, pulled out a journal and began the messy process of untangling years of developed bad habits and behaviors.

Within that two-week practice, I discovered several pivotal areas of my life of which I was previously unaware. The first was that my self-compassion sucked, and I didn't know how to speak to myself kindly. I had spent so much time pushing myself to greatness that I had forgotten how to be kind on the journey. Secondly, I learned that my critical self-talk was connected to my parents and a childhood of adopting a lot of unhealthy beliefs about myself and what success should be, rather than what it actually is. I was so overly ambitious that I would sacrifice my health, relationships, and obligations to pursue it, to the detriment of the rest of my life. The third thing I learned was that I had to forgive myself for all my misperceptions before I could move on. I dedicated an entire page in my journal to write down everything I decided I needed to forgive myself for. I have copied that page here so you can see what my process looked like and the approach I took. I kept it about me. I let go of any blame from external sources and pulled all that energy back into figuring out how I had created this mess for myself. The following section is what came from that practice.

FORGIVENESS PRACTICE

- *I forgive myself for ALL the negative patterns I have been living in that have kept me feeling stuck.*

- *I forgive myself for ALL the false beliefs and limitations I have entertained about everyone I love and care about, including myself.*

- *I forgive myself and others for ALL expectations I had that have led to my disappointments.*
- *I forgive myself and others for ANY & ALL pain I may have caused as a result of my trauma and my healing.*
- *I forgive myself for ALL the times I was unable to remain in grace, where it caused myself and others pain.*
- *I forgive myself and others for ALL the reactionary interactions that shadowed love and caused tension, fear and mistrust to grow in its place.*
- *I forgive myself for not trusting that I know best, what I need for my highest growth, and to be my very best self.*
- *I forgive myself for not being able to speak the transcendental language of love, which has created tension, bad feelings and separation.*
- *I forgive myself for not knowing how to comfort myself and others when love would have served better than reaction.*

More personal stuff & some seeds of wisdom

As you can see from the journal entry above, I went right to the source, me. I read this page every day for a week, then I decided to get a 9-5 job. My logic in this was that I still had much to learn before I was ready to work from home, and I was dedicated to saving my relationship with my partner so we could navigate these transitions together, and in a healthy way. Obviously, I did not want a 9-5, I wanted to be self-sustaining and be the boss of my own financial success. I wanted to be the self-empowered business woman, the Warrior Godess of internal strength and discipline. However, I could tell that my mental and emotional health needed a lot more work before that would be possible for me. So instead of fighting against reality, I went to work for a grocery store while I got myself together. Needless to say, the relationship with my partner improved (for a little while, until about October) and I felt better about myself overall. The job was physically demanding, and I got in shape as a result, which was a big bonus, and something I could not have anticipated prior to the decision.

Allow Yourself the Process even if it's Painful

I spent a year sorting myself out and, in the summer of 2020, I was hit with yet another deep realization that shook me to my core. I won't go into the nitty gritty details here because I believe that our stories are important and valuable and should be shared with ONLY those who are deserving of hearing them. Furthermore, this book is NOT about me, so I am only sharing stories that relate to the material in this book to provide examples of how I personally used them in my own life. I will say that in May of 2020, my partner left me, moved back to his own land, and I was on my own for the first time in about seventeen years. The reason for our separation is less important than the results of it. That time apart gave us both some well-needed space to work on ourselves. I was certain this wouldn't be the end of our story as a couple, and we still talked to one another through messaging as we both got clear on what we each needed. I used forgiveness a lot during this time because I knew that the practice is less about the other person and more about creating peace of mind for myself, so I could remain in a stable emotional state. It is a key component in learning how to regulate emotions and deal with conflict resolution. Forgiveness gave me the tools I needed to make it through to the other side of our separation, which lasted until August.

I spent a lot of time with my sister and her family during these unsteady months, and she was the only person who was able to help me with the constant anxiety, panic attacks and sometimes hourly waves of intense emotional outbursts, whether it was tears, fear, or gremlins, she was always a phone call away and she literally saved my life. Suicidal thoughts are something that one cannot, and I believe should not, try to sort out on your own. It wasn't the separation that spurred this, but an internal aspect of myself that had been revealed to me that I was certain I would be unable to live through. I spent some of that time in a near catatonic state because it was so difficult to face the reality of ME and the dissociation I experienced separated me from my children, family and friends. This was my breakdown/breakthrough that nearly broke me but didn't; my sister's understanding, support, and non-judgmental advice kept me here on the planet and in my body. My gratitude practice will continue to include my sister and the role she played in my healing, probably for the rest of my life. I know the power of energy transference and I continue to intentionally send her love, strength, and gratitude. She is one of my greatest teachers in this life.

Trust the Process

There is a process to our healing. It's a journey. If you look at a road map for any state, you can see all the features, scenic roadways, large and small towns, bustling metropolises, and long expanses of desert in between facilities. Your life is a road map, and its constantly changing landscape as you move through your own trials, challenges, and joys. This metaphor has served me well in figuring out what I need to prepare for, when I can make spontaneous trips and when I have to just ride it out until I get to the next checkpoint along the way and refuel. And sometimes I get to wildcraft native medicines or seeds in roadside ditches and a rare, secluded oasis.

We must learn how to navigate our lives as if it were an entire planet that is ready to be explored. Using the road map as a metaphor can be helpful in recognizing how diverse we are as individuals. There's a lot to see and not all of it is pretty, but all of it can be mapped out so we can understand our own landscapes and travel through them with conscious intention. Forgiveness is something that can help us with that. You may have deserts where there used to be a forest because you damned up the water from some glorious river so you could install a power plant. You still have to travel it and see it realistically, so self-rejection/condemnation doesn't take hold. Avoiding those parts of ourselves is only going to make our situation worse. Forgiveness is the opposite of avoidance. It shines a light on the fact that even though you can't change the past, you can choose how you use the past to make your present and your future a place you want to travel to and live in.

SEVEN steps to true forgiveness

Step 1: Acknowledge

Acknowledge the hurt. Who hurt you and why did they do it? What is the context of the situation, and how long ago did this happen? Or perhaps you were the perpetrator and need to turn inward. Self-compassion can make acknowledgement easier.

Step 2: Consider

Consider how the hurt and pain has affected you. The word "consider" is key here because it involves thinking before deciding. Before you decide on whether you will forgive this person, consider the negative feelings you've acquired since the incident.
How has the pain changed you? How detrimental was the person's mistake to your life or someone else's?

Step 3: Accept

Accept that you cannot change the past. No matter how much you wish this pain could be reversed, it's time to admit to yourself that your anger toward the person won't redeem what they have done. It is during this step that you must thoughtfully consider whether you want to forgive. Again, if you committed the act that needs to be forgiven, you must accept that you were, at one time, capable of causing so much pain. Are you that person now? How have you changed and what is different? Are you still capable of repeating such detrimental mistakes? Accept it, regardless, and then decide what you need to do to move forward in a healthy direction.

Step 4: Determine

Determine whether you will forgive. This is when the forgiveness process will either begin or end. This decision should not be made lightly, as it will determine the future of your relationship with this person. Are you unforgivable? Is anyone unforgivable? Where does that belief live within you? What values shaped that belief? Determine to get to the bottom of it so you know how to proceed.

Step 5: Repair

Repair the relationship with the person who wronged you. Before any act of forgiveness or reconciliation, if you want to rebuild the connection you used to have with this person, you'll need to work on repair. In most cases, you will be the instigator of this repair, but if you have thoughtfully engaged in the previous 4 steps, then there is a higher chance of success.

Note that you are repairing the relationship, not restoring it. It will likely take more time for the relationship to return to normal, whatever that may look like to you. Acts of repairing can include kind words, simple gestures or even gifts.

Repairing internal conflict over something you have personally done is no different than if you were interacting with another human being in the external world. You must figure out how you can repair the relationship you have with yourself. This is tricky, but not impossible. What do you need to do to forgive yourself? What do you need to believe, and who would you need to become?

Step 6: Learn

Learn what forgiveness means to you. Up until now, you've probably thought that forgiveness is more for *their* benefit, not yours. But once the relationship is on the path to restoration, and you've given yourself time to accept the reality of the past, it's clear that forgiveness is a way for you to find closure. Closure can also bring peace of mind, and you need that if you have any chance of learning from your failures. Remember, there is valuable information in failing, so take the time to learn about yourself so you can restore the divine connection you have with ALL of life.

Step 7: Forgive

Forgive the person who wronged you. In some cases, this will be silent. You may be compelled to verbally forgive the person, even if you do not expect a kind response, but if you have followed through on the previous steps, then their reaction won't really matter. What will matter is that *you* have found a way to let go and move on.

Forgiveness can lead to feelings of understanding, empathy, and compassion for the one who hurt you. Forgiveness doesn't mean forgetting or excusing the harm done to you or making up with the person who caused the harm. Forgiveness brings a kind of peace that helps you go on with life. If you have been the perpetrator that needs to be forgiven by YOU, then the only way you can truly forgive yourself is by changing behavior. If you repeat the unhealthy and damaging behavior by creating another incident in the future, then you have not learned the lessons that were screaming at you to be acknowledged, considered, accepted, and repaired. You deserve to move through life gracefully and have empowering interactions with others. You have to be the one to make changes that will ensure that happens for you.

Letting Go

Psychologists generally define forgiveness as a conscious, deliberate decision to release feelings of resentment or vengeance toward a person or group who has harmed you, regardless of whether they deserve your forgiveness. Forgiveness does not mean forgetting, nor does it mean condoning or excusing offenses. Forgiving oneself rather than focusing on what other people may have done can be a big steppingstone on the road to recovery from internal disempowering behaviors. Remember that you are at the center of every experience you have, every interaction you participate in, and every single belief or narrative/story you create about it. Forgiving yourself for misinterpreting something, staying in a bad situation, or even something unintegral that you've done, is personally rewarding. Letting go of some of these transgressions by removing anything external as the source of blame can send a powerful message to your subconscious. This kind of internal repair can be subtle, but it is also interesting to note how much resistance can come up when we practice methods of self-investigation. Your internal roots need room to spread, they need food to thrive, and fertile ground that will feed you in the years to come. Forgiveness in this form is nourishing for your roots. When you are strongly rooted in the reality that you are the source of all the power within you, miracles not only become possible, but they also become real. Letting go of the need to outsource reasons for our angst can steer us in a direction that leads right to the heart of our own power. Our Hero lives there, and this is exactly the kind of language that they respond well to. This form or forgiveness creates accountability, and our Hero loves that and wants to make us feel safe while we are investigating all these hard truths about ourselves.

The Roots of the Tree: Forgiveness Practice

- **Journal Practice:** Write out your own list, or use the one provided, of forgiveness insights from recognizing what surfaced when you decided you are enough (in chapter 5). Remember to keep your forgiveness sentences focused on yourself and how you have either been the cause or progenitor of your own suffering rather than implicating blame on anything outside of yourself.

- **Art It!** Allow yourself to let go of false beliefs. Roots grow in the dark and we often don't see the foundation of what is holding us up. Our own roots need proper care, and letting go of blame, shame, guilt, and projection of any external sources can give us a chance to let those roots thrive. You are rooted in something, that's a given. This practice is designed to transform the source of what feeds your roots. Nothing outside of you is powerful enough to impact how you grow. Draw an image of a tree trunk where it touches the ground. Draw a line across the page. Under the line draw a series of root structures and name each one of them. These are the foundational beliefs that are moving you forward. These are what give you stability in times of struggle. You deserve to feel good and have a solid foundation that will hold you up during any storm, this is hope and resilience as well.

- ❖ Some of the beliefs that empower me are "I am always enough with NO prerequisites", "I am beautiful AND smart", "Failure has information I NEED and is my friend", "I am forgivable for anything" ... And I have many, many more.

- ❖ **Art Practice:** Use colors and shapes to convey how you feel when you are at your BEST. Saturate the page in color and images. NO WORDS this time! Just visual feedback. You have used enough words so far. Give your mind a rest by creating an abstract page that visually reflects feeling good. Sometimes feelings have no words, just shapes, colors, and vivid images. Let go of trying to define your feelings, just let them be something fluid and aetheric. It's okay to not always have words, sometimes we use way too many words anyway, and improperly I might add. When you look back on this page it can be a calm, tranquil reminder of what feeling good looks like.

WEEK 8

Shame & How It Shapes Your Story

"We live in a world where most people still subscribe to the belief that shame is a good tool for keeping people in line. Not only is this wrong, but it's dangerous. Shame is highly correlated with addiction, violence, aggression, depression, eating disorders, and bullying."

-Brené Brown, Author of Daring Greatly: How the Courage to Be Vulnerable Transforms the Way We Live, Love, Parent, and Lead

OH, the Stories we Make up and Tell!

Have you ever thought about what your story is and how it has shaped you? Do you have more than one and why is that important? Shame is a topic that many people don't want to discuss. Depending on what shame is attached to, it can be difficult to analyze without help. In the chaos of the daily grind, we are generally unaware of how shame plays a role in creating the stories that we tell. Shame can shape and form our critical thinking. Every person has their own experiences; however, they are not always unique to us. The human experience has existed for how many years now? In all eras, throughout history, we have been having experiences. Therefore, what you are going through internally is probably more common than you want to admit. Even though we have overall similar human experiences, they are relative to the specific conditions we have undergone individually. Now, think about it this way. You do not live life in a vacuum; therefore, it is the exchange with other people, places, and stimuli from the outside world that develops every aspect of who you are.

From birth to seven years of age you are a sponge that is absorbing every ounce of external stimuli that you encounter. To have any consciousness at all, you must have something to become conscious of. The real key here, to understanding ourselves, is that we *must* create stories to function in our 3D reality. We need personal stories to interact within the parameters of our world. This is a blessing because that means that we get to write them ourselves. The beliefs we have learned, the programs we have accepted, and the conditioning of our youth, have all played a role in how we learn how to be human beings. It helps us engage within the framework of our social worldview.

We have all probably been shamed for exhibiting naughty behaviors as children. That was valuable to us because it taught us what our immediate environment expected from us. This form of discipline (as with anything in life) can be taken to an extreme level and used as a form of abuse by authorities that have had influence over us as children. Overall, though, I think most of us can remember at least once when we were disciplined through shame as a means of teaching us what appropriate behavior should look like.

Shame at a young age can be detrimental because it creates a limiting perspective about what we can achieve on a larger scale, outside of the acceptable world we were conditioned to live within. Shame gains power when we avoid speaking of it. So, when we "stuff" experiences and interactions and even traumas from our youth, it keeps us firmly shackled to it. We can't let it go and move on because we haven't gone through the process of disempowering that shame story. It's a story too, and it's more powerful than you might think. It has a way of taking over empowering stories you've created by tainting them with self-criticism.

Self-criticism is a way of keeping us tethered to belief structures and socially acceptable behavior. I say that not to tell you that it is a "good" or "bad" thing; it simply is. You gained values, morals, and social cues through this programming that self-criticism reminds you of daily. To put this quite simply, it keeps you from doing anything that society would frown upon. That can be a "good" thing, when used with some conscious intention. Sociopaths have not gained from the social shaming structure and value systems that have been passed down from generation to generation. They miss some key components that prevent them doing things that go against socially acceptable behaviors. That can be a "bad" thing.

We must get into the evolution of shame as it relates to altruism in how tribal peoples in social groups survived and thrived. There were rewards for exhibiting altruistic behaviors that benefited the tribe and consequences for being a "taker" or not reciprocating cooperative behaviors; this is shame. It has had its utility in our evolution and how we train our young.

According to research and science, plants feel no such thing. They have been observed screaming when cut, reacting negatively to touch, and even communicating with one another via their root structures, but shame is not a function in the plant kingdom that we know of at this time. Essentially, plants do *feel,* but it is not in the same way that humans do, and we are barely scratching the surface of why they feel and in what capacity. There can be incredible therapeutic benefits in placing ourselves theoretically, through visualization, in the body and mind frame of a plant. In my research I have not yet come across others who use this method of therapy to help patients struggling with mental health, but I have personally used this practice to realign myself with the highest form of existence that is removed from societal pressure and stresses. I am introducing this practice in this chapter for you, reader, to use and learn firsthand how soothing it can be to "transplant" your consciousness into another life form for a brief period. Plants are incredibly complex in how they synthesize food using the energy from light. Their cellular structures have evolved over millions of years of adaptation to environments and stresses. We can use that to our advantage by connecting with them in a new way. This might sound ludicrous to some people who have not developed a language to express themselves from a broader perspective, one in which extends their connective energy field to other forms of life. As dumb as it might sound, there is utility in removing ourselves from our human experience to understand ourselves on a full spectrum scale.

The way to "transplant" our consciousness is through meditation and visualization. It helps to have a subject with you that you can use as a visual example. I have many houseplants, but I have done this practice with trees growing in nature far more easily. A public park, wooded area or remote forest are good places to find a tree you can connect with. Sit down in a comfortable position and close your eyes. You might even want to touch the tree with an open palm before beginning and take a moment to slow your thoughts. Once you're ready, you can take a few deep breaths, clear your mind, and become aware of the sounds you hear all around you. Are there birds singing, leaves rustling, a breeze blowing? Use these external sources of information to tap into the consciousness that is a tree. This environment has been its home its entire life. It is very familiar with these sounds. Are there insects nearby? What do you think it sounds like at the top of the canopy? What would it feel like if the branches were your limbs? If your hair were the leaves, how would that feel on your scalp when the wind brushes your face? All these questions can lead you towards a sense of calm introspection. This kind of meditation is thoughtful. Instead of trying to push away your thoughts you are using them to help put yourself into the mindset of the tree. They are slow growing, dance in the wind, and have synergistic relationships with the rest of their environment. As you ease deeper into this meditation, you may begin to feel yourself experiencing life differently. You may feel the blood pulsing through your veins, or the way your breath presses against your skin as your belly and chest expand and contract. All these mindful observations are how we can connect with our own bodies as well as imagining how the tree is experiencing its own existence. I really enjoy this meditation practice as it is extremely grounding for me. If you'd like to try it yourself sometime, I encourage you to branch out and give it a go.

Science has already revealed that we are energetic/magnetic creatures and "glow" when we are in excitable states, and the light dims when we are in a grounded state. The light spectrum that humans have access to prevents us from being able to see this glow, but it is there. I wonder sometimes which beings on Earth can visually see our glow and how they use it to their advantage. An intriguing thought indeed. (Masaki Kobayashi, 2009) This science is well established, so it is not a new concept I am presenting here. I bring it up simply to illustrate that we know very little about our place in the world in direct relation to other life forms, and how we are perceived by them and one another. Our connection to plants and cultivation of them has proven to reduce stress, elicit a sense of calm and tranquility and most of us know that "grounding" is the practice of walking barefoot on the Earth to discharge negative energy. There is even a practice of horticulture therapy that utilizes the relationship between plants and people to help reduce anxiety and stress and alleviate symptoms of depression through the act of gardening. If you don't have a plant in your home, I encourage you to get one, and see what kind of relationship you can cultivate with this kind of life form. It is quite magnificent in its simplicity.

Moving on now, it’s time to talk about how self-criticism and shame are linked. We have discussed what self-criticism is and how it's related to shame. Can you see how you developed some of the stories you continue to tell? These stories shed light on what our values are and how we use them to our benefit and detriment. Our values are the foundation of what we believe is right or wrong with the world and with us. So, we shame what we hate and praise what we love. We virtue signal what is in alignment with our positive values. We become aggressive and hateful with anything that is out of alignment with our positive values. We put what we consider negative traits, behaviors, beliefs and values into a box and label it as “unacceptable”, “intolerable”, “inappropriate” and “undesirable”. Society has a long list of these negative traits that we collectively agree with (and it seems to be growing exponentially). This can be beneficial for social groups to interact with one another because without them, how would we know how to behave “when in Rome?” This is a phrase many of us are familiar with because we grew up with it. As a child you learn the differences in places by going to friends' houses and learning the “rules” of their household, their dos and don’ts. Broaden that teaching, and you can see how we have developed rules as families, communities, cultures, and nations. Shame is a method of teaching what is not acceptable; however, the lasting effects can give rise to insecurity, inadequacy and guilt over small infractions, people pleasing and perfectionism. These can lead to severe social anxiety, introversion, depression and even PTSD if the shame was given in an abusive or traumatic form.

We live in a dualistic reality which means we have life/death cycles, good/bad ideals, positive/negative energies (like a battery), up/down and on and on with the contradictions and opposing realities we figure out how to navigate. Before going further into shame, let's get really clear on exactly what self-criticism is.

Addressing Self Criticism and Shame

"I AM NOT GOING TO BE THE CAUSE OF MY OWN SUFFERING"

Comparative Self Criticism: comparing oneself to others and finding oneself lacking. Basing self-esteem on the perceptions of others (externalizing).

External comparison is a way of judging how well or how poorly we are doing in life by comparing ourselves to anything outside of ourselves. We all do it, however it is not beneficial when we use that comparison to find fault with our own journey. We can acknowledge where others are in comparison to ourselves without deciding that we are less (or more) than. We are not them so we cannot gauge our successes or failures on the image we see in other people. There's a lot we don't know about them, so our perception will oftentimes be incorrect or lacking context to understand how they reached the point they are at now. We cannot compare ourselves to anything external because it is not an accurate representation of where we are currently.

Internalized Self Criticism: the feeling that one cannot possibly live up to personal ideals or standards, or the belief that one is deficient in some way - thus even success can be viewed as a failure. (Internalizing)

When the Gremlins say, "It's all your fault", use constructive statements to address only what is your fault, like - "I reacted badly which created a domino effect in everyone else's mood. I can manage my reactions better."

Self-critical tendencies have their roots in childhood. These earliest bonds with our parents, often authoritarian relationships where rejection is present, can be the source of our self-criticism. Internalizing our flaws has some serious side effects. We do it because it is easier sometimes to find fault in ourselves, rather than others, but we don't use it constructively most of the time. The example above is a way that we can internalize constructively. Saying "I just do everything wrong and I'm not going to get any better" is a destructive example. We tell ourselves a lot of lies/stories based on misperceptions. The problem is that our brain believes everything we say to ourselves. So internalizing criticism can lead to larger problems like the ones below.

Self-criticism becomes self-doubt

Chronic or excessive self-criticism may contribute to mental health concerns such as:

- Depression
- Social anxiety
- Body image issues
- Feelings of worthlessness
- Self-blame when things go wrong
- Difficulty asserting personal needs
- Exhibiting submissiveness in relationships out of fear that voicing an opinion will lead to criticism
- Feelings of failure
- Guilt and shame
- Perfectionism
- Eating and food issues
- Self-harm

I presented this list to my daughter (age 16 at the time) when I discovered it in an online article on CMT (Compassionate Mind Training) (Scotland). I asked her to check how many of these she has experienced, either in the past or presently. She had checked every single one of them. I had too. I was surprised because she carried herself confidently and moved through the world with what I had perceived as a stable internal foundation. This facade should have been easy for me to see through because I was in a similar place emotionally when I was a kid. I seemed quite fine, confident, and sure of myself as far as everyone could tell. When, in fact, I was overwhelmed, anxious and in many situations felt out of place and alone.

Self-criticism is something we brushed the surface of in our chapter about gremlins. It's dangerous because it sets the stage for larger mental health issues. The last one on the list is self-harm. I want to illustrate in no uncertain terms that there are far more forms of self-harm than we understand or pay attention to. If we were aware of and attuned to these red flags, then it would be much easier to identify people experiencing a variety of mental health issues.

Self-harm can take the form of:

- Food addiction to something detrimental to your health
- Staying in an abusive situation
- Addiction to substances
- Saying cruel things about yourself, either in public or alone. This is often brushed off as self-deprecating humor, which is often not as funny as it sounds
- Chronic self-blame, as this deteriorates your resolve and resilience

None of these listed are recognized as self-harm, as they are not intentional forms of self-injury. They are on the list of mental health disorders and can be symptoms of a larger issue where coping mechanisms have kicked in and the person needs something to relieve the pain. Self-harm can also be a means of feeling something, anything, to combat emotional numbness. It releases endorphins and therefore the act of harming can feel relieving.

I place these under the umbrella of "self-harm" because you are harming yourself internally, in ways that no one else can see. I believe this is far more dangerous than cutting your skin, because you are not getting as high of an endorphin release, therefore you are not using them as a conscious coping mechanism, but more as an automation. To another point, when you cut, there are scars that other people can identify. When you're self-deprecating, there are no visible marks for others to look out for, no physical evidence. When you blame/shame yourself mentally, each and every day for something, anything, you leave marks on your psyche, like bruises in the mind. To put it differently, you are stomping through your mental garden destroying anything that produces valuable fruit. You're taking your shovel and ripping the flower beds to shreds. No one knows you're doing it! There are no visual symptoms to recognize the behavior. Later you might feel bad about it. You sit at that garden's edge, sorting out all the broken bits by yourself, crying over the pretty flowers you chopped to pieces. No one sees that either. It hasn't left a mark on your skin so it can't be addressed by anyone who would be able to help you. That's one of the key reasons that mental health issues are so undertreated in our world. Where's the mark? While you are busy abusing yourself, smiling at the people you pass by, they have no clue about what is going on inside of your head. You're a wreck and can't reach out, so you dive deeper into self-abusive/harmful practices and habits that spiral to a dangerous level. Sound familiar at all? I know it was for me, and I had no idea what I was doing to myself all the time.

Full stop here!

Take a breath, you just walked through a really painful truth with me. Take another one, because my goodness I commend you for taking the time to get to this part of the book. It is not easy to admit that we are the source of our own suffering because it's so much easier to point the finger at something in front of us, outside of us. Take another breath just for good measure. I will too. There we go, inhale… exhale… now we're ready to keep going.

There are many ways to rewrite this behavior, many avenues that are in alignment with how you heal. Resistance is part of healing as well. Many of the things we want to resist are the very things that will lead us to the highest growth. In the previous chapter we talked about forgiveness. I intentionally put it before this one because I think it is important to understand how to forgive ourselves BEFORE we talk about shame. We had to be able to forgive ourselves for our terrible behavior first since we have a whole lot more to talk about here.

THERAPIES TO ADDRESS SELF CRITICAL TENDENCIES

- PRACTICE SELF-COMPASSION
- KINDNESS AND UNDERSTANDING
- MINDFULNESS (NON-JUDGMENTAL AWARENESS OF ONE'S THOUGHTS AND FEELINGS)

Mindfulness: Is likely to further one's ability to self-validate and challenge negative thoughts. Focus on constructive and useful self-critique: behaviors rather than chronic defeatism.

Compassionate Mind Training: Encourages you to be compassionate towards yourself and others. As a result, you learn to manage your moods. Specifically, to gain knowledge on how to decrease anxiety and negative self-talk. Also, how to increase self-acceptance.

(DBT) Dialectic Behavioral Therapy: DBT therapy includes specialized skills training that can help you increase your ability to accept yourself and your situation, and self-acceptance is the gateway to self-compassion. - (Grouport, n.d.)

Self-soothing Practices: Practicing self-kindness by doing nice things for ourselves in moments when it feels contrary (like the automatic need to self-criticize) can help repair the strained relationship we have with our internal world. Repeat kind, compassionate phrases to yourself. Say it either aloud or in your head, as many times as you need. These examples can give you some ideas of how to do that:

- *"I'm having a rough time right now, but I've got a 100% survival rate to make it through this."*

- *"I'm feeling so defeated. I'm strong and this pain is here to show me something I want to see."*
- *"I'm trying hard even though I feel like I fail, and I'm doing my best and that is enough until I can do better, I am determined to do better."*

Do intentional acts that are self-soothing

- SIT WITH YOUR PET
- LIST FAVORITES
- VISUALIZE A PLACE THAT FEELS GOOD TO YOU
- PLAN AN ACTIVITY
- TOUCH SOMETHING COMFORTING
- LIST POSITIVE THINGS
- LISTEN TO MUSIC
- TAKE A BATH OR A WALK

Depressed people can have problems processing anger and dealing with conflicts. Self-criticism is a form of safety behaviors/strategies. They are not maladaptive schemas or cognitive distortion. They are linked to safety and self-protection. Paradoxically though they increase the sense of internal threat. Self-reassurance lowers depression. Self-compassion can reduce the sense of threat and create feelings of safeness. Feeling safe is vital in moving away from a detrimental and disempowering situation so you can reestablish a sense of security. When we feel safe, we are more likely to think rationally about what is really going on rather than being swept away by the story we are telling ourselves about what is happening.

What is Your Story (Stories)?

We have all experienced moments in life that we recall again and again. Many times, we recall them because they were traumatic and left a negative impression on us. We talk to our friends. We repeat it a lot. What if I told you that it changes every time we bring it up? The original experience remains exactly as is, and yet, every time we speak it aloud, our mind adds to it, changes it, and updates it, even years later. So how can we be sure that we are conveying a memory with accuracy when our mind makes these kinds of updates? We can't, and that's the problem with sharing a story repeatedly.

Dr. Joe Dispenza has uncovered some shocking evidence about the brain and how it catalogs memories and creates new neural pathways when we change the way we look at, think about, and behave around "our stories". His research is quite extensive, and the scientific community, as well as the spiritual community are seeing some correlating parallels when it comes to his research. The mind-body connection is one of his greatest findings and has revealed that when we connect the two in a conscious way, we can deliberately make adjustments, and sometimes profound, and seemingly impossible transformations in our personal lives. Thinking + feeling = experience. When we learn how to steer our thinking and feeling in a way that aligns with the truth of our divinity, the world is suddenly much more malleable than we were taught. We scratched the surface of this concept in an earlier chapter. (Dispenza D. J., How To BRAINWASH Yourself For Success & Destroy NEGATIVE THOUGHTS! | Dr. Joe Dispenza, 2018)

Do you believe you can change your story? If you could, what kinds of changes would you consciously make to it and why? How would that help you live better in every "now", since whatever it is you are relaying took place in your recent or distant past? Your stories are collections of memories that you repeat (usually) verbally to other people. Your stories are also the beliefs that have shaped your personality, habits, and behaviors, and are indicative of what your value structure is. These foundational memories are the source of your current worldview. They can be rewritten, rescripted, and upgraded to reflect where you want to be, rather than where you think you are right now. A story can be useful because if you find yourself repeating it, there is something to gain from having it surface in recurring cycles. Perhaps there are some insights you've missed, and so it arrives again to get you to see a valuable aspect of your ever-expanding consciousness. You would be surprised by the many ways our subconscious tries hard to communicate with our conscious selves.

Stories are one way that we do that. The gap between the conscious and subconscious is one thought removed from connecting the two. That thought is the deliberate action of figuring out what messages are being relayed to us by asking the right questions.

So, what are the "right" questions? We ask ourselves a lot of questions but are they always helpful in getting beneficial answers? Well, not always. The best questions lead to answers that will help us resolve an issue.

Let's imagine a situation where someone shunned you after a conversation you had with them, and you don't know why. A good question for example is this: "In what way did I cause this situation to occur?" That takes all blame off the other person and frames it in a way where we can locate some aspect of our own behavior that we could potentially improve upon. An example of a less functional question would be: "Why did they react that way when we were just talking?" This kind of question has no answer. We can justify any reason for the other person to behave in any way. This kind of justification leaves no room for self-improvement or self-reflection because we can only assume what is going on in the head of the other person, whereas we can get to the root of our own motivations instead. It can be useful to understand the motivations of others, but it is not practical to frame a situation in a way that blames someone else. Regardless of what has taken place, we have made the choice (conscious or otherwise) to put ourselves in the situation where the interaction occurred, therefore it is better to determine our own motivation so we can figure out why we ended up there, and what it is serving for us. This approach can help us determine what it is we are doing that is potentially holding us back from being our best selves. It is also highly dependent on the value we place on the interaction. Perfectionists and people pleasers have a habit of always blaming themselves, even when they are not at fault. So, the functional question I mentioned above may not be helpful to a people pleaser. They would then have to ask themselves "What level of importance have I placed on this encounter and this person?" Because our sense of value matters as much as our motivations.

There might be some people who disagree with this kind of thinking, and that is fine. From my experience I have discovered that every single interaction I have ever had in my adult life has been orchestrated by me, either consciously or subconsciously based on exactly where I was at during the time. I could have learned from these interactions much faster, and not repeated uncomfortable encounters, had I used this method. However, I was unaware of the power I had in the moment because blame was taught to me at an early age, and I used it. Expanding our toolkit and understanding can give us insights that dramatically reshape the options we have to work with, changing the way we interact with others.

I want to express the importance of the effects our stories have on others. The human condition can be overwhelming at times. It can be tragic and devastating. A tragic story with a happy ending can help other people overcome adversity in their own lives because they can see the example of how temporary it was, and that there is light at the end of that tunnel. This is encouraging to keep moving forward in the face of adversity. Inspirational stories are motivating because we all have an innate desire to thrive in this world. We share our stories to encourage others. We share to support our own journey of growth and healing. We share so that people can see our example and find their own way through a trying time. Our best stories are the ones that light up the darkness and lead the way for others to come back into the light, as well as giving us insights on areas where we can personally grow through self-reflection. Have you ever been so grateful that a friend shared their story of how they overcame a personal tragedy? Was it just what you needed to hear? Was it the driving force of change for you that made it possible to get out of your own darkness? We need our stories. Some of them. We need to know the difference between the stories that empower us and the ones that disempower us so we can optimize the best parts of our human experience. Our bodies will show us which ones are which by displaying health or disease. It is now known through science that what you think transforms into what you feel, and your body is the indicator of how well your mind is working. It can also inform us where we need to do the work because where there is dis-ease, there are often thoughts at the core.

Personal Story

I have so many that it's difficult for me to pick just one. I was driven by shame and guilt for so many years that I unconsciously played it out in many of my relationships.
Here goes. I will share what happened in 2020, not because it is the most recent example I have at the time of writing this book, but because it was the crucial moment of realization that something was terribly wrong, and I needed some serious life reflection to get the most out of my life expression.

My partner and I were having communication issues for about nine months, from October of 2019 to May of 2020 when he finally decided to leave me. Somewhere within that nine-month span, I had an extremely volatile breakdown. I had been using an audio recorder to document our conversations so I could gain some insights on where both of us were coming from to see if I could locate the source of our communication issues and whatever else might be getting in the way of us loving each other well.

During this particular interaction (of which I am certainly not proud) I was crying and screaming in the same breath. I was so emotionally reactive that I could not logically reason with anything taking place. He was uncompassionate and I will add, rightly so. My behavior was pathetic. I was so desperate for him to understand me, to hold me, to comfort and console me, that I had deteriorated to the child-like tactics of a full-blown tantrum. My heart was pounding, palms sweaty, eyes streaming, and I'm sure my blood pressure was so high, I could have popped a vein if it had escalated any further. He stood stoically in the doorway, angry and unresponsive to my emotional outburst. We said some things back and forth that I personally am not proud of, but he was right. I needed to calm down, look him in the face, have an intelligent conversation and drop the tears. I wanted to hate him so badly for what I considered at the time as "shaming" me for where I was at emotionally. I wanted to point out how unempathetic he was being, how wrong he was, and that he just needed to love me through it. In reality, what I needed was to go within, search for the part of myself that was so hurt and soothe myself. I needed to stop insisting from him all the things I needed to do for my own comfort, and I needed to be honest about why I was so emotionally volatile.

In short, I had grown up with a narcissistic mother. I people pleased my way through childhood, and I had become a perfectionist on the outside and an overwhelmed mess on the inside. I spent weeks at a time in a deep depression. I was unresponsive sometimes, crying for my lack of resolution. I felt disconnected from my partner and that affected our love life. We couldn't reconcile the deep seeded issues that were being brought up by being in a relationship together and it felt permanent and "unfixable" at the time. I felt that there was something inherently wrong with me and he felt equally "not enough". We were between a rock and a hard place and banging our own heads against the boulders as well as each other! It was the darkest time in our relationship. It had us both feeling gaslighted, manipulated, insecure, disrespected, and unfulfilled. I cannot speak to what he was going through internally, because that is HIS story, and this is MY story. I can say he felt all those things because that is what he expressed to me. What internal work he did, I have no clue, but I can tell you with certainty that I had the Villain and Hero reversed and it was destroying me from within. All the while I kept finding fault in everything he was doing while claiming to be in a place of spiritual growth and intellectual acumen.

That is one of my most shameful stories, and it might not seem like much on paper as you sit here and read it. You may feel no attachment to it whatsoever, no emotional squirming over it. I can assure you that I have moved beyond this place because it no longer brings me pain to discuss it. As an adult who has gone through many self-help practices, knowing the material and tools to keep myself in alignment and function as a stable person… I had totally lost control of myself. I share this one because I think it's important for everyone to understand that it is not about how much you know. Healing is not a onetime fix or an accumulation of wisdom and spiritual insights; it is a practice of maintenance that we must undergo on a daily basis to keep ourselves "right" inside. A series of stressful events, circumstances that are out of our control, and environmental factors that bring us to our knees can lead us, quite quickly I will add, to a place of complete mental breakdown regardless of how strong we seem to be. Do not think that the "strong" do not struggle. I was told my entire life how very "strong" I am, how "courageous", how "resilient". These words mean nothing when you are going through something that you feel is breaking you. During those times, we need solid daily practices to keep our minds from eating us from within. Like an auto-immune disease, our minds can do incredible damage if there is something being brought up to look at and we can't or won't see. A naughty child who feels like they aren't being seen will often act out in negative ways to get any kind of attention they can. Your "stuff" does the same thing. If the feeling(s) ignored, it will give you negative feedback so you can't pretend it doesn't exist, and it will escalate to whatever means necessary to get you uncomfortable enough to address it properly.

How can Plants Teach us about Shame?

Plants are unconditionally loving. You will not encounter a plant that will put you down, highlight your faults, or degrade you. The highest form of love is where we can sit honestly with ourselves and others without judgment, fear, and the need to make someone else wrong for something going badly in our lives. This is why we feel so refreshed and renewed when we spend time in nature. Nothing in that environment criticizes us for being who we are, flaws and all. The trees are just being trees, the grass is being grass and the flowers are blooming, not for our benefit, but because that is exactly who they are. Interacting with that perfect expression of existence can help guide us towards determining when we are doing the same, and when we are out of alignment with our true selves. Who has ever looked at a plant, even one growing on the side of the road in a ditch and said to themselves “Look at that stupid plant! What was it thinking growing right there? How dare it just take up space that doesn’t belong to it?” Said no one ever. Yeah, we have pulled out weeds that were intrusive because they were in *our* way. They were hindering something *we* were trying to accomplish, they disrupted *our* sense of order, but *they* weren’t doing it to intentionally upset us. It was not a ploy to get our anger to flare up, and it had nothing to do with us in any way. *Our* sense of control is what drives us to determine whether a plant is in our way, not their presence.

Have you ever gone out in your yard, garden or to a public space and just appreciated a plant for being exactly where it was, growing particularly beautiful, and thriving in its natural environment? If you haven’t, I highly recommend trying this practice. I tend to notice trees that are shapely, swaying in the wind, and standing tall, even under adversity. There is something fundamentally soothing for me about the way trees grow, the hardships they endure, the life they support, both in their branches and the flora around the base that prefers the shade provided. Trees have always been a symbol of a perfect incarnation for me, and I use their example in many aspects of my life. They can take hundreds of years to grow, and one decision (to cut them down) can change the landscape in an instant. Where a tree once sprouted from a seed, impacted the environment for a hundred plus years, someone decided that it was “in the way” or “an insurance hazard” or just an “eyesore”, and can take a chainsaw and remove it from the landscape. This choice has benefits and detriments all in one. It could be necessary to remove a well-established tree which has become overgrown and might endanger your home if a branch were to fall on the roof. What will that do to the yard, the creatures that have relied on its presence, and the ground flora that will no longer have the protection of its shade? It is not just removing a tree; it is altering the ecosystem that tree created by its presence.

I hope this metaphor is unfolding in your mind, like a curly fern at dawn. We don't always understand the impact other people have on our lives. We don't see the way they are affecting our environment, and perhaps we are unaware of our own participation in affecting the environment of others. Is our presence beneficial? Have we become overgrown in someone else's story? Has someone become so well established in our lives who had provided shade and shelter but now threatens our roof with damage if a storm were to brew? Just because they have been with us (or conversely us with them) for long periods of time, does not mean that it is still beneficial to remain there. Changing with the times and recognizing when we have outgrown our environment can make the transition of shifting our perspective much simpler, more honest, and a little less frightening.

To add to what I mentioned before, plants unabashedly take up space. They are not afraid to grow in even the most obviously unwanted places. We are not like that most of the time, because if our presence is unwanted, we either leave or are forced out and move on to a place more desirable, satisfying and fulfilling. This is always true right? Not quite. Sometimes we don't leave our environment simply because we don't know it's an option. We end up living in substandard conditions that do not water us, do not provide adequate sunshine, or get beaten up by harsh weather. You may know nothing other than the ditch you are growing in, the one that fills with water during a rain, and is dry for extended periods of time. The one that is exposed to harsh chemicals from the cars driving by, how could you imagine that there is another plant just like you? Right across the street, behind a row of trees and buildings there is one that was intentionally planted by a gardener who waters, prunes, fertilizes and speaks kindly to it on a daily basis. It is exactly like you! However, the growing conditions in those two environments are very different. Look around, determine your surroundings, and assess where you have chosen to root and what is growing around you. Your environment plays a vital role in your wellbeing. Plants do not feel anything about where they take root. They simply are where they have sprouted and will be there until they die. We have the power to choose, but first, we must see where we are growing before we can move on. We must become aware, without judgment, shame, or criticism of all the ways we have had an impact on our environment and how it has impacted and shaped us as well. Become the objective observer and your vision will clear.

This is one possible approach toward complete freedom. Again, the plant does not feel shame for itself. It grows where it has rooted, and it lives in that place regardless of the surroundings that shape it. Allow yourself the grace to stand back without the lenses of contempt. Evaluate yourself in complete honesty and you will be like the plant that knows it takes up space, has needs, and is worthy of thriving. You may choose to remain where you have sprouted. There may be untapped resources around you, and thanks to your new mindset you can see them now. As you assess yourself and your surroundings, new and wonderful possibilities will creep out like vines from dark and shadowy places. Pruning the Mind Garden has opened the path for some of these plants to see sunshine again. A struggling weed-vine might seem unsightly at first as you examine it. Perhaps, as it gets more attention from you, it may grow into a passionflower or jasmine, and only when it blooms will you understand its value in your garden. These hidden treasures are everywhere for us to find! Do not dismiss a plant that is ugly, yellowing, or covered in bugs. It got that way possibly because of neglect, not always because it is "bad". With proper care and attention, it can become a flourishing member of your beautiful Mind Garden.

Whether it is sickness you have been experiencing, depression, anxiety, or any other dis-ease that is keeping you from thriving, you can be sure that there are signs around you and within you that will point to exactly why that is happening. I was surprised to learn that after two months of off-and-on health issues, and tracking my symptoms, I might have had an ulcer. The symptoms lined up, so I checked the "Heal your Body" book (Hay, 1976) . Ulcers = Worthiness issues. Have I mentioned worthiness before? Oh yes, I have. And I will say it all again before the end of this book. I thought I had "healed" that issue. This just goes to show you that we must work on ourselves every single day. It will keep coming up until every part of your life is in alignment with your highest self. Is that possible? Only for short periods of time because you are living in a 3D reality, and it requires you to engage with it as a 3D component. Your highest self is not a 3D component, and we can sync up, be in alignment with, and visit it from time to time, but we live HERE, and can use the connection with our highest selves as a barometer for wellness. Body scans, meditation, practices of calm, self-compassion, boundaries, mindfulness, gratitude, forgiveness, honesty etc. These tools can align us. Do not get the idea that you will heal once and be done. You are alive and will never be done while alive. That's part of how this game works. Accepting every single place we are at, at *any* given moment, is part of what makes this life worth living.

Pruning: Addressing Self-Criticism and Shame - You are more than the story

❖ **"I will not be the cause of my own suffering"** Write this header at the top of a page in your journal. This is not an affirmation. It is a determination. An affirmation is something we WANT to be true; a determination is something that we have decided to MAKE true. This determination is another steppingstone on the path. In what ways are you the cause of your own suffering? Leave everyone else out of this practice. It's all you. Time to get honest and prune the branches, limbs and weeds that are getting in your own way. You can add to it anytime you recognize a behavior, habit, attitude, thought, belief, addiction, pattern, or critical self-talk that contributes to your own suffering. Prune them away by writing them down. Shame cannot live in the sunlight. These are your "branches" and extend towards the sky. When you prune the dead ones away, it gives more energy for new shoots to bud, and reach even higher than the ones you clipped off. Pruning can be painful, you are the shears and the branches simultaneously, so experience it from every perspective. Be kind to yourself during this process and try not to overthink any of it, you'll just wear yourself out. Go slowly and let it develop as it unfolds.

- **Art it! Write it!** Your Hero and Villain are miracles within you! Use two opposing pages, and make a collage, list, or use other expressions of how these two have been influencing your life. Be sure to include the (internal) and (external) ways you have seen them show up for you. Are they in their proper place? Are they friends or foes?

- **Journal Practice:** You are powerful beyond measure and your story has value. Pick a story, any story about yourself. Make sure it's an honest one and write it out. It can be one paragraph or three pages. It's up to you. The practice of writing your story (and there are many novels worth within you!) is a way of putting shame into perspective and letting go of what no longer serves us. It can be painful to admit certain things about ourselves and rereading it might bring up the emotions associated with it, but that's okay. One day, you will be able to read it with nothing but gratitude for the treasures it brought you.

WEEK 9

Resilience & Weathering The Storm

"Do not judge me by my success, judge me by how many times I fell down and got back up again."

— Nelson Mandela

How Resilient Are You Really?

What do you know about resilience? Is it a word that you grew up with or a new concept to you? Would you be surprised to learn that resilience is attached to shame through self-reflection of a past shameful experience?

The definition of resilience is pretty straightforward and tells us everything we need to know about why it's important. It's our ability to bounce back from trauma, stress, and challenging situations. It's how quickly we recover. For some people this comes easily. It may be easy for some people to shrug off a challenging event in retrospect, but what about in the moment? Can we use resilience during a challenge and how will that change the way the situation affects us in the long term? We discussed how DAAT, (dysfunction, anxiety/abuse & trauma) can have lasting, detrimental effects on our well-being. If we could experience something that is perceptibly traumatic, anxious, or stressful and practice resilience *during* the experience, as well as afterward, it can help rewrite what we think about that moment and change the direction of our awareness. Therefore, instead of an external stressor, we fortify ourselves with a strengthening inner knowledge. This is characterized by our ability to bounce back. How quickly we recover is directly correlated to how much resilience we have.

Imagine this scenario. You are at work, and you are not doing your job to the best of your ability. Let's say that you are having some troubles at home, which has you distracted and moving a little slower than usual. Rather than being approached with empathy and understanding, your boss comes to you with criticism over your performance. You already felt bad about something else, and now you have another thing to add to the plate of concerns that feels like it's going to bury you if it gets any bigger. This can be overwhelming. A healthy response to a situation like this is, "I know I'm not my best today, but I will do better tomorrow when I've gotten a good night's sleep or talked to my partner about that thing that was bothering me"; or whatever it happens to be that has your attention divided in the first place. This is healthy guilt, as we mentioned in the previous chapter, and is the foundation of resilience. Let's say instead that you take on the thought that, "I am failing at home, I am failing at work, I am just a complete failure!" This is an example of shame and we discussed that in the previous chapter as well. The definition of resilience is this.

re·sil·ience,
/rəˈzilyəns/

1. the capacity to recover quickly from difficulties, toughness.
Ex: "The often-remarkable resilience of so many British institutions"
2. the ability of a substance or object to spring back into shape; elasticity.
Ex: "Nylon is excellent in wearability and resilience"

Resilience then, is what shapes us during challenging life events. I am going to jump into the forest now. Follow me for a moment. Consider a forest of baby trees. They are thriving. They are growing in their perfect habitat and are healthy. A one-hundred-year storm blows through, devastating the landscape. These baby trees are laid flat to the ground, not broken, but bent. Their life force and the will to live is so powerfully strong that they will continue to reach for the sky although they have just suffered a severe, life-threatening event that has changed them forever. These stands of trees, twenty years into the future, all have a bend in their trunks in the same place and are all growing in what appears to be a deformed way. The event has left its mark on them, it re-shaped them for the rest of their lives. Is this a trauma? It could be considered so. Some of them will die because of the experience. Not everyone will make it out alive. To the trees that do survive, it was a setback in which they had to put forth a massive amount of energy in repairing the damaged part of themselves so they could continue doing what they do best, continue living. They do not look at deformity as a mark on their character, an ugliness, a social stigma, or a trauma because they experience no shame. They don't look at it all, they just keep living through it, slowly straightening their trunk, reaching for the light of the sun every single day, digging their roots farther towards the water source, and thriving however they can.

As human beings with the capacity to analyze, we take on a lot of misperceptions about our situations, tragic life events, and circumstances that change us. We listen to outside voices and influences that tell us "You have been traumatized" or that we are "weakened" because of a harsh life experience that tested our resilience. Your ability to bounce back is proof of the fact that you have survived 100% of the experiences you have already gone through in your life, not 85, not 30, but a full 100% of your experiences have been survivable, because you are still here, and you are reading this book. We can put PTSD in this section as a long-term side effect of survivability. This is because, as humans, we catalog all our experiences so we can recognize patterns. Patterns give us the knowledge of whether something will repeat itself, and if it was an undesirable experience we will avoid it at all costs. We will even look for evidence of it arising again so that we can avoid it. However, this is backward thinking because whatever we focus on, we get more of. Therefore, we need to be like the tree that is not looking around for another event to break it and it is not waiting for the next storm as evidence that the event will repeat in its lifetime. It is also not wary of other potential threats just because it went through one already. It is only looking to the source of life that will make it stronger and able to thrive.

Science is beginning to understand that highly resilient people are some of the most optimistic and objective. They have an ability to see what went right and focus on that. They investigate their memories and aren't replaying what was perceptually traumatic, but are seeing how they lived through it, and what lessons were available to them to move forward in life with strength and a fortified sense of self. Victimization of ourselves begins with a series of beliefs that we are structurally, foundationally, and ultimately flawed, which will give us some kind of disadvantage in life. These are some of the identification badges we wear and show off to people. Optimistic people rarely feel this way because they live by the understanding that they are adaptable, and that all life is suffering anyway. So why make it worse by adding to that suffering by looking at life as though there are no roses among the thorns?

All life is suffering

We must look at this from a realistic vantage point to see it in its proper place. Buddha knew this fundamental law of the Universe. We are pleasure seeking creatures, so the opposite of pleasure would, at least to my understanding, be suffering. Therefore, we resist suffering at all costs because pleasure is so much more… pleasurable. Let me remind you though that some of our greatest advantages in life have come from our ability to suffer "well" and live through it.

History has also taught us a lot about suffering and how it is advantageous to our survival regardless of how devastating it was at the time it took place. One example is the utility of living through the great depression, which was indeed a tragedy and killed many people. This event produced the kind of parents that wanted better for their children than what they went through. They wanted their children to experience pleasures that were not available to them. So, it can be true that hard times make strong people. I will venture to add an opinion to this statement, regarding good times. You may notice that we are in "good times" now, with pleasures available to us at the touch of our fingers, connectivity without leaving our homes, nourishment, and amenities that are abundant, and we have the resources to indulge in pleasurable activities whenever we like. I question then, have good times created weak people? This question plagues me because I see the death rates from suicide on the rise, the mental health crisis growing, and our youth in a state of limbo and confusion over how to proceed in a world that is offering them so much on-demand pleasure. They are overwhelmed. They are perhaps not suffering enough (or in the right ways), not uncomfortable enough to see that the pleasures they are privileged to enjoy have come to them on the backs of a resilient population who came before. If they are not learning resilience through metered suffering in some form, how will they develop problem solving skills, conflict resolution, and fortification of their inner beings that are constantly reaching towards the sun (i.e. goal oriented progression)?

> *"Hard times create strong men, strong men create good times, good times create weak men, and weak men create hard times." --from postapocalyptic novel "Those Who Remain" by the author G. Michael Hopf*

Some of the greatest truths have been revealed by the creatives of our society. This quote is one of my favorites because it illustrates a cyclical structure that our society and consciousness moves through. It may not be one-hundred percent accurate but stands as an instructive metaphor to help us recognize the patterns of our human drives that fluctuate between pleasure and suffering. It is a guidepost for us all to understand the relationship between the two and why we need both in our daily lives to live to our fullest potential.

Get comfortable with being uncomfortable

There are many self-help books that will tell you to think positively, do your affirmations and focus only on the good so you can live a better life. This is not the message I want to instill in people within these pages. I won't go so far as to say that it is the wrong way to look at it. I believe wholeheartedly that it leaves out a key component of what we need to live a complete life, free of the restrictions of limiting belief structures and social expectations and reflecting what it means to be a truly divine human being on this planet. When we do not allow ourselves the introspection required to fully embrace our suffering as a part of our human experience, we miss out on some vital universal truths that might just make us the people we want to be and create a world we want to be in.

I have studied the research on a concept called "toxic positivity" that has become well known to us today. (Samara Quintero, 2019-2022) It is the dismissal of suffering. It is the blatant removal of our innate need to embrace our struggles and encourages us to overlook anything that isn't bringing us pleasure and satisfaction.

There is a danger in this kind of thinking. For one, it doesn't give us a chance to process our emotional states in a realistic way. Secondly, it tells us that if we are not happy all the time then there is something wrong with us. This is so destructive to our overall wellbeing because it is, at its root, shaming. How can we be happy all the time? In short, we can't, and should never think that is an attainable goal. I want to point out here that we can cultivate happiness, and that we must! The cultivation of happiness is the practice of embracing our struggles and looking at them with a resilience mindset. We know what makes us happy, and often these are circumstantial and external experiences. Happiness is a mindset as well as a practice. We really can choose "happy" over other feelings that come up. This kind of choosing is what resilience is at its core. It is the choice to be happy regardless of our situation but it also accepting our suffering as a necessity. It is living through our suffering by developing skills that will fortify our resolve. Just like the trees that were misshapen by the tragedy they suffered; human beings can still reach for higher goals regardless of whatever life has dealt them. It takes practice to get to a place where you can experience hard times and be happy about it. Gratitude is one practice that we have highlighted already, and a core tool in the cultivation of happiness because it puts our experiences in proper perspective. Through the suffering, we can still be grateful for what we DO have, rather than what is currently disturbing our peace. Allowing ourselves to experience uncomfortable emotions and let them run their course is healthy and normal. If we don't give ourselves a chance to feel unrest, upset, unsatisfied and other overall unpleasant emotional states we may not be able to feel the ecstasy and bliss of joy, gratitude, and love to its fullest. We are dualistic, and we are resilient. We must accept that we will experience hard times and understand that it is temporary.

Some Research on Resilience

Dr. Ginsburg, child pediatrician and human development expert, proposes that there are 7 integral and interrelated components that make up being resilient – competence, confidence, connection, character, contribution, coping and control. (Gallaty, 2013)

Resilient people are aware of situations, their own emotional reactions, their own behavior, and the behavior of those around them. By remaining aware, they can maintain control of a situation and think of new ways to tackle problems. In many cases, resilient people emerge stronger after such difficulties. According to the research of leading psychologist, Susan Kobasa, there are three elements that are essential to resilience: (Jill Haupts, 2020)

Challenge – Resilient people view a difficulty as a challenge, not as a paralyzing event. They look at their failures and mistakes as lessons to be learned from, and as opportunities for growth. They don't view them as a negative reflection on their abilities or self-worth.

Commitment – Resilient people are committed to their lives and their goals, and they have a compelling reason to get out of bed in the morning. Commitment isn't just restricted to their work – they commit to their relationships, their friendships, the causes they care about, and their religious or spiritual beliefs.

Personal Control – Resilient people spend their time and energy focusing on situations and events over which they have control. Because they put their efforts where they can have the most impact. They feel empowered and confident. Those who spend time worrying about uncontrollable events can often feel lost, helpless, and powerless to act.

Another leading psychologist, Dr. Martin Seligman, says the way that we explain setbacks to ourselves is also important. (He talks in terms of optimism and pessimism rather than resilience; however, the effect is essentially the same.) This "explanatory style" is made up of three main elements: (Seligman, 1990)

Permanence – People who are optimistic (and therefore have more resilience) see the effects of bad events as temporary rather than permanent. For instance, they might say "My boss didn't like the work I did on that project," rather than "My boss never likes my work."

Pervasiveness – Resilient people don't let setbacks or bad events affect other unrelated areas of their lives. For instance, they would say "I'm not very good at this," rather than "I'm no good at anything."

Personalization – People who have resilience don't blame themselves when bad events occur. Instead, they see other people, or the circumstances, as the cause. For instance, they might say "I didn't get the support I needed to finish that project successfully," rather than "I messed that project up because I can't do my job."

Dr. Cal Crow , the co-founder and Program Director of the Center for Learning Connections, identified several further attributes that are common in resilient people: (Crow, 2019)

- *Resilient people have a positive image of the future. That is, they maintain a positive outlook, and envision brighter days ahead.*
- *Resilient people have solid goals, and a desire to achieve those goals.*
- *Resilient people are empathetic and compassionate; however, they don't waste time worrying about what others think of them. They maintain healthy relationships, but don't bow to peer pressure.*
- *Resilient people never think of themselves as victims – they focus their time and energy on changing the things that they can control.*

How we view adversity and stress strongly affects how we succeed, and this is one of the most significant reasons that having a resilient mindset is so important.

How Do We Implement It All?

The fact remains that we're going to fail from time to time. It's an inevitable part of living that we make mistakes and occasionally fall flat on our faces. The only way to avoid this is to live a shuttered and meager existence, never trying anything new or taking risks. Embracing suffering and being compassionate with ourselves is the most useful way to embody a lifelong sense of resilience so that we can come through any struggle and overcome a defeat with grace and stability. The components listed by Susan Kobasa illustrate all the necessary parts that make up the whole in understanding what exactly we need to do to execute this in our daily lives.

Personal Story

In July of 2018 I met the love of my life. This was a beautiful time to be celebrated. The pleasure that came of this meeting, the creative abundance that flowed out of both of us was prolific and powerful. It was one of the most wonderful times I can recount. Rewind just three months earlier to April, and I was reaching out to my ex to see if we could spark a relationship after seven years of separation. We dated for only a couple of months and although it was "good" I knew, with a heavy heart, that I had made a terrible mistake. I had grown during that time apart and done severe pruning work on my Mind Garden so that I could be a better person than I had been in our relationship of five years. We had gone through an unofficial marriage ceremony, had a son and were highly destructive and dysfunctional during our time together. It didn't matter how much we loved each other (if we were capable of truly loving, given our dysfunctions), our interactions were bringing out the worst in each of us. So, it was easy for me to recognize that I had done the work to overcome those parts of myself that had been holding me back. He had not been focusing on the same and was essentially the same person that I had been with before. I had to tell him that. It was so hard to express that I was not the same person, and that I could not go back into a relationship with him and that I had made a mistake in trying. I apologized for my misperception and moved on.

He was unable to move on though. In September, he learned that I had found a new partner. He was angry at first, and then wrathful. In November of 2018, we went to court. He filed many false accusations against myself and my family, and it nearly tore us apart. William, my partner, who I've mentioned several times already, took this in his stride. His compassion for the situation and his love for me and my family shone through every action he took during this incredibly hard time. It traumatized us all while we were going through the hardest parts of it. I will spare you the goriest details, just know that although it tested all of us in many ways that we could not have anticipated, we have all grown stronger together because of the resilience we created through intentional practices. I made sure to engage my children in fun activities even when I was so stressed with paperwork, court dates, the uncertainty of possibly losing my son, my mother being forced to leave her home for a year over false (and heinous) accusations, and the constant threat of my ex and his aggressive verbal attacks and accusations against me. We still made life good. We intentionally found pleasurable moments to fill the crevices of our suffering, so that we could soften the blow, cushion the hard edges closing in on us, and buffer the pain. It felt like applying a band-aid to a severed limb, but it worked. Every time we countered the stress and pain with satisfying activities and connective moments, we all released some of the fear and anxiety of the overall experience. It was temporary, but effective.

This process of uncertainty lasted for four years. After the court ruling was in place, we still had to interact with my ex as outlined by the judge. Afterall, he is still the father of my son, and it was determined that to maintain a meaningful connection between them, they needed time devoted to that. So, I was still communicating over email, arranging parenting time and discussing our son's needs. The PTSD I suffered lasted through 2021 when I finally put my foot down, gathered up all the evidence of his inflammatory interactions and went back to court for a final time. I had reached a point where I couldn't even open one of his emails without experiencing a panic attack. I knew this was unacceptable and that I needed to get a grip on my own reactivity. I chose to see it differently. Instead of valuing anything he said to me (mostly about what a terrible mother and disgraceful human being I am) I was able to empower myself to reach out to the court system on my own. With the help of a lawyer, the support of my partner and the resilience I had gained from the first experience, I went into it with an inner strength that fueled every action I took to end this destructive pattern of communication once and for all.

My poor lawyer. I have a great deal of empathy for him as I tried to convey from the very beginning just how volatile this situation would be. He initially expressed how he was fortified to handle it from a professional standpoint, but as the case progressed, he became more and more flustered as everything I pointed out to him began playing itself out. He told me that my ex was the most belligerent individual he had ever experienced in a personal and professional setting. “I know, I tried to tell you”, was all I could say. I understood what we were dealing with, and it had nearly broken us the first-time round… but it hadn’t. My lawyer also kept wondering why the court system was responding the way it was, (which I had expected as well, given the history of our case) regardless of my ex’s blatant belligerent behavior. The judges overlooked much of it and moved forward as if it were perfectly normal to get screamed at in their own courtrooms. September of 2022 was our last court date. So, this is still quite fresh in my experience. I am now fully empowered in my ability to navigate my feelings regarding my ex. I no longer have the PTSD rise within me when a communication is made. I no longer sink into anxiety over what might happen, over the uncertainty and danger that I felt would destroy us all. I am at peace, knowing that I did everything I could (even throwing a ridiculous amount of money at it) and that I can rest easily, because I showed up, did the work, made no excuses, and pressed forward in the knowledge that I was strong enough to carry the weight of returning to court for my family and for our future. I survived it, and so did everyone else. Therefore, my survival rate is still at 100%, and my resilience is strengthened. The bonus of this is that I am more peaceful, loving and kind instead of embittered. Is this a victory? No. In my experience on this Earth I have consistently been an advocate for the men. My studies in reading The Myth of Male Power by Warren (Farrell, 1993), and other works that highlight the plight of men in the family judicial system, I had determined to never create a debt slave out of my children's father. The fact is that my ex, however terrible his behaviors and actions have been, is now a debt slave of the state for the rest of his life (because he will likely never pay off the money the state determined was appropriate) because of my actions. This is a bittersweet win. On the one hand, my son will be provided for in the way he deserves to be, and financial opportunities will now be available to him that were not previously. On the other hand, my ex now lives in the statistics of fathers who have had their lives ruined by the judicial system that enslaves them financially. I do not feel "good" about this. I am the Hero and the Villain embodied in one determined choice made for the safety and sake of my family. My final thought is this. I include my ex in my gratitude practice now when I used to "need" to hate him.

How this Changes the Landscape of your Mental Garden

Any gardener will tell you that when a storm is approaching and your fruit trees are blossoming, you must protect them, or they won't bear fruit. If a flood is on the way, sandbags are a useful method of deterring water that could wipe out a year's crop. If frost is imminent, and you have immature tomato plants, the wall-o-water can be put over them to keep them from freezing. Gardeners deal with a wide range of adversity in ensuring the success of their crops. They use a variety of methods depending on the situation they need to overcome. Your Mind Garden is fraught with all kinds of challenges that will test your resolve in reaching the outcome you desire. If you slack in one place, the consequences will be visible, and oftentimes immediate. The long-term effects mean more work for you because the process of rebuilding is harder than the process of preventing. Resilience is not only the way your plants weather adversity, but the preparation you give them to weather it well! Your garden is teeming with life, and it can be easy to overlook an important step in the process, creating setbacks.

I will confess that in the process of learning, I have personally killed more plants than I have successfully grown. I mean this in the most literal way. I have planted so many seeds, tried to grow trees and other things, a lot of them in fact. You could say perhaps that I've failed a lot. Instead of seeing this failure as a reason to stop trying, I troubleshoot what potentially went wrong and make appropriate adjustments the next time around. I have a dream to plant a forest on our land. Do you know how many trees make up an entire forest? Neither do I. I know it's a lot though! Therefore, to meet that goal, I need to keep going, every single day. I can't just take a day off from watering my seedlings because I didn't feel like it, or I was sick, or I thought that something else would be more satisfying in the moment. I have an aim that I am shooting for, a goal that requires the proper dedication and commitment. This means that I must be unwavering in my approach to seeing that goal through. When I plant a tree and the cows eat it, it's dead. Start over. However, there WILL be a forest there! It's up to me and ONLY me to keep planting until I am standing under the canopy of tall trees with leaves filtering sunlight through to the Earth at my feet. This is my truth. I can see myself standing underneath them, feeling the shade of their magnificent canopy, and bathing in the satisfaction of my ongoing effort. I may never see some of these trees reach maturity, but that is not the goal. The goal is only to plant a forest, and I am already doing the work today, to make that a reality in some unnamed future.

Your mind is this way too. When you commit yourself to the goal of tending your Mind Garden as the focus of your desire, the results within you will become tangible. You may not even see the progress you've made, but those around you will look upon you and make comments like "Your skin is clearer", "your eyes are shining", "did you lose weight?" (Even if you haven't) "what's different about you?" "Wow, you look really good today". These are all recognitions from the external world that your mental garden is flourishing. Take them for what they are. Acknowledge them and use them to your benefit so you can see the progress you are making through the eyes of others. We are not experiencing life in a vacuum, and we need this confirmation from the Universe that we are succeeding! External validation in this form can be the most useful because we are not seeking it out. It shows up only as a reflection of what we are doing for ourselves. It sends a visible ripple into the world and sets a shining example to others around us that internal peace is possible, powerful and has worldly impact on our nearby environments. I am adding an additional quote here because I feel it represents the core of what I am trying to convey in this entire chapter.

> *"To suffer terribly and to know yourself as the cause: that is Hell." -Jordan Peterson, from the book "12 Rules of Life: An Antidote to Chaos".*

Strength Training: Resilience Practice & tools to weather the storm

- **Journal Practice:** Write out one story in your life that was impactful in a disempowering way, that STILL AFFECTS YOU NOW, regardless of how many years have passed. Flesh it out and get the details of it on paper in your journal. The more detail you use the better, because this will aid you in determining how to weather a future storm that may arise.

- **This story CAN** have a happy ending, and you will be creating that new and empowering ending by writing out some of the practices that are highlighted in this chapter that you can use to reframe the story you just wrote. Give it time to evolve. It may not come to you immediately. This will be an ongoing practice of rereading your story every day for the next week and picking out insights from it that you can use to develop a new outlook on what it can mean to you now. You have the power to use the experience to your benefit instead of your detriment moving forward.

- **(Optional Journal Prompt)** The art of resilience, redefining your inner strength. What situations are you prone to internalize and how have they "misshapen" you? (Like the trees) These can be as simple as not getting a text back from a friend or as complicated as a childhood issue that has left a kink in your growth somewhere. It does not matter about the severity of an experience; it is gauged on the severity of your feeling of the experience. Where you hold the most extreme feelings, is where resilience is lacking.

- **(Optional Journal Prompt)** Where is your "Sun"? Meaning: What do you do for yourself that has you striving toward a satisfying goal that can get you out of the mindset that you have experienced a trauma that is breaking, rather than simply bending you? These are the practices you do that can pull you out of extreme emotional states. These self-soothing acts and goal-oriented tasks are the sunshine that provides context to your suffering. Praise them and bring awareness to them so you can use them more intentionally. Emotional regulation begins with knowing how to alchemize your experiences.

WEEK 10

Your Value Structure Develops Your Purpose

"To stand up straight with your shoulders back is to accept the terrible responsibility of life, with eyes wide open. It means deciding to voluntarily transform the chaos of potential into the realities of habitable order. It means adopting the burden of self-conscious vulnerability, and accepting the end of the unconscious paradise of childhood, where finitude and mortality are only dimly comprehended. It means willingly undertaking the sacrifices necessary to generate a productive and meaningful reality (it means acting to please God, in the ancient language)."

-Jordan Peterson, from the book "12 Rules of Life: An Antidote to Chaos".

Accountability is Harder Than You Think

What is responsibility? We talk a lot about it in this book and how important it is, but do we really know what it means as a core value?

re·spon·si·bil·i·ty
/rəˌspänsəˈbilədē/
noun

1. the state or fact of having a duty to deal with something or of having control over someone.
Ex: "a true leader takes responsibility for their team and helps them achieve goals"
2. the state or fact of being accountable or to blame for something.
Ex: "The group has claimed responsibility for a string of murders"
3. the opportunity or ability to act independently and make decisions without authorization.
Ex: "We would expect individuals lower down the organization to take on more responsibility"

This definition tells us that accountability for our actions, control over our internal structure, duty, and independently making decisions without authorization are the key elements we need to live responsible lives. My mother used to say to my sister and I as children, that I never fully understood as being a value introduced into my psyche: *"Take responsibility for your thoughts, deeds and actions"*. A kid only kind of understands what that means, and then is shown countless examples of how it works in their lives.

If you think a thought, one which is detrimental, you will experience lasting pain from adopting a misperception. If you commit a deed (a conscious or intentional action) that is treacherous, you will pay the consequences of being considered untrustworthy. If you act in a way that goes against your integrity or aim, then you will suffer as a result.

The flip side to this concept is the reward system associated with this value. If you think a beneficial thought, you will see the direct result in your positive outlook on life. If you commit a deed that is in service to your mission, others, and yourself, you will be satisfied by having mental peace and a purpose. If you act within your integrity, other people will know you are dependable, trustworthy, and honest.

Responsibility is a core value but there are many, far too many to mention in one chapter. They are given to us by external environmental factors, conditioning, and influences. These help us determine our aims in life, what we reach and strive for, and our beliefs associated with our judgment, motivation, and work ethic systems, to name a few. There are personal values, character values and work values. Schwartz and colleagues have theorized and shown empirical support for the existence of 10 basic individual values. These are: (Schwartz, 2012)

CONFORMITY	TRADITION
SECURITY	POWER
ACHIEVEMENT	HEDONISM
STIMULATION	SELF-DIRECTION
UNIVERSALISM	BENEVOLENCE

These values range across cultures and are the most common among all the values we could name. There are many, but we will focus only on these ten in this chapter for simplicity. For example, selflessness and altruism are values, as well as humility and compassion. The ten main values listed above give us a broad spectrum to work with so that we can see how we aim and strive, and how our drives and motivations are rooted in our value system. When we define value, we get this multifaceted perspective of the internal workings of an individual. This is the complex core sense of self that builds our character, integrity, and convictions. Your values have shaped you so completely that they have become a part of everything that you do and more importantly, your personality. Whether you are influenced by others or not, whether you are in a group or alone, your values are an essential part of your soul. That may sound like a stretch, but as I flesh this idea out further it may become clearer to you as to why I claim such a bold statement.

val·ue
/ˈvalyo͞o/
Noun

1. the regard that something is held to deserve; the importance, worth, or usefulness of something.
Ex: "Your support is of great value"
2. a person's principles or standards of behavior; one's judgment of what is important in life.
Ex: "They internalize their parents' rules and values"
3. estimate the monetary worth of (something).
Ex: "His estate was valued at $45,000"
4. consider (someone or something) to be important or beneficial; have a high opinion of.
Ex: "She had come to value her privacy and independence"

We have learned through repetitive action, input, and stimuli throughout our upbringing what to value in life. If your parents made you feel unlovable, it may be more difficult to value yourself. If you were in an environment where physical goods were very important because your parents accumulated a lot of worldly possessions, then you may have learned the value of "stuff". Perhaps you had a religious upbringing and learned the value of God and going to church, having a community at your back, and supporting you through your faith. There are many values, and expressions of those values. Some of them intersect and are complementary to one another, while others conflict within you. Let's say you are in a situation like this. You are in grade school and your friend is in a fight. You want to help them, but if the value of security has been more established than courage, then you will not be able to intervene because you lack the courage and value your own safety over others. Your security is more motivating than your courage. It is not "bad" to be this way. It just points to the values you have adopted and now live by. Another good example could be that you made a mistake at work (I will raise my hand to this one) and it created an unavoidable conflict. Do you take accountability for what you did to create it, shift the blame by pointing to another person's failures, or deny that it is a problem to begin with? These are three different sets of values and three different ways of dealing with the same scenario.

Personal Story

While working in a grocery store, one of my duties is to place orders for our department. There is a book with bar codes and descriptions that I would have to calculate how much product we would need to get through to the next order, in short it's intuitive. Well, mistakes are made, even by my boss. So, one time I missed the bananas because I didn't see it on the page. We had none on the display and customers kept asking why we had no bananas. I was telling them that I did not scan them and that we would certainly have them in a few days when we placed our next order. I apologized for the inconvenience this caused them. My coworker heard me saying this and came over to me. She told me that I didn't need to tell them that I had made the mistake and gave me options of several other things I could blame it on. I replied to her that I knew it was my mistake. I was very aware of the fact that I didn't scan that product and it was indeed my "fault". I did not feel guilty when I explained this to the customers. I simply stated what had happened, with a sheepish smile on my face and shrugged my shoulders.

I was taken aback by my coworkers' ease in shifting the blame. Because I had been taught to take responsibility for my thoughts, deeds, and actions, it hadn't occurred to me that I could just blame someone else for what I had done. I didn't feel shameful for having made the error, and I wasn't trying to absolve myself of the mistake.

This told me a lot about her value structure and belief system. My integrity wouldn't allow me to lie to my customers, and they were usually kind to me, and understanding when I shared the truth about my blunder. I made many mistakes at that job, and I have had to own up to them. Some I would rather not have made and others where it would have been more beneficial for me to shift the blame, but it just didn't feel "right" to me, so I didn't.

Right and Wrong

Oh boy. This is a big bag to unpack and lay before you. We all know the concept of right and wrong. We have been taught what is right to do, and what is essentially wrong. We know about good and bad, light and dark. This contrast within our dualistic world has been well established. As I mentioned with the Hero and Villain, it's not always as black and white as that. There are degrees and a spectrum (words we have all become familiar with these days) because what is right for one, is wrong for another. A popular quote is "What is normal for the spider is chaos for the fly." This plays into shame, our values, motivations, in other words, why we do the things we do. We want to be right. We do not like being wrong. Our brains cannot make us wrong.

Historically, if you were wrong, it could kill you. Thcrcforc, we have been conditioned through generational accumulated learning that we need to be right, and about the right things. Being right is intimately tied with feeling safe. Wrongness gets you exiled, shamed, painful experiences and death. Have I gotten your attention? Human beings are still just apes (I say this sarcastically of course), regardless of how well civilized we purport ourselves to be. We have all been in a conversation with someone who needed to be right. Maybe it was you, or me, but we can agree that this has happened before. It is likely that the person who was so convicted in their "rightness" needed to assert a sense of safety in some part of their lives that was playing itself out within the situation. Their need to be right could even be a method to establish a sense of control within the chaos. Perhaps their beliefs were being challenged, or they valued authority who could say the perfect thing and correct any error, or they were insecure about something and needed their "rightness" to get them back to a stable internal foundation. We can't guess their "why", only our own, but we can always be sure that rightness and safety go hand in hand.

The Way of Mastery (Foundation, 2004) is a book about self-mastery through the channeled teachings of Jeshua Ben Joseph between 1994-1997. This comprehensive book covers many of our value structures, beliefs, and conceptualizations of reality through metaphors, practices, and meditative techniques. It offers a different way of viewing ourselves and the world. There is an interesting question within it, that has been echoed by many and made into a multitude of memes online. "Would you rather be right or happy?"

That's black and white too, because of course we all want to be right AND happy, don't we? Why not, that would be fantastic! The likelihood of achieving both may only be possible through deep self-introspection, self-reflection, and non-judgmental interaction with all aspects of our reality. That's a tall order. Be content with one for now. You are either right, or you are happy, and call it good enough for a moment while we dissect the parts and pieces of why this is.

When you are "Right"

To be right, you must make somebody else wrong. To assert your truth in this way, you must dismiss all other possibilities. The law of noncontradiction states this:

"The law of non-contradiction is a rule of logic. It states that if something is true, then the opposite of it is false. The law of non-contradiction states that contradictory propositions cannot both be true at the same time and in the same sense. For example, if an animal is a cat, the same animal cannot be not a cat. Or, stated in logic, if +p, then not -p, +p cannot be -p at the same time and in the same sense."
-Wikipedia

I had to chew on this for a long time after a conversation with a Facebook friend who used this against me to win an argument they proposed in a post. No one, except him, no matter how clever or intelligent or thoughtful, or philosophical would have been able to be "right" because of this law. It can be used to prop up your sense of rightness/pride/ego/superiority if that is what you need because you cannot argue any statement against the first one that is proposed as true. Nevertheless, it cannot make you happy. Because he made a statement, this law tells us that it is irrefutable regardless of any logical discourse against it. You probably won't come across this in regular situations with people, but it does happen sometimes in less obvious ways. Dare I use the example of abortion. This is a topic under great scrutiny and the core of many conflicts in our social structure currently. Abortion cannot be both beneficial and detrimental at the same time according to the statement made above. This is the law of either or. I will now illustrate how abortion can be both, and how nearly any situation can be both.

(Potentially Triggering Concepts!)

The pros of abortion are that if a medical condition arises during a pregnancy, there will be safety measures in place that will not threaten the life of the mother. Also, in cases of rape where an undesired pregnancy occurs, the pregnancy can be terminated to ensure the quality of life for the victim. Abortion was a concept in our human experience and history long before our civilized age. It was considered witchcraft to use medicinal herbs (called emmenagogues) that would expel a fetus from the womb in the early stages of pregnancy.

The cons of abortions are that it can be used as a form of post-contraceptive (much like the morning after pill) where a woman can make choices that are not in alignment with her goals and a correction is required to maintain her methods of living and conducting herself. There is also the potential for abuse in this area where it becomes a moral issue of serial killing the lives growing inside of a pregnant woman when this is repeated as a consistent practice by an individual. Their body count used to refer to how many men she has slept with, now it is a question of how many babies she has "expelled" from her uterus.

I know this might be triggering for some people to highlight such an inflammatory topic in this book, but it is an extreme example on purpose, because although I am personally against abortion as a choice for myself, I can see the utility it can have in a responsible society, and the detriment it can have in an irresponsible one and how individual choice, lifestyle, belief, and motivation all play a part in the value structure associated with this topic. I highlight many of these factors I am presenting in this chapter. Both examples I have given above have their value, however according to the law of contradiction, only one of them can be right. This is where the systemic controversy occurs that robs everyone of their happiness. Because which one is right? In my mind it is not as simple as that and needs much deeper contemplation and consideration before we make a determination that will impact millions of people. This is a generational issue that will span lifetimes because of the impact it has on us as human beings, our social structures, and our values, now and for generations to come.

Moving on now

When you are "Happy"

Some would say that happiness is fleeting, temporary and flawed. I can't argue with that directly, but I will present some ideas that can perhaps change the way we think about happiness. The excerpt below is a good example of how happiness can be an unattainable goal when we treat it as a condition in life rather than a way of being.

> *"If I could just make a little more money, then I would be happy. If I could just find that special someone and get married, then I would be happy. If I could get that promotion, then I would be happy. If I could finally own a home, then I would be happy."*

Taken from: The Law of Happiness: How Spiritual Wisdom and Modern Science Can Change Your Life. (Cloud, 2003)

We chase pleasure and satisfaction. That is undeniable. Happiness is not a value, so why am I taking so much time to discuss this with you? Happiness is characterized as the emotional state of well-being, feelings of joy, satisfaction, contentment, and fulfillment. We all want that, right? I taught my children that the definition of success as I understood it was going to bed at the end of the day HAPPY. For me it is that simple. It is not about seeking after something I don't already have; it is about cultivating the feelings of satisfaction in my daily life so that I go to bed feeling them. It sure makes waking up the next day a lot more fun.

Happiness is a symptom, in my opinion, of a well-tended Mind Garden. It can mean the difference between a "have to" and a "want to", or a "get to". I "have to" go to work, or I "get to" go to work. I "have to" pay my bills, or I "want to" pay my bills. This is an overreaching outlook on life as much as it is an emotional state of being. Everything we do as human beings is coupled with an emotional marker. Therefore, if you are coupling happiness to your actions, thoughts, and practices, you can guarantee a much more fulfilling life. Another fact about happiness is that although it can be fleeting because something terrible might come up to pull us out of our happy place, we can always call upon it again and again and again. It is an unlimited wellspring. We can turn the tap on for happiness and pour it into our wells without needing to elicit our Alchemy Shop Keeper for another "dose". Happiness is the practice of bringing momentum to that which we value.

Of course, we are not going to be happy ALL the time. Aiming for such a ridiculous notion is completely contrary to the fact that life is suffering. If we tried to be happy all the time, we would make ourselves miserable, and we have! Toxic positivity is at the core of this misguided belief. We can be happy that we are alive, we can be happy that we have a roof over our heads, and we can be happy that we are (somewhat) healthy. However, it is NORMAL and realistic to accept when we are NOT happy and allow that to run its course. We are NOT happy when someone we love has passed away. We are NOT happy when we get fired. We are NOT happy when something goes terribly "wrong" in our lives. We can be grateful as a practice in these instances so that not being happy does not throw us into a tornado of other associated feelings that can disempower us, cause us to blame others and act out in reactionary emotional states.

Values that Aim

In the list of ten common values, it is easy to see how some of them have played a role in our lives. It is not always easy to understand how they have impacted our choices and personality though. This chapter is about how your Mind Garden is growing, specifically reaching for the sun, reaching skyward, the new, tender shoots that climb upwards to gain nourishment. Your values aim you. Whether intentionally or not, you are still aiming at something. Instead of unconsciously aiming and ending up with all the things you don't want, intentional aim is like archery, you learn how to shoot accurately. When gardening, if you understand what and when soil, fertilizers, pruning, cyclical rhythms, harvesting and water are needed, the results are far more fruitful. When you aim, everything makes more sense, the results are achieved more efficiently, and you are more satisfied with the effort because you will likely fail less if your aim is on target. I didn't say you won't fail, but you may fail less often. I have broken down the ten core values here by adding some of the attributes that correlate with them, the aims that they strive for. This will give you a much clearer idea of how you have been using them, how they have shaped you as a person, and how you can use them intentionally.

Conformity: Aims at social connection, acceptance in the group mind, respecting authority, steering a group project forward, team building, alignment with beliefs and behaviors that support your goal.

Tradition: Aims at maintaining unity and longstanding practices, comradery, team building, motivation and momentum, meaning, structure, solidarity.

Security: Aims at safety, stability, integrity, honesty, observational skills, situational awareness, dependability, consistency, repetition, certainty.

Power: Aims at momentum, action, doing, achieving, gain through work, focus, risk, contribution, leadership, initiative, innovation, progress, accumulation of a skill, knowledge, or a position.

Achievement: Aims at learning, acquiring skills or knowledge, commitment, dedication, focus, driving potential, motivation, passion and desire, challenge, risk, determination, and courage.

Hedonism: Aims at stress relief, pleasure seeking, creativity, fulfillment, satisfaction, meaning, avoiding pain and suffering.

Stimulation: Aims at feeling sensations, tactile experiences, intellectual, physical, mental, and emotional, action, movement, focus on an experience, creativity, memory, group activities, community.

Self-Direction: Aims at internal discipline, self-motivated learning, personal pursuits, internal fortitude, initiative, independence, time management, self-awareness, personal growth, personal development.

Universalism: Aims at understanding universal truths, inclusive of all without differentiation, general widespread value, social order, internal placement within the world as a whole, concepts and practices that have general positive outcomes for all people, sustainability.

Benevolence: Aims at kindness and compassion, goodwill, being well-mannered, optimism, seeking positive outcomes and practices, recognizing virtues, civility and altruism, selfless acts of service, for the good of one, the group, or all.

The above list breaks down some of the traits, expressions and behaviors that are associated with these core values and how they are translated into thoughts and actions in the world. We all possess varying degrees of every one of the values on this list. The aim of a value is determined by how we use it. We can have a higher amount of benevolence and a lower amount of power, etc. These values give us purpose. Purpose is the driving force that moves our lives forward. Purpose is the momentum of a value structure and how it is executed in real time.

Plants and Value

Do plants have values? Not that I'm aware of. Why am I bringing it up then? WE place value on plants for the differing characteristics they possess. Could we go so far as to say that the characteristics of those plants are values? Not to them perhaps, but to us, absolutely. If you want shade, you look for a tree, if you want medicine, you seek out Echinacea for example. If it is beauty you want, then a rose or lily might be your aim. Every plant has utility, utility is a form of value. We would not be so excited to find a cactus when we want shade, and we would not look for a tree if we are seeking out wildflowers for a bouquet. So why do we seek anything that is not in alignment with our aim, purpose or even our values?

It's easy to see when we have examples that remove us from our daily lived experience of running children to school, managing our working week, and making dates with our significant other. While we are immersed in our lives, sometimes the value can elude us. When we are challenged, the value can feel downright abstract. When we are clear and calm and focused, those values take on a crisp, fresh, and applicable form that we can use to our benefit.

What we deem important, we focus on. What we make a priority is directly in alignment with our values. We can say that we value people and friendships yet forget to text someone back for three days. We can say we value a good work ethic, but not be able to meet our own personal deadlines outside of our jobs. We can even say that we value family time, but when something comes up spontaneously that interferes with the fun we planned for, we may drop the plan and go with the spontaneous event that came up. So, regardless of what we say, it is what we deem important in the moment where our values live. We can determine what those values are based on what we prioritize.

That's easy enough to understand, I believe, so I will leave it at that for now. When you know your values, the image of your purpose becomes sharper, and the details are easier to see. Your values will change as you age. You probably don't value the ice cream truck at forty as much as you did when you were five. Although you might be secretly hoping that a taco truck will cruise your neighborhood one day, sigh… at least I do sometimes. You didn't value a clean house when you were ten as much as you do when you become a parent. Values are meant to change and update themselves because we are ever changing creatures and our aims change as we age. Our purpose develops as we grow and experience more of the world. Purpose is what you live for. It is a noble pursuit and worth our attention because without it, it is easy to wander aimlessly. This can be a dangerous and faulty way of moving through the world because it leaves too much room for us to do more harm than good.

We are goal-oriented creatures. Without goals, we lack meaning in our lives. Without meaning we miss out on the value. Without understanding the value, we don't see our purpose and without knowing our purpose, we set ourselves up for consistent failures regardless of how well-meaning we are at approaching life.

The mind garden's purpose and value

Your Mind Garden is designed to grow everything you have accumulated in your life experience. It is there for you to tend consciously. It's set up by you, laid out to cultivate everything you will need to be able to reasonably feed yourself (mentally and emotionally and spiritually), stay at peace, challenge your skills, and bask in your divinity. Your Mind Garden is designed to be a paradise within you! It is time to start valuing it. You value it by making it a higher priority than you have been. Your subconscious has been a higher priority than your conscious mind, otherwise you might not be seeking out a book that is telling you to stop abusing yourself with your past. Your past is a vital aspect of everything you have become, and the accumulated life experiences belong solely to you, and are worthy of your love and attention. By taking responsibility for yourself in all areas of your life, you are asserting your own divine value by making yourself a priority.

You deserve the very best in life, and it is your responsibility to make sure that you have the best. No one else can do that for you. No one else can even see your Mind Garden! You are the ONLY one allowed in there and you are not allowed in anyone else's Mind Garden. When you focus on the things you have control over and stop ruminating on everything you don't, the amazing potential of divine oneness that resides within you will be able to shine right through your eyes and reflect in the outer world as you become more in sync with the truth that is your highest self. Universal Vibration is the alignment with the ALL. The ALL is what encompasses everything we interact with in our reality, (whether seen or unseen) and is the underlying structure of everything. Quantum physics has a name for it too. Religion calls it something else. I call it Universal Vibration because everything, I will repeat, everything is vibrating. The desk I am sitting at, the cat on the bed, my body, the spike mace resting on the top of my desk in front of me. Yes, I have a spike mace in my office, it inspires me.

Let us not get confused by assuming we are entitled to anything. We are not. We are only entitled to that which we give to ourselves. Nothing in the external world is ours for the taking, we have to work on the Mind Garden to discover our place in the world and how we can BE valuable. We are worthy with no prerequisites. We are NOT entitled.

Reaching High: Developing Purpose with your Value Structure

- **Journal Practice:** The 10 Values list gives some examples of how we use them in our lives. Write down what is important to you. It does not have to be any from the list provided. You might include

Prosperity, Abundance, Playfulness, and so on… With this list, think of all the areas where you prioritize those values in your life. Perhaps playfulness is a big part of your family time and without it, would lack meaning. The values you list have meaning in your life somewhere.

- **Art it! Write it!** Make PICTURES! Take photos of people you love, things you enjoy doing, your pets even, (print them out) and label them with a "value" word. Your pet might have "comfort" written over their head, or your partner has "LOVE" in bold letters. Make it fun! Use as much room as you need for this practice. Once you start, it might be hard to stop. If you can't print… use magazine photo representations of those same things and even title them with the names of the person, place, or thing they are representing a well as the value word associated with the image.

WEEK 11

Definiteness of Purpose. Your Life, Your Way

"Until a man selects a DEFINITE PURPOSE IN LIFE, he dissipates his energies & spreads his thoughts over so many subjects & in so many different directions that they lead not to power, but to indecision & weakness."

-Napoleon Hill

I Define the Parameters Of My Existence

What is a definiteness of purpose and how does it differ from purpose? What are the rewards that accompany definiteness of purpose? Napoleon Hill wrote the book (Think and Grow Rich, 1937) . It has garnered attention from many influential people throughout the years and is making a resurgence in the minds of people in the twenty-first century with the revised and updated audiobook freely available on YouTube. I mention it here, because this concept is not my own, and credit is deserved where it is due. This fundamental concept is what has birthed the belief that "thoughts are things' and that we have some control over them and can mold our reality in a way that shapes our experiences favorably. Napoleon Hill gave a list of benefits and consequences regarding the principles he outlined for success. They are parallel to Ralph Waldo Emmerson's philosophical concepts of life.

> *"Emerson is often characterized as an idealist philosopher and indeed used the term himself in his philosophy, explaining it simply as a recognition that plans always precedes action. For Emerson, all things exist in a ceaseless flow of change, and 'being' is the subject of constant metamorphosis." - taken from the internet encyclopedia of philosophy. (Brewton, n.d.)*

We discussed the concept of aim in the last chapter and how our values help us aim more accurately. Definiteness of purpose is like sharpening and fixing all the tools in your shed. You need shovels with good handles, pruners with sharp blades, rakes that have all their tines straight, and quality hoses that don't leak. When you get definite, you take every tool available to you and repurpose them to their finest quality. Every gardener understands the value of tools in good working order. If you use a busted hoe with a wonky handle, it takes twice as long to do the same job. If you dig with a shovel that keeps losing its head because it's got a loose screw, it can be frustrating to have to stop and keep putting the end back on to finish your project. Trust me, it's not ideal. You probably don't realize it, but every time you go willy-nilly through life, wishy washy, wandering like the good intentioned village idiot, you are using your tools badly and in piss-poor condition. I know, that sounds harsh, but I assure you, it couldn't be more accurate.

Your life, your way, means that you've got to go above and beyond what you know in order to get something different from what you've always had. "If you always do what you've always done, you'll aways get what you've always gotten." Thanks mom. You're brilliant once again and I could probably fill a book with quotes from you. We need a strategy. It takes that aim we talked about earlier. It has to do with responsibility and resilience. It is all about rewriting that script you've been replaying in your head since childhood and finally stepping into a life that suits your soul. It means being uncomfortable too. The trick is to remember that you are worthy of grandness and deserving of having connection and meaning, and quite capable of surviving so far, so why not go a step beyond that and start thriving in a life that fills you with all the desires of your heart?

The learning zone can be painful because it stretches us to ask questions about our current state of being. It demands that we go beyond the comfort and safety of our familiar ways so we can "become" something greater than what we know. It is pursuit. It is ambitious to do this because the requirements are not easy. Everyone is familiar with the transition between a caterpillar and a butterfly. The caterpillar hatches, eats constantly until it forms a cocoon, then literally turns to soup inside a shell. Its molecular structure transfigures itself into a creature with wings! That's downright miraculous if you ask me. Then it painfully breaks through the cocoon, must learn how to use its wings before it can fly and is in a lot of danger in this fragile in-between state. You can't help a butterfly out of the cocoon because it will never be able to fly properly if you do. I learned this as a child and the metaphor stayed in the forefront of my mind my entire life. We are all caterpillars and butterflies and transmogrify our character as we develop into ourselves.

"The expectations of life depend upon diligence; the mechanic that would perfect his work must first sharpen his tools." -Confucius

Passion and Creativity

One of the components of thriving is the requirement of passion. Yes, yes, you are passionate with your lover, no need to explain that to me. That's easy. You want it, right? Apply that feeling to the pursuit of greatness. What burning passion do you have tucked away in your shirt pocket that you haven't been sharing with the world? Are you afraid it's too big, too daring, too much, too extra? It's not, and that's the point of this chapter. Nothing you can dream up, get passionate about, and pursue is too big for you. The idea is to aim as high as you possibly can. No need to get overwhelmed, we understand you're not quite used to thinking so big and that's okay. Just as it has taken time to prepare your Mind Garden, introspection to sort through your issues, effort to feel your innate worth, and some faith to believe in your Universal Divinity, it will also take some determination to do this next step. Breathe it in, the life you desire, with every grateful inhalation. Breathe it out, everything that is YOU, that is standing in your own way of it.

Now is not the time to get sentimental about all the issues you are clinging to that keep you stuck. No one likes changing, birthing is painful. Transition is messy and transcendence is lofty. Who would you need to become to embody the person you imagine in your dream life? You not only have to figure out what you WANT to do, you also must get really clear on what you are willing to GIVE in return. Let me explain this. "You can want in one hand and shit in the other, which one weighs more?" This is an old saying that I grew up with and I still remember it because, for most of my life I repeated it like a mantra anytime I wanted something I thought was bigger than I deserved to get. I was guilted into believing that I wasn't worthy of wanting, but not only that, also that my wants weighed less than shit. That hurts and simply is not true. My wants may have been childish and unrefined at the time, a bit out of touch with reality, and not grounded in logic and reason, however they still had merit. I wanted to be an artist when I was a kid. That's a cool dream to have. In my twenties, I was legitimately an artist that made and sold Digeridoos, gourd rattles, mandala paintings, and any other object I could get my hands on to paint. I was a mediocre artist with little skill for the craft and I own that truth. I have no shame tied to it anymore. What I hadn't realized then, is that writing is an art too, that I am far better at it, and more passionate about pursuing it. I also have developed the skills required to be a writer, whereas I was unable to master the subtleties of painting. I spent years writing down every crazy thought in my head in journals. I still have them, from somewhere around 2009 consistently, but I have found others from as far back as 1996. It's no joke. I still have them. The stack is about two feet tall, and I have read them repeatedly throughout the years, identifying patterns of behavior, thoughts, beliefs, and conditioning that I had not (at the time of writing them) understood on a conscious level. When I told you earlier that I am my own best guinea pig, I was being one hundred percent honest. As my own therapist over the years, my writing has gone through several upgrades. I managed to autodidact myself into a state of peace and reason that seems pretty well balanced these days. But enough about me. I am only an example, there's more.

The kind of purpose I am outlining in this chapter is that of clear and direct action. We must act on and take calculated risks that will allow our passion to be seen in the world. It is frightening to imagine that you are capable of great things when you have been told your entire life that you won't amount to anything. It can be terrifying to pull yourself up and face the challenge head on, defying all social norms, cultural programming/conditioning, and your own belief structure to make the life you know you deserve. This is not entitlement or ego talking either. There is real humility in discovering your definiteness of purpose because you also must know what you are NOT good at and own that truth. You cannot be a master welder tomorrow if you have never welded anything in your life. You must begin somewhere. A board game cannot be won if we do not play. A skill cannot be mastered unless we give it time and energy. Health and wellness cannot be achieved by engaging in unhealthy activities and behaviors. We cannot become who we are meant to be by remaining stuck in everything we are not.

Therefore, the concepts I have compiled in this book have all been transforming your internal landscape by replacing the programming/conditioning (plants) with an updated version of YOU that can get out of your ego long enough to sync your physical body with your etheric one (the higher self, the divine aspect of you that lives eternally as a state of evolving consciousness). You've got to develop a sense of confidence in yourself, and you must do it in a humble way to achieve the passionate desires of your heart that are obtained through skill acquisition. Realistic understanding of your capabilities and level of willingness is required in attaining any goal you desire. What you are willing to do is mirrored by what the Universe can co-create with you. If you are unwilling, nothing in the energetic vibrational field can penetrate your reality. That is not an opinion (although there are many of those in this book) it has been scientifically proven. I mentioned Dr. Joe Dispenza and his research in previous chapters. His book (Becoming Supernatural. How Common People Are Doing The Uncommon) highlights the ways in which this statement is true. This book can be taken as quite controversial by some because it focuses on ancient wisdom techniques that have been run through scientific methods and tested in controlled studies. The controversy is in recognizing the unseen realms as a tangible force that works within, and alongside, everything we do in 3D reality. Bruce (Lipton, n.d.) is another forerunner of this concept. He has been on the world stage for enough years that many have heard his name, but he has not received accreditation from the scientific community who find his claims to be contentious in the field of epigenetics. I find his works to be insightful, inspiring, and quite rooted in a realistic pathway for self-responsible living. There is a saying, that if we cannot taste, touch, see, hear, and feel it with our physical senses then how do we know it's real? Because it's all measurable!

Your progress is also measurable. Consider your position before reading this book. Where was your mental state before the first chapter? How has it evolved and adjusted as you have been moving through your Mind Garden as a cultivator of your own thinking? No one else can see your garden; they can however see your behaviors, your actions, and your lived experience, which is a physical representation of what is going on inside of you. That is measurable progress that the world can see. We began developing your definiteness from the beginning of this book. To be definite, is to act deliberately. Your purpose is that which you are personally responsible for sharing with the world in a way that no one before you has. It is unique to you, and the experiences that have shaped you personally. It is your fingerprint in the tapestry of life and the world needs you in it, being you, the only way you know how to. So, to act deliberately about what you are personally responsible for is the path to a life of clearly outlined action, in a direction that aims at a goal you find valuable and worthy of pursuing, which will benefit all who encounter it.

LET'S BREATHE AGAIN SHALL WE...

INHALE A LONG AND STABLE BREATH. HOLD THAT!

FEEL IT WITHIN YOUR CHEST FILLING YOU UP.

EXHALE NOW, SLOWLY, DELIBERATELY.

FEELING YOUR RIBCAGE CONTRACT AS THE BREATH IS RELEASED.

Ah. Sometimes we just need to take a break, breathe in, and let ourselves feel whatever is moving through our body. This is exceptionally helpful when we are learning something new, as it grounds us in the present moment. Our brains are making so many connections, and at such high speeds that we are scarcely aware it is taking place. When we pause to breathe, we connect the mind and body so we can fully experience what we are learning.

Moving on now

I pointed out the importance of self-responsibility. Jordan Peterson, in his book, (12 Rules for Life, an Antidote to Chaos), lays out what those rules are and why we need them. They are all available online for free, so I included just the heading of each of them for your reference here. I removed the body of text that describes them, simply because I would prefer you read it directly from his book, as he adds context to each that would be too lengthy to include here and honestly, he wrote it better than I could describe for you in a single chapter. Below are the titles of his rules:

1 STAND UP STRAIGHT WITH YOUR SHOULDERS STRAIGHT.

2 TREAT YOURSELF LIKE SOMEONE YOU ARE RESPONSIBLE FOR HELPING.

3 BEFRIEND PEOPLE WHO WANT THE BEST FOR YOU.

4 COMPARE YOURSELF TO WHO YOU WERE YESTERDAY, NOT THE USELESS PERSON YOU ARE TODAY.

5 DO NOT LET YOUR CHILDREN DO ANYTHING THAT MAKES YOU DISLIKE THEM.

6 SET YOUR HOUSE IN ORDER BEFORE YOU CRITICIZE THE WORLD.

7 PURSUE WHAT IS MEANINGFUL, NOT WHAT IS EXPEDIENT.

8 TELL THE TRUTH. OR AT LEAST DON'T LIE.

9 ASSUME THE PERSON YOU ARE LISTENING TO KNOWS SOMETHING YOU DON'T.

10 BE PRECISE IN YOUR SPEECH.

11 DO NOT BOTHER CHILDREN WHILE THEY ARE SKATEBOARDING.

12 PET A CAT WHEN YOU ENCOUNTER ONE IN THE STREET.

I personally like number twelve, having been a cat lover my entire life, and the funny thing is, he talks about dogs through most of the dissertation on this rule, it cracked me up. As you can see, these are simply guidelines for a well-adjusted life. The headers are far less interesting than the actual content and I would like to encourage everyone who has taken the time to read this book, to venture into the 12 Rules for Life, as I believe it to be an academic, intellectual perspective of the concepts I am proposing here. His language differs greatly from my own and his ideas are well formed. He has a brutal way of dishing out truth that I think we all would benefit from hearing.

As we have illustrated in these pages, we must know what we need to do to be “good" at being human. We’ve got to treat ourselves with importance and understand that our vision for life should be greater than those imagined for us by others, and we need to consider ourselves worth helping. When you lay out a plan for your life, in whatever detail you can put on paper, you are treating yourself like someone who is worth helping, having, and honoring. You are treating yourself like you deserve to be here and take up space when you practice the art of personal growth (which used to be referred to as “self-help”, and perhaps still is in some cases), because personal development is a right that every single human being on the planet has. Mental health is a human issue. Mental illness is an individual issue. We all have mental health, just like we have physical health, we just pay less attention to it because it isn't important until it breaks. Hm. Let's start doing some preemptive maintenance on our humans so we can get the optimum performance out of this vehicle. You’re a vehicle. You wouldn’t forget to change your oil in your car, or the brakes. You change your windshield wipers so you can see in the rain. You make sure your tires are in good repair. Do the same for your human and you will see the same kinds of results. If you wait till it breaks, the repair is a lot harder, and more expensive.

A Note on Self-Help/Self Improvement and Personal Development

Self-help books have been a concept in its earliest form from an Ancient Egyptian genre called “Sebayt,” an instructional literature on life (“Sebayt” means “teaching”). A letter of advice from father to son, The Maxims of Ptahotep, written circa 2800 B.C., advocated moral behavior and self-control. These are not new concepts, and recently the self-help genre has gotten a bad rap as some have coined the term "toxic" to describe something that is unhealthy, undesired, or unwanted in our lives. Doing too much self-help can become "toxic" say some people, and I have always lived by the opinion that too much of a good thing can become detrimental, therefore everything in moderation. Moderation is the balancing act we do on the stage of life. Juggling our balls of relationships, learning, feeding ourselves, thinking, goal setting, creating passionate pursuits, doing nothing in a meaningful way, and the list goes on and on. Moderation is beneficial to keep your life stable, and sometimes we need to tip the scales in one direction or the other for a short while so we can delve into an aspect of life more fully. We will not always achieve balance and that's okay too.

Obsession over a pursuit can also be healthy when we are gaining specialized skills because this is a sprint and not a marathon. It is temporary and not long term. If we tried to obsessively pursue "a thing" for the long term, we would burn out and lose momentum for it. Our endurance is only as good as our ability to keep pace. Therefore, part of the journey will be a sprint, other times it will be a walk, and we must accept the fact that there will be moments when we feel like we are crawling, making barely any progress at all. The cycles of our lives must be honored because it is all there to teach us something. Self-help was designed to get people the tools and resources they need to overcome a personal issue "by themselves" - hence the name. It is always beneficial not to demonize something we don't fully understand. Have you ever heard the saying, "Know thyself"? This level of self-mastery requires you to engage with yourself and "help" YOU become the fullest human being you are capable of. Within this scope, I think it is only fitting to share with you another valid statistic. I would really like to drive the point home here. This sums it up in a language that most of you will understand.

> *"85% of rich people read two or more education, career-related, or self-improvement books per month, compared to 15% of poor." (S., 2020)*

Do you see why that is important? In general terms, the rich are into self-help and educational material, and the poor are not. Doesn't everyone want to be rich? We hear it all the time in our social circles. "If I only had more money.... I could... I would..." The goal of this book is not to make you rich. That may end up as a beneficial side effect of doing these practices to stop abusing yourself with your past, because as I have mentioned before, once you begin treating yourself like someone worthy of your own help, you start to feel differently about what you're capable of achieving. So, we all want **more** money, **more** stuff, **more** love and connection, **more** meaning, **more** time. We are so consumed with the concept of *more* that we overlook the power of quality. Humor me here. Read it again but this way. So, we all want **quality** money, **quality** love and connection, **quality** meaning, **quality** time. It FELT different when you read it, didn't it? We have gotten so lazy with our language that we have replaced "quality" with "more" in an ever-consuming age of technology that offers us more of everything at a lower quality in an overstimulating, instant gratification package that doses us with dopamine without really satisfying our needs.

What the heck does this have to do with my definiteness of purpose? I'm so glad you asked. Quality is the standard by which we determine its level of importance in our lives. Do you need to read it again? To break that sentence down even farther, we can say that quality is the satisfaction we seek by pursuing pleasurable activities. Now, wait a minute. I used different words and said the exact same thing. Have you noticed in your life how easy it is to say something two, three, or four different ways, and have it mean the exact same thing? Therefore, definiteness is so important. If you say I want more money, the universe interprets a lack. If you say that I want quality money, the universe interprets the standard by which the money is coming to you. Maybe you are a janitor and feel it is a lowly position, but the pay is good. (I personally believe that anyone in the service industry is of high importance to our society and many go widely underappreciated.) You want quality money, not just more of it, you want a job that honors what you are capable of, rather than wasting your talents on a profession that is not asking the most of you and challenging you to reach your potential. You may be perfectly happy being a janitor because it is a stable position that pays you well. You might not have greater ambitions. AWESOME. Do that and feel good about it! Only pursue when you are in a state of discontent. Don't misunderstand me here. I'll say it this way. If you have any part of your life that you are not satisfied with, there is room for growth there. Does that make sense? It boils down to what we believe about ourselves, our job, our time, and the energy we use to engage in the activities, and with the people we choose. Beliefs again Dannielle? Why does everything always go back to beliefs? Can't we move on from beating that dead horse already?

No: We will not move on when it comes to beliefs

We will recognize that everything is a belief, even the context within the pages of this book. They are my beliefs, the compiled collection of beliefs of authors, visionaries, authorities in specialized fields, neurosurgeons, scientists, spiritual gurus and more! Belief is what shapes our reality. So, let's start believing that we are a person of value and worth helping. Let's do ourselves some favors by writing out what we believe we are capable of, what we believe we deserve to accomplish, and what we believe it will do to benefit other people. We have spent a long time within this book identifying all the reasons, beliefs and thoughts that have shaped us and some of the disempowering practices that we have been using in our lives preventing us from living our true divine purpose. Now that we have gotten a lot of that out of the way and opened the possibility that there is a whole lot more within you than you might have previously believed, we are going to take it to another level by intentionally stating what we have to offer the world. Have you ever thought about writing a personal mission statement? If you said, "no that sounds stupid", then humor me by indulging in the potential benefit of participating in the concept below.

A Personal Mission Statement

This practice is what every business must do to show the world why their company has value. You have value just by being you. (I'm reminding you in case you forgot. Wink!) You have potential welling up inside of you, and you are no different from a business that has to convince the world of its value and why it's necessary. Your personal mission statement is a testament to what you can offer, but it is also a guidepost to what you are capable of, and why you personally were born to the family you have, the environment you grew up in, and the trauma and suffering you have endured. It shows how all of that in such perfect alignment has produced YOU to do and be exactly what the world needs. As we have gone through the process of unraveling all that you are, this next step will provide direction to the new concept of you that has been forming throughout this course. Developing your personal mission statement is a process and it has parts to complete so you can see the path your life has taken to lead you to the most fulfilling and meaningful life that supports who you really are, rather than accept everything you've been told about yourself that has kept you locked into a life that suits others.

Let's Begin

We want to keep it short. Your personal mission statement should only be one sentence long. This statement is so important because it is the true you, so be true to yourself. Your mission statement should reflect your greatest passion and what you believe your long-term purpose is in life. It will not be executed immediately but is an ongoing series of choices that you will have to make to remain true to this purpose. You probably won't have one as you are reading this chapter. Don't fret over that. You aren't supposed to. You are still marinating in self-help soup, fermenting, ripening, transmogrifying. Give it time and be kind to your journey.

"Definiteness of Purpose means we must have a clear understanding of what we want, and it must be a burning desire and passion for us. When you have

a definiteness of purpose you will not be distracted by anything that takes you away from pursuing this purpose."

-NAPOLEON HILL

To create your major definite purpose, follow the steps below:

Step 1 – Determine Your Specific Desire

Your desire is the driving force of whatever action you will take in determining your life and its mission. It is up to you to figure out what you have to offer that is in alignment with your soul's desire.

Step 2 – Establish the End Date

This is a concept that Napoleon Hill highlights in his book "Think and Grow Rich". It has utility because it sets up your mind to prepare for it happening on the expected date. I want to mention here that there are differing perspectives regarding this, and Abraham Hicks has an interesting point to make when considering how to use this effectively. She says that when you *generalize*, manifestation is slow and steady while it is being created. The more *specific* we get to our desires, the quicker they will begin to appear in our lives. This is a powerful example of how specific and non-specific goals reach an end result, and how quickly they appear. So, giving yourself an end date is a way of telling the Universe exactly when you expect to see the results appear in your life. If you are unclear about your desires, **do not** give an end date until you know what you will need to do to become who you must be to get to that end date.

Step 3 – Determine the Price

What are you willing to give? This is a simplified version of the give and take of life. We must give something to receive, therefore we must be absolutely clear on what we are willing to personally do for our definiteness of purpose to manifest in the world. This could be learning a skill, offering a service or product, helping in your community, writing a book, etc.

Step 4 – Make an Imperfect Plan

Lay out a plan. Don't be concerned about making it perfect right now, you've got to get the ideas on paper and read them to yourself so you can refine it as you understand the journey of how that plan will execute in your daily lived experience. If your goal is to become a writer, and yet you have no writing skills, you will need to learn the skills applicable to the field you are entering. You will need to learn about publishing, grammar, formatting and plot lines, character development and a slew of other important factors that will guide you to the goal of becoming a writer that people will want to read. Your plan must include all the steps along the way that will get you to your goal. You must figure out if you are even good at it. If you persist and find yourself taking far longer than someone else, it means that it just doesn't come easily to you. It may still be worth pursuing if you are determined to take the time, or you can use this gauge to shift your pursuit to something that comes more naturally to you. The skill sets might come easily and are more rewarding to pursue. The first step is starting somewhere. Again, don't try to get it perfect as you will need to update it while you learn more about the process of "getting there".

Step 5 – Write A Concise Statement

This statement is like your definiteness of purpose but differs in its utility. This concise statement is a declaration of your passion and your willingness to pursue it. Taking the imperfect plan, you can weed out any unnecessary words or lines that do not line up exactly with what you are trying to accomplish. This revision condenses your plan into a workable statement that is achievable and something you can use as a guidepost to get you to your result.

Step 6 – Reading Your Major Definite Purpose

The importance of reading your purpose is to make sure you remain in touch with your aim and why it is important to you. This is *your* definiteness of purpose and be sure that you read it every day to keep your focus on what your overarching aim is, so that your plan is in alignment with it, and you are taking the appropriate steps to achieve it.

Step 7 – Changing Your Identity

You will have to become the result of your aim to achieve your definiteness of purpose. This requires you to change your habits, behaviors, actions, thoughts, and lifestyle so you can step into the life you are creating as the new version of you who has all those things you are reaching for. You must become the person who already has those things through intentional choices made daily, creating incremental growth in the direction of your aim.

Definiteness of Purpose develops self-reliance, personal initiative, imagination, enthusiasm, self-discipline, concentration of effort, and conflict resolution, which are all prerequisites for the attainment of material success. According to Napoleon Hill, your definite major purpose should be like reaching for the stars. But, according to the rare recording of (Hill N.) speaking on the subject, it DOESN'T have to be "sound." Hill emphasizes that the point of your definite major purpose is to develop an unwavering focus on one particular thing. This laser-like focus clears the path for only that which you are aiming to achieve. We began this chapter with a quote from Napoleon Hill pointing out how we sometimes move through life in a way that zaps our energy, discourages us, and weakens our ability to create when we do not have the passion to lay out a definite plan for our lives. Throughout this chapter we have highlighted the method for developing a sense of purpose that can carry you through whatever struggles, rejection, sense of failure, and even the sneaking doubts that may arise as you begin to pursue with laser-like focus.

Manifestation Principles

Abraham Hicks said during one of her talks that manifestation can be done intentionally in two ways because we will find ourselves, usually, in one of two states of being. Since we mentioned this concept before, it's time to flesh it out for you. (Hicks, 2022)

General Manifesting: For Feeling Better

We can ask for generalized things to appear in our lives. Example, "I need some rest time so I can think properly about how to proceed. This rest time should not interfere with my job or relationships in any way and give me the insights I need to pursue what I am after." This sounds specific, but it is not. You have specified that you need rest time, and you have made it clear to the Universe that it must not interfere with your life's activity in any way. It can come to you now in any way it sees fit, to give you the time and space you require. When we are not quite sure of exactly what we need and when, this is a good way to get into the flow of Universal time so you can allow the process to unfold organically. If you are feeling stressed and not sure how to proceed, putting basic guidelines down for your manifestation will give you the time you need to get clear on what it is you really want. If you just said, "I need rest", you might manifest sickness so you can stay in bed for three days. This is NOT what you are aiming for, I would hope, but it often happens.

Specific Manifesting: For Faster Results

The more specific you get; the faster manifestation will arrive in 3D reality. If you need something to arrive quickly and you are clear on your intent, then you can ask the Universe to give you exactly what you need and when. We will use our earlier example and adjust it for this purpose. *"I need a day off work THIS WEEK so I can focus on writing the next chapter of my book. I have a deadline to complete, and I have been working my 9-5 job consistently, and I have not been able to pursue my creative endeavors that are meaningful for me. I am dedicated to completing this chapter in the time off I will be given, and I have outlined the structure of this chapter so that when the time does become available, I will be at my highest creative level to produce the results I am after."* As you can see, we have a goal in mind already for the "rest time" we are asking for. We have a plan, and we NEED the Universe to provide the space to put that plan into action. We tell the universe exactly what we are willing to give when the time becomes available and, in this way, we have been highly specific about how we will use the time we are asking for. When we give a date or a time frame to accomplish a mission, the manifestation can't help but to make sure that it takes place quickly within the parameters we have laid out.

You can apply this example to anything. Just keep in mind that general and specific manifesting will achieve different results. Definiteness of Purpose is about specific results. We have shown you how you can lay out a plan, set your dates, financial compensation, what you are willing to offer, and give all the details you can to bring it into 3D reality with the quickness you require. Some of the first chapters have been geared more towards generalized manifestation as we sorted through all the issues that have gotten in the way of us being definite.

Personal Story

I told you that when I was a kid, I wanted to be an artist. That was a generalized purpose. I achieved that to a degree. I was successful with the art that I pursued at that time, and I did make a career of it that was willy-nilly, inconsistent, and overall mediocre. I had not taken the time to get clear on what kind of artist I wanted to be, and how it would benefit my clients. I had not known at the time that I could ask for specific things to manifest them quicker and with greater clarity. My twenties were a disappointing example of the starving artist. I got the book "Think and Grow Rich" at this point in my life. I read it three times in ten years. One thing always stood out to me every time I read it. "Between the ages of forty and sixty, you are at your height for success." I took this in subconsciously and let it marinate in my unconscious mind. I hadn't realized at that time that I had unintentionally set my time frame for success to occur at the point when I turned forty.

At the age of thirty-nine, I had my breakdown/breakthrough. This incredibly challenging time in my life opened the way for me to let go of everything that had been holding me back from becoming highly successful with my pursuits and goals. My dream of being an artist stayed with me, and I have seen it transform as I evolve and experience more of life. I would not have been able to write this book had I not gone through the process of disentangling all the places where my energy was conflicting and contradicting everything I wanted to create in the world. I needed to break open before I would be able to understand my definiteness of purpose. I needed to get to the heart of my soul and sweep away the basement floors that had, for so many years, been cluttered with all the disempowering beliefs I have carried with me through life. I needed to discover my Mind Garden and create a completely different blueprint for its highest growth. I hadn't known about fertilizing and pruning and weathering the storm through resilient practices.

Failures, even minor ones, would cripple me and inhibit my progress. I would descend into deep bouts of depression that could last for several weeks or longer when I would undergo a failure. Failure has always been my kryptonite, because perfectionism is the mechanism that allows failure to become shameful. There must be something wrong with me because I just fail at everything, regardless of how knowledgeable I am, how much I study or practice, or how much I throw at it… I will always fail. This lie ruled my life for such a long time that it took a Universal intervention to shake me up enough to get myself out of my own way.
What is my definiteness of purpose now? Oh boy, I know it and I live it every single day!

> "MY DEFINITENESS OF PURPOSE IS TO EXPRESS MY DIVINITY IN A WAY WHERE OTHERS CAN SEE THEIR OWN."

That looks like a generalized statement because it can be pursued in a wide range of ways. However, I could not be more specific, and as you can see, you want your definiteness of purpose to be a "one-liner" that can be easily translated and read out loud every day. This is your laser focus. If you do anything in your life, you can read your statement and see if your action lines up with it. My one-liner requires some of the values we discussed earlier. Integrity, humility, leadership, universalism, conscientiousness, and courage, to name a few. It requires that I let go of judgment of myself and others, view the overall picture rather than scrutinize circumstances and individuals, remain humble and make sure my ego is in balance with my goals. The ego must pursue, so to pursue this without getting a big head helps me to remember that I am no more special than the mother walking down the street, the grandmother in the wheelchair, the mechanic who is covered in grease from working on cars all day, the veteran propped up on a cane. We are ALL special to the ALL that is, and the ego will try to tell us otherwise, weaving a false sense of importance into our work and our mission. What I know is that if I do not say what is in my heart and mind, someone else will, and most of the content of this book is compiled from what many other people have said before me. It is not mine, therefore I cannot own any of it, I can only be a conduit that it can flow through, to the hearts and minds of others, who like me are practicing being our best selves always.

My definiteness of purpose encompasses being an artist! All the dreams I had as a child are being lived out through me, now that I have narrowed my focus into exactly how I want to manifest my art. That is a beautiful gift to myself that I am grateful for every single day. It is my compass, my north star, and the guiding light of all my actions. I fall short and forget myself of course, but because I can read this statement every single day, no matter what circumstances take place in my life, I can always compare my every action to it (rather than others), so that I know I am being true to my mission in life. We cannot compare our progress to anything or anyone outside of ourselves. We can and must compare our progress to every one of our yesterdays and act accordingly. "Comparison is the thief of joy", said Theodore Roosevelt, and Mark Twain phrased it this way. "Comparison is the death of joy", which means the same thing. Both individuals understood a fundamental truth about human nature, which is that our ego wants to compare to external sources, however it is more useful for us to compare only that which we can actually measure; ourselves.

Definite Plants!

Nothing arrives by accident. I have observed a phenomenon in nature that has been confirmed by other people I know but is not a scientifically proven theory. In the White Mountains of Northern Arizona where I live, we have a lot of different kinds of weeds that thrive in this environment. Being the chatty person I am, I talk to a lot of people from all walks of life. One year, we had mullein and horehound take over the fields and the roadside ditches, pop up randomly in people's gardens unwanted and along any stretch of earth that they could get ahold of. That particular year (2018) we had a widespread issue of lung ailments that plagued the locals. The persistent dry cough that would not go away after a cold, harsh lung condition with heavy mucus discharge and asthma was inflamed in people that don't even get asthmatic symptoms normally. Mullein is a specific remedy for the lungs, and it will soothe, coat, and subdue a stubborn cough. It is so gentle that even children can take it in large quantities and can be used as a fomentation for swollen glands. Horehound is best known for the candy that was popular in the 50s and 60s. It is a very bitter herb and has a way of expelling even the most stubborn mucus from deep in the lungs. These two plants grew in abundance the year we most needed them. That was not a coincidence. The next two years in a row (2019 and 2020), we had wild lettuce do the same, and its common uses that have been documented are pain relief with its milky latex and providing restful sleep, which seemed to be exactly what this community needed. The next year we had camphorweed (2021) when the symptoms of covid left people experiencing unexplained pain even while they were resting and the development of rheumatoid conditions that traditional medicine couldn't touch with enough efficacy to provide relief. Camphorweed is for this kind of pain when applied topically.

These are only a few examples of the definiteness of purpose plants have and how they have evolved alongside us. As a culture, we don't understand that language anymore as a whole, and I have dedicated my life to this pursuit of what used to be considered "occult knowledge" of the Earth and I call myself a "Witch" because I choose to learn this language and understand how it can benefit us all. Plants communicate quite well with us; their messages are sometimes so blatant that it is impossible to ignore. As an Herbal Witch, I have been able to predict what ailments will arise the next year just by observing the wild plants that grow in our area. This would look like magic to some people, but it is just a language, a specialized skill that has taken me forty years to develop and there is nothing magical about it at all. It is rooted in science more than spiritualism if we want to split hairs about it. Plants are so definite in how and where they choose to grow that Siberian Elms can turn a vacant lot into a forest within five years' time. I have seen this occur in our area as well. A plot of dirt grew into a flourishing forest that housed birds, insects and smaller groundcover plants that would bring nourishment back into the soil and combat erosion. We can learn a lot about ourselves and our environment by looking at the plant kingdom and how it conducts itself naturally, wildly, and without shame or fear of failure. They know exactly what is needed in an environment; even if we have forgotten how to recognize that, they still show up, do the work, and grow purposefully regardless of our human ignorance. We must honor ourselves by doing the same.

Sharpening your Toolkit: Definiteness of Purpose - Your Life, Your Way

- **Journal Practice: Art it!** Write it! Write a list of all the words that you WANT to define your life. These are the tools you are sharpening; just by naming them, you bring it to the forefront of your awareness.
- This is a form of self-love and self-care. You are about to do something kind for YOU! Are you ready?

- **Write out** some adjectives that define the life you are creating with your new mindset and skill acquisition. Some of the words I have chosen for my life are magnificent, magical, fantastic, playful, excellent etc.

- What tools/skills have you always had within you that are available right now? White them down. What tools/skills do you still need to become the person that will be able to execute your mission? Write them down.

- **Write out** your personal mission statement: What is it that YOU can offer to yourself and the world that is unique to you? Write your plan first. Make it messy! Then condense it down to a single sentence. Read it every single day! This may take time to formulate. Don't rush yourself but do push your resistance so you can find it and begin living it!

WEEK 12

In Full Bloom. Harvesting the Fruits of Your Labor

"I challenge you to make your life a masterpiece. I challenge you to join the ranks of those people who live what they teach, who walk their talk."

– Tony Robbins

Your Development is Personally Tailored

Did you know that the reward for your hard work goes widely unnoticed by the outside world? I may have mentioned this already. The progress you make for your personal growth has fruits that are ripe for picking. These fruits of your Mind Garden are the culmination of every season you have dedicated to the care and maintenance of your internal world. There will be outward signs that society will celebrate with you, but the overall benefit of all this progress on the journey you're making will be seen most in your daily lived experience, not in the praise you receive from others.

There is a term I have become familiar with recently called "destination addiction" and it happens when we lose track of the magical journey and focus on the outcome as the "goal" for our efforts. We must, of course, celebrate our victories. It is the way in which you celebrate these milestones that will determine what you get out of the journey. We have been cultivating a garden throughout the pages of this book, with the practices you've been engaging in. Every gardener knows that there are seasons that have specific requirements for your plants to thrive. Each season takes a different level of effort and has their own rewards attached to them. Harvest time requires that we continue forward with the same diligence we have applied in getting to this chapter in this book. There will still be much to do! So don't sit down yet, kick off your shoes and think the work is over. Just because you get to benefit from your hard work does not mean that you need to stop taking action at this stage in the game.

Timing is Everything

Our lives move very much like the lifecycle of a garden. Some of your plants are perennial, or annual, may multiply by rhizome and root, or rely solely on seedheads to produce next year's crop. All plants have their own cycles, and each one has a window of harvesting opportunity specific to their needs. Poplar buds must be harvested during a very short window in February before they open as flowers. If that window is missed by even a day (and I speak from experience here!) They burst open in fluffy, cottony flowerheads that can no longer be used as a medicine. They've gone to seed. The buds no longer exist in the form that would have produced the medicine that plant offers, sad face for an opportunity lost. Camphorweed is ready for harvest over a two-month period at the height of summer. Every single day new blossoms will open that can be popped off and collected. The leaves are covered in glittery terpenes that are sticky to the touch. This plant has a long harvesting window and will require you to be vigilant in collecting or you will end up with a lot of seedheads and no flower tops or sticky leaves, which will result in a massive outcropping of the plant the next year, and you missed out on harvesting the medicine when you had the chance.

Everything we have been working on has its own cycles and will be ready to "collect/harvest" at specific times. We can miss opportunities if we are not paying attention to the cycles that are natural to us, as individuals. Some people will see results quickly in certain areas and can capitalize on their inner work after brief stints of effort and action. Others may see slower progress and will be required to take extra care and attention in the process of harvesting their hard work. There is no one size fits all for any of this. I have pointed this out before too. Just because you did one of these practices during a period of your life, and it came easily to you at the time to get to the satisfactory harvest quickly, does not mean that the process will be identical as you continue down this path of growth and discover new areas of your personal development that require your attention. Give yourself the opportunity to move through each of these phases in their own time. If you rush the process, you may miss out on valuable information that is right in front of you. Just like those poplar buds that need to be checked daily to collect them at the height of their medicinal potency, you will be given chances to practice what you have been learning. These may not always be obvious to you in the moment, when your kids are screaming at one another and all you need is for them to stop right now, no questions asked, BECAUSE I SAID SO! However, if that is not the loving reply you want to offer your children, then you have the chance to choose differently, get creative and curious, and seek out these situations to practice your newly derived skills. Harvesting is all about seeing the benefits of your labor. Every time you choose to use a skill that has bloomed in your Mind Garden, you are harvesting your hard work, transforming your life in each moment you choose differently from your automatic/default mode that was built on the programming, conditioning and environment that has become most familiar to you. It can be awkward at first, and that's okay. No one is handing out medals here. You must reward yourself this time and it will be blissful when you do! Gold stars on your chart for every time you get your timing right. There are no penalties for an opportunity lost, you will get another chance to try again, so keep your eye out for it, it's on its way!

What Am I Harvesting?

You are a plant, remember? (Several at any given time in fact.) You spent seasons in your garden, digging, pruning, watering, fortifying the banks, preparing your tools and now your garden is thriving! But what are you actually harvesting when it's all happening in your own head? When we have an external garden, the progress is easy to see and the material world is instantly gratifying when we can walk our physical body into nature, cut the stem of a plant and hold the food that WE grew. The plants are there to touch, and we can literally see the zucchini peeking out between broad, serrated leaves. We know what to do with that zucchini once we pick it. It's going to be dinner! We understand this on a primal level because we have been interacting with our external world for millennia, and the social, genetic blueprint is firmly established in our DNA. So, what about everything we can't always see? What about the behaviors, the habits, the sneaky thoughts that derail us, the judgements, the hard emotions? What about those intangible things that we have been discussing throughout this entire book? Harvesting your "fruits" is about knowing when you are in the cycle to get the most out of your work. When are the concepts most potent in their medicinal qualities that will benefit you and others?

The answer...

When you are able to move through the world without succumbing to it

Well, that's a broad and general statement, isn't it? This is not evergreen. Meaning that it will ebb and flow throughout your journey rather than being a static force that will remain with you forever. Hopefully I am not bursting any bubbles here by pointing this out, but you will need to continuously, and forever, as long as you are alive, do the work. You may need to revisit practices as a reminder of the process. Harvesting these concepts, we have been going over is an ongoing journey because we have been working in many parts of our Mind Garden and they all require our energy, attention, and constant care. We're important, remember? We are absolutely worthy of our time and attention. We get to treat ourselves like the valuable assets we are and change with the seasons of our own lives so we can be our best selves in every season. There will be storms, floods, blights that take you out, and bugs that eat your medicinal plants. You have learned the tools and skills required to overcome all these obstacles, and now we will reveal what your fruits actually are and how they benefit you.

STABILITY

Inner stability, or the foundation on which you stand firmly rooted, is one of the harvests of doing this work. You have a foundation of practices that keep you upright in hard times. You will need this during challenging interactions, when you might be predisposed to a reaction of anger. You are harvesting STABILITY every time you emotionally regulate in a way that is contrary to a past preprogrammed, negative/disempowering reaction. When you have an internal foundation of calm, you will interact with the world very differently than you used to. STABILITY is the grounding force that keeps you mentally prepared to engage in circumstances and situations that test your calm. This is like a pond of water that is still. There are people in our lives that cast stones into our ponds, getting a "ripple" out of us, an emotional reaction that they are comfortable and familiar with. When you harvest STABILITY, you will notice that it is much more difficult for people to get a "rise" out of you. Your language has changed, so you now know how to defuse a situation rather than inflame it. You bring calm to the moment by being truly present for whatever is happening and offering only the divine correct action that will keep the moment in a state of peace. Offenses occur less in your life, given or received. Offense can only happen when you are not on an even footing. STABILITY is the landing pad on which you can stand true in your mission and purpose without faltering at a slight breeze of doubt and criticism from the outside world. When you have an internal doubt and criticism, you can ground yourself in this harvest and know that you are standing firmly rooted to a solid and stable foundation that you built.

SELF COMPASSION

It is easy to elicit sympathy from the external world when we are experiencing some form of adversity. The harvesting of SELF COMPASSION is when we go inward and offer ourselves the voice we most need to hear. Instead of running to another for the words of comfort we so desperately long for, we have become that voice. We harvest SELF COMPASSION every single time we soothe our anguish with nourishing thoughts, practices, and actions. We have become the most loving individual in our own lives. We have become someone worth loving and giving our attention to in a loving way. We no longer berate ourselves; we no longer tell ourselves the lies that make us shrink away from our dreams. We are the most valuable and loveable person in our lives because SELF COMPASSION has moved from being a concept, into a daily practice that we engage in frequently. This harvest is long term, and the potent medicines will be most luscious when we are at extremely low points in our lives that test our worthiness and our lovability. For some, that may need to happen daily until they get better at harvesting STABILITY. For others, it may only be necessary to harvest this when they have gone through an unexpected tragedy. Whatever is correct for you, you will know when it is most needed in your life.

THANKFULNESS

THANKFULNESS, as we mentioned earlier in this book, is the deep appreciation for something important to you. As you have been learning to pay attention to yourself, and learn the importance of your varying aspects, THANKFULNESS is the harvest you get when you are fully satisfied by your process. This is especially potent during times when we want to question "why is this happening to me?" because we have learned that when we are thankful for even the bumps on the journey, we can enjoy the scenery with greater satisfaction. THANKFULNESS will be beneficial to harvest in the moment you think you want more than you have. Yes, it is necessary to dream and aim large, but we cannot envy or covet another's achievements. If we find ourselves longing for something that takes us away from being present in whatever process we are experiencing, we can harvest some THANKFULNESS to remind us that we are right where we are needed most and the victories we have experienced up to this moment are steppingstones, and more will be coming. We need not dwell on them or how long it seems to be taking us to get there. We are already here. We have arrived. THANKFULNESS is evergreen. This conifer will never lose its leaves throughout the winter and that is a valuable asset to draw on ALL the time, as some of your other plants are not as bountiful and hearty.

MOMENTUM

There will be times along this journey when we just don't feel like doing what we know we need to do. We know, we know we know, but we choose not to anyways. This can be thwarted by harvesting MOMENTUM in the moments when we feel despondent towards life and lose sight of our aims. This is not always tethered to achieving. Sometimes we will need MOMENTUM just to get out of bed in the morning. Reminding ourselves what our purpose is, and why we are here, can drastically increase our MOMENTUM during trying and difficult seasons. Without this driving force, we wander willy-nilly through our garden and can't really enjoy anything we have grown there. It lacks meaning and value. MOMENTUM is the catalyst that can change your "I can't" into "no one can stop me" and this might involve creating a playlist of music that gets the fire pumping in your blood, saving and listening to a motivational speech or speaker, or a compilation of motivational quotes. It might look like writing down in your journal all the reasons you want to do a particular thing that you have lost MOMENTUM over. MOMENTUM, once harvested, can transform apathy into excitement, lethargy into energy, and melancholy into synchronicity. We make our own luck in the world with our determined actions and MOMENTUM is the driving force that sets up synchronicities in our favor by opening a space within our awareness that shows us the path. The path is always laid out before us, but it becomes overgrown, distorted, and landslides block the way at crucial turning points. With MOMENTUM in our bag of harvested goodies, we are aware of what lies just beyond the bend, just out of reach, and we move towards it even when we aren't close enough to see it. We can do anything. We can be anything. We can accomplish anything when we remember to harvest MOMENTUM at the right time.

FORGIVENESS

This is a hard one for many people and it has a narrow window of opportunity for harvesting, much like the poplar buds. It is something that requires diligence and practice to get our timing right. FORGIVENESS can be most useful in times when we feel wronged by another. An instant, a flash, a blink of an eye is all the time we really have to harvest this powerful medicine. When something inflammatory has just come out of a person's mouth, that is the moment we harvest FORGIVENESS. We quietly and instantly forgive the other, and our response will be that of the highest love we can express in that moment. Can we do this after the fact? Of course, and we often do as we are learning how to harvest this fruit. However, it will be slightly shriveled and not as potent, perhaps it will have lost some of its "flavor" if we wait too long. FORGIVENESS is one of the most potent medicines we are growing in our Mind Garden and the greater awareness we give to this plant will determine just what we are capable of harvesting from it. When we harvest FORGIVENESS instantly, rather than retrospectively, we also harvest STABILITY and THANKFULNESS simultaneously. That is a rare gift indeed and worthy of our attention! There are other potent combinations within our harvesting capabilities that we will learn to capitalize on, and you will learn to recognize them as you practice but let me say that this combination yields the highest and most potent medicine in our Mind Garden by far! The rewarding satisfaction that comes by harvesting this in the moment is truly blissful and felt within the body, which is why I am asking you to pay special attention to it.

FORGIVENESS, when applied to oneself, and harvested in moments during which we are the recipient, is much more "forgiving" in its window of potency. We can retrospectively forgive ourselves at any moment if we are sincere. We will make choices that we are not proud of, tell white lies that do no real harm overall, but might leave us with some unwanted gremlins or guilt. FORGIVENESS harvested for us kills a gremlin like bug spray! The effects are not always immediate and may need reapplication through journaling or self-care practices. I assure you it is worth the time you give to take special care of this plant in your Mind Garden. You will need to harvest it repeatedly, and the cycles in which it will be available vary based on the environment you are living in.

HONESTY

We all know why HONESTY is important. Have you ever considered it something to harvest though? Probably not. I have always thought of HONESTY more as an action rather than a result. Harvesting HONESTY comes with great courage. This plant is beautiful like a rose but has very long and dangerous thorns. This plant in your Mind Garden has developed in a way that protects itself from YOU! How so, you are wondering? It has had to adapt to a lifetime of your lies, and the lies you adopted from others. It has evolved into a formidable and tangly tree-like bush with fruits on the highest branches. It does not matter what your background is either. Even those of you who grew up in the most integrous environments, where this value was cultivated, will still end up with a tangly bush of HONESTY. Society has had its way with you, and HONESTY had to adapt in order to survive. Just the thought brings tears to my eyes! This is one of the most beautiful plants in the garden, regardless of how gnarled it has become over time.

Let me assure you of this though; the more you harvest HONESTY, the more you will notice that this plant will transform from a jagged, thorny, and dangerous mess into a luscious and delicious, juicy, food bearing tree, laden with ripe fruit for you. HONESTY has been described as a double-edged sword because sometimes it is not warranted by others but needed in order to establish boundaries that keep you safe, even though it can come at a terrible cost to you. HONESTY can be harvested in times when your values line up in such a way that it would not benefit you to tell the truth but would benefit a greater purpose. It can be challenging to harvest this at the right time without cutting yourself on the thorns. It is almost impossible in fact, but worth the effort you put in, to ease past the dangers and get right up to the highest dripping fruit of HONESTY during times when you would rather shy away and shrink. You must be bold in life to achieve your aims. HONESTY is the reward that is so satisfying to sink your teeth into, it is the ambrosia fruit of your garden! The food of the Gods. I cannot express enough just how delightful it is to be able to walk into a situation with HONESTY in your harvest bag, stand true to yourself and watch the scene unfold in unexpected ways. We are ninjas at covering our asses and playing it safe, but ninjas are not seen. They move through the darkness for a reason. HONESTY is the bright, white light that shines even when it is not wanted. It can burn, and sometimes it must burn away whatever is being covered up, whatever is being intentionally looked away from. Harvest HONESTY when you cannot back down but be a considerate cultivator because if you are not conscientious you will get shredded with the thorns as you reach for this fruit!

DILIGENCE

You already know about how we are constantly referring to consistent, persistent, and careful effort put forth in attaining your goals, dreams, desires, and passions. Conscientiousness is another word that means the same thing. DILIGENCE harvesting is how we reach our passionate pursuits. It is most valuable in times when we want to procrastinate. Procrastination can mean a missed opportunity, a delay in your manifestations, a roadblock on your journey. DILIGENCE can be harvested when you have your phone in your hand, and you have scrolled for five minutes too long. This plant is simple, shrubby and its flowers are aromatic. They have an alluring aroma of promise that lingers in the air. They almost whisper "come breathe me in and you will be satisfied!" DILIGENCE flowers are the sweet nectar of pursuit. This shrub flowers throughout the warm season. There is always a winter in the garden, so you will not have these blooms available ALL the time to draw you back to your projects, and that must be honored. We've got to flow with our own cycles and knowing when to harvest DILIGENCE and when to rest can make the difference whether the quality of your work is worthwhile. When you cannot harvest DILIGENCE and must sit down and relax, harvest THANKFULNESS instead because it is evergreen with rich coniferous leaves even in the snow.

ACCEPTANCE

Sometimes we need to sit with ourselves during uncomfortable and difficult emotions that disempower us. Positivity is applicable during times when we are ready to be happy. ACCEPTANCE is most valuable to harvest when we need to give ourselves the support to be exactly where we are, with no judgements. ACCEPTANCE is like an old friend who shows up with chocolate and tissues when we are entrenched in feelings we would rather not have. Emotions can get the best of us at times, and ACCEPTANCE is the salve that will make healing easier. Can we just push through them? Probably, but it is not always wise to just shove through an emotional disturbance because we may miss some of the valuable information that is trying to come through it. We are told that strength is a virtue, and that being strong is valuable. Being vulnerable is also valuable because it teaches us conflict resolution on a micro level. When we can harvest ACCEPTANCE and eat of this bitter fruit, its healing properties have long lasting effects that we might not recognize immediately. With practice and time, it will get easier to be with ourselves in discomfort, to ride the natural waves of life, to allow whatever is moving through us to simply be what it is, and to be okay with it until it has run its course.

GRIEF

You read that correctly. GRIEF plays a huge role in growth and is often misinterpreted as something we must avoid. Think of it as the healing rains that water your Mind Garden. It is the reprieve from all your pursuit and achieving. I don't know anyone who has looked at GRIEF in this way and discussed it like I am sharing with you here. GRIEF is so packed with nutritional information that we all need as we move through life, that we literally cannot live without it! If you had to take a hose to water your Mind Garden all the time, it would become an exhausting and laborious chore. We welcome the rain when it comes in the seasons of our daily lives. Any gardener will tell you how satisfying it is to look out the window and watch the blessing of sky water descend on the gardens they have worked so hard to establish. They can sit back, relax, and enjoy the moment because they know that their hard work is now in the hands of a higher power. They know that natural water will reach deeper and penetrate the roots of their plants in a way that hand watering simply cannot do. GRIEF is the reprieve from your efforts. Harvest GRIEF whenever you have extended yourself too far, given to the maximum of your abilities, or been in service to those around you so thoroughly that you must turn inwards and stop.

We all know how painful GRIEF can feel when we are experiencing it, so why would I include it as one of your harvested fruits? One incredible benefit of tears is that chemicals from our brains are released when we cry. There are different qualities of tears. (Miller, 2021) When you learn to lean into GRIEF, you can benefit from understanding the temporary nature of all that is. GRIEF teaches us that there is a timeframe for everything we see and do. We only get so many days with the people we love. Loss is a part of every life. We only get so much of a good thing, and it must ultimately end at some point, so that something new can fill the space. GRIEF fills all your little trenches and basins with life giving water that will soak deeply into the Earth. It washes away anything that has accumulated in your paths and mosaic walkways meandering through your Mind Garden. It cleanses the air and helps new shoots come up from the fertile soil. GRIEF is truly a magical fruit when we can harvest it for our benefit. It is bittersweet to taste but fills the belly like no other food can. When you feel completely empty, GRIEF can be harvested to fill you back up. Harvesting GRIEF this way can transform what might have become a depressive state, into a healing hiatus. It is the retreat you have been asking for, so welcome it with open arms, let the rain flow down (and the tears if necessary), and watch the plants in your mental garden beam with verdant life. You deserve this, and just as monsoons never last forever, GRIEF too shall pass, and there will still be work to do once the clouds break.

As you can see from this list, we have a very special garden in our minds. You will add to this list of course, as your mental garden is filled with plants that YOU put there intentionally so that you can harvest exactly what medicines and fruits you need most in life. This is a minimal list of "fruits", and I encourage you to do some contemplative introspection so you can determine which other "fruits" grow on the plants you are cultivating.

Personal Story

I have been a hardcore journaling maniac for most of my life. Thanks, mom! This has given me the opportunity to review my past from an observer's perspective. One time in 2015, while going through my journals from 2009 I noticed that I used the word "stuck" to describe where I was at. Well, in a 2011 journal I saw the word again, and again, and again. I'm like "how the hell can I be so stuck for this long without moving through whatever this 'stuckness' is?" Well, it was in my 2013 through 2015 journals as well when I peered back though those in 2019. What the hell? I was really racking my brain trying desperately to figure out what was going on. That was my first mistake, desperation. While I was poring over my problem, I remembered the course I took in 2013 from Brene Brown, The Gifts of Imperfection. In that course she talked a lot about self-compassion, something that an overachieving perfectionist like myself is not naturally very good at. I have been exceptional at praising others, and advising others, and being a soothing presence in the life of other people that I care about. I could not, however, regardless of how many times I revisited that course, figure out how to say nice things about myself, and give myself the love I wanted. Fast forward to 2019 and I've lost my job, as I explained in a previous chapter. I was looking for something that would help me cope with the loss of my meaningful work while I grieved the identity change that took place when I no longer had the number one thing in my life that brought me the most joy and fulfillment. It was so much more than a job for me. I found an article online (thank you, Google) about CMT, compassionate mind training, and I began doing the practices they discussed in the article (of 20 something pages, it was a small book!)

This brought up a whole slew of shit from my past. My childhood had been speckled with so many dysfunctional influences that I absorbed like a sponge. I had no clue for so many years that I was carrying around all this baggage, weight, conditioning, programming, and beliefs that were robbing me of being able to feel worthy to be alive. I felt like I was an existential failure for most of my life, and had a few sources (not many, but enough) that reaffirmed that belief for me. With all the support I had from a multitude of other sources, I could not believe them when they told me I was a good mom, I was loveable, I was strong, I was … (fill in the blank of virtuous external praise). My mind could not accept these forms of praise because of an underlying belief in my general unworthiness due to shame I had taken on in childhood. Ouch. What the flying fuck? I was outwardly the most confident, independent, capable, healthy and successful human being that many of my friends knew. They told me so. However, because of this underlying and insidious thought pattern that ruled my life, I had lived in a "stuck" place for nearly forty years. I experienced an existential crisis when this revelation sank into my awareness and marinated in the conflicting parts of myself that were at war with each other. My unwillingness to believe differently, and my willingness to change for my betterment were at odds with each other like a couple of testy siblings. They fought over who would take supremacy in my belief structure.

Compassionate mind training is all about the way we speak to ourselves, and I had been a terrible boss, friend, lover and confidant for so many years that it was going to take a miracle to talk myself out of the negative and disempowering language I was using with myself. So, slowly, and deliberately, I started a new journal. I dug into what effect the aftermath of a narcissistic mother had on a grown child (me) and in what ways that shaped my beliefs about myself. Now, I talk about my mom a lot in this book, she has amazing qualities, and is one of the most amazing human beings on the planet (yes, I'm biased) and I have seen her transform herself over and over again, wearing so many hats it would make your head spin to try to keep up with it. She's human too, and if you ask her, she will tell you that she is very "bad at being human" "God's dumbest child" and a "slow learner" who thought she needed 2x4 therapy to learn anything that would have lasting positive effects in her life. She has finally dropped the 2x4 therapy and I can hardly express the dramatic and positive changes it has made for her.

Can you see why I might have some issues? When I started looking at my mom without the lenses I had put on to frame her in a way that suited me, it was pretty painful at first, and I chose to create some distance between us while I figured out what to do with my newfound knowledge, which I had no idea how to implement. My progress was slow, and my breakdowns were frequent because I had not learned how to emotionally regulate properly as a child. Emotions were important growing up, so much so that we had a pillow and a bat we could use whenever we were angry so my sister and I would stop shredding each other like feral cats whenever we got mad at one another. We had the Heal Your Body book to recite mantras of affirmations that never really meant anything at the time, but I tell you what, as an adult I remember it! And it was a valuable practice even if it was missing some key components and context. My mom had the tools she was equipped with at the time, and she tried her hardest to give us tools that she wasn't given. I commend her for that! She knew that emotions were important even though her entire family exiled us because we were the "heathens" of our entire family lineage, my mom was "crazy" for wanting us to be emotionally healthy and "you make it too good for your girls" were some of the things she was up against. I cannot imagine how difficult that journey must have been for her. Which is why I understand how she passed down so many dysfunctional behaviors that I have had to swim through (like an expansive ocean) while I felt like I was drowning for most of my life. The roller coaster ride of my fluctuating emotional state made sense to me in 2020, and I no longer felt "stuck" by the end of that year. I have not used that kind of language to describe my situations and circumstances since, and I will never again consider myself "stuck", regardless of what I am experiencing.

I know this story is longer than the others, and that is because the value of it in regard to our "fruits" and the cultivation of our Mind Garden is one of the most important teachings in this book for the reasons I describe above. We cannot choose what our parents pass down to us. We don't get to pick our emotional and generational inheritance. What we do get to do is sit down with it quite intentionally, and sort it out, piece by piece, loving every single item with tears in our eyes as we decide what we want to keep and what must be thrown away and painfully dug up (or set on fire with lots of gasoline, as my sister so thoughtfully conveyed to me once). This is the job of every adult child. This is something that is not widely taught in our world, and this rite of passage into adulthood could be graceful if we only understood this concept. Our inheritance is not chosen, the "plants" our parents put in our Mind Garden were given to us. We must take the shovel to some of these, a chainsaw, shears, a bulldozer (and a cup of warm tea) and figure out what is crowding the garden and not helping us grow. It is laborious! My goodness, that's why we go to therapy for gosh sakes. We pay people to give us the tools to do just that. We also must recognize the gems of everything that went RIGHT! All these plants have shaped our empowerment, our stability, our personality, and everything we love about ourselves. Those are our inheritances too and tending to them intentionally will cultivate the strengths that we were given by generations of ancestors. These ancient plants in the Mind Garden are sacred! They sometimes go unnoticed as ordinary, and we have even dug a few of them up mistakenly because we thought they were of no use to us. Thankfully… if they were useful, they are prolific in reseeding themselves, so we never lose them. Now you know what you can do for yourself, that costs no money at all. What it costs in time, energy, your diligence, and your willingness to uproot even the pretty plants will be priceless when you see the results. Remodeling our garden to suit US as grown children is the responsibility of every single adult human being on this planet. I personally believe that children and teenagers can also benefit from these practices because the earlier we identify our problem areas, the better. Teenagers have very few resources and a stubborn resistance to doing what is best for them. But they are magical creatures! Teenagers are incredibly resourceful and will find ways to thrive in even the most terrifying environments.

In Full Bloom: Harvesting the Fruits of your hard work

- **Journal Practice: Art it! Write it!** Fruits are your mental food. If you don't plant it intentionally, then it will grow like a wild field, yielding whatever. You are not living a whatever life. You are living an intentional life. You read the list of "fruits" in this chapter. Add to them! Think of some fruits that you can harvest and eat during situations that are challenging for you. Remember to write the ways that your fruit will aid you, as I've illustrated. It takes introspection to decide how the fruits will benefit you and when you will need to harvest and eat them. It's your garden, you get to design it however is most beneficial to you.

- **Journal practice: Art it! Write it!** Art page of healthy habits you are maintaining throughout the duration of this course. Over the past 12 weeks we have done A LOT of work! I am so proud of you for getting to the "end" with me. Out of all the practices we did, which ones came easily to you? Which ones were met with resistance? Write them down and see if you want to revisit any of the practices with fresh eyes. Then commit yourself to a sustainable practice of adding them into your daily lived experience.

WEEK 13

Living to the Fullest Means Accepting What IS

"The untrained mind keeps up a running commentary, labeling everything, judging everything. Best to ignore that commentary. Don't argue or resist, just ignore. Deprived of attention and interest, this voice gets quieter and quieter and eventually just shuts up."

-Plato

Divinity is the Source of your Power

What would you have to believe in order to KNOW within every fiber of your being that you are complete AS IS? You are not a used car. You are a divine spark of the ALL that the entire universe contains. I am reminding you of this now because we are nearing the end of our journey together, reader. I feel honored to have walked this part of the path with you. We have gone through forests and valleys, across rivers and fields, through swamps and deserts, and have ended up here, at home, in our collective divinity. As you have hopefully discovered throughout the duration of this process, you are infinitely wise, infinitely loveable, and infinitely worthy of creating the life that suits you best. Most importantly, you are absolutely whole just as you are right now, in this moment. You were completely whole when you opened this book for the first time, regardless of what anyone may have told you. There is nothing that can diminish you from being exactly who you are in any given moment, and that is a beautiful thing to always remember. Just because you have gone through experiences that have traumatized you, scarred you, and left you with deep wounds, does not mean that you must remain in a broken mindset.

Why do we feel the need to identify with everything we think is broken about us? This is never who we truly are, and often during some of our most challenging emotional states, we shine brightly for others as a beacon of light to their wounded experience. This divine spark that shimmers through our eyes is often referred to as our soul.

"The eyes are the windows of the soul." -William Shakespeare, Charles Darwin, the Bible, Leonardo De Vinci, Cicero (many people have been accredited for this quote)

The eyes can reveal everything, and nothing if we are so entrenched in our own pain that we cannot see beyond the suffering within ourselves. But I know, beyond the shadow of any doubt, that you have had a miraculous moment with another human being, where you looked into their eyes and saw the perfection of the cosmos resting there. It lives inside of all of us, my beloved, all the time, without fail, regardless of your personal tragedies. This is where we reiterate how much you have done for yourself. How far you have traveled to adjust certain outcomes in your life, how willing you have been to accept new thought forms, tell better lies (that slowly have become truths) and step into worthiness with both feet eagerly. I just want to say, good job. I am so proud of you! You deserve to be praised for all the victories you've achieved during our time together. You may think that you are just reading a book and gaining insights into living, techniques, and practices for daily accountability for yourself, digging gardens in your mind and picking fruit. I am going to tell you something that may or may not be profound.

You are engaging with the ALL of creation every single time you cultivate yourself in harmony with the vibration of the universe, which is exactly what you have done by reading this book. To align yourself with the frequency of creation is to be in sync with your highest self, the one who is always waiting for us to show up and be our best selves regardless of the circumstances. Our highest self will never stoop to our level, so it is up to us to raise our vibration so we can meet in the place where all things are always possible.

Enough with the esoteric and frilly jargon of spirituality. It feels good to affirm certain things, so I wanted to take the time to share that gem of wisdom as we bring this chapter of our journey to a close. I have prepared a list of extended practices that can take you further on this journey towards self-discovery and self-mastery. We began by asking questions, better questions than the ones we were taught, and we will conclude by giving you some "extra credit" if you choose to participate in it. This is not required of course and will only benefit you if your willingness lines up with the work. It is, after all, a choose-your-own adventure here on Earth. So, I have offered a wide range of exercises, journal work and other practices that might be "fun" to indulge in. Fun, being a relative term because as an autodidactic human being (self-learner, remember) I often find that learning new things is quite fun for me, and I seek out “the new” every chance I get.

You Live, You Learn

As long as you are alive, you have the option and ability to learn new things. You can develop more skills and build your knowledge of worldly and internal affairs. Your attention is valuable, and you “pay” in the form of attention to anything you focus on. You buy in to anything which receives your attention, so be wise in what you are consuming with your attention. If you pay attention to everything going wrong in your life, you will only see what is wrong with the world at large. That is the power of attention. When you “pay” attention you choose what to buy into, so you will seek out anything that you have paid for. It's transactional by nature and a valuable asset that we often misuse, under misguided ideals and beliefs, and sheer ignorance. It is easy to focus on something we paid for, like that recent movie, or a shirt, or an expensive piece of musical equipment, how about that car… you’re going to be quite focused on that car while it is still new to you.

Since we are paying with our attention, we may as well get something valuable in return. You pay for goods every single day and it feels completely normal. You even pay for classes and educational materials that will help you learn skills. Paying with attention is something we don’t pay any attention to at all! We choose to pay for all sorts of things that are contrary to what we want. If we bought a product online and they sent us something other than what we paid for, we would return it and request a refund. We don’t get refunds on our attention. It's a one-way, one-time deal, and we keep whatever we paid for because it’s non-refundable. The folly with this is that we oftentimes have no idea what we are paying for, or why, for that matter, even though it's our attention we are giving as the currency. This is so ludicrous a notion, that once it came into my thinking, I became hyper aware of everywhere my attention wandered. And wander it does! We must constantly pull our attention back into focus because it drifts off into all sorts of inquiries. We fantasize, daydream, worry, analyze, organize, categorize, stress, evidence collect, sort preferences, accumulate biases, etc. Our attention is all over the place when it is undisciplined and unsharpened. It's a tool too… and could have been added to our chapter on sharpening tools, but I have included it here because I want to thank you for the attention you have paid to the concepts I have compiled in this book. I appreciate the attention you have paid in exploring this journey with me while we walk the path together. It has been a beautiful journey so far.

Learning your way, and on your terms, is solely in your own hands, reader. You have a huge world at your fingertips and an even larger world between your ears. You are a multidimensional being, you live in the seen and unseen realms at all times. If you don't believe that you live in unseen realms, then where do you go when you close your eyes? Where do your memories live? Where do your daydreams come from? Can you touch your thoughts? These intangible features of our everyday lived experience are just as real as your hands, feet, children, and friends (and the table at your bedside). They are inseparable parts of us that deserve our attention as much as our 3D reality. Our attention is our currency, and we are worthy of this investment.

This is the part where you get to go back through the journal you have been filling over the duration of this twelve-week course. I told you that we would revisit some of the practices we did in earlier chapters, and I wouldn't want to disappoint you by not including them. Below I offer a list of indulgent, and extended ways that you can gain even deeper insights from the work you have already done. Cool huh? I'm always seeking out new ways I can use my already existing practices to get more out of my work. Every time I use the word "work" I mean "fun" because for me, learning more about myself is incredibly fun! We are amazingly complex beings, and science is learning more and more about us every single day as they test the limits of our reality and how we all fit into it. I'm kind of a geek like that if you haven't already figured that out.

One Tree in a Forest of Billions:

YOU ARE A PLANT AND YOUR LIFE MATTERS

- ❖ You took a picture of yourself in the very first practice in this book. Look at the work of art you made and reevaluate your initial judgements about this person. Has anything changed? What do you see now? Have you developed a new language to describe this individual? If you want to, make a new page, using the SAME image you did in the beginning. Use your new skills to define this person NOW, twelve weeks later. You might just grin the entire time!
- ❖ In **chapter 1** you did your first SOC practice (Stream of Consciousness writing). This is the time to go back and read it. Now that you can view it with a fresh perspective, are there any insights that can help you determine what your next steps are? Do you still do this practice now? If not, why? If you have kept this practice going, in what ways do you find it useful? SOC writing can be a powerful tool for reaching our subconscious and unconscious mind. If you want to be able to recognize patterns that are consistently holding you back in life, this can be one of the most reliable methods for hearing the voice within you that speaks just under the surface of your intentional thinking. Another way you can use SOC writing is to get a red pen and circle all the words that are disempowering, limiting, and contributing to the decay of your Mind Garden. You can highlight phrases, especially if you do this practice consistently, and notice what you write on repeat in your SOC sessions. You can turn this around by re-writing the stories, redefining the words you use and replacing some of those words with better ones. Words that reflect the life you WANT to have, rather than the one that keeps you feeling "stuck", "sad", "alone", etc. Remember to be patient and allow time between the writing and reading part of your SOC sessions. Trying to interpret immediately can be a frustrating and fruitless exercise.

- ❖ You wrote out some questions **during week 1**. Do you think you could go back and answer those questions now if you haven't already? Have you gained any insights that will help you transform them into better questions? Try it. It might be fun to go back and reread what you initially wanted and contemplate in what ways you have updated those questions.
- ❖ **In chapter 2** you wrote down your triggers and how you dealt with them badly. Do they still bother you? Have you developed new ones? Have you healed any of them? You can either go back to that original page or start a new one and update it with your newfound insights.
- ❖ **Chapter 3** was all about connecting our body to our mind through movement practices. Do you still exercise every day? twice a week? Four times a month? Do you remember how much movement means to the plasticity of your brain and extending the learning window? 18 minutes a day protects our cognitive function. See what other kinds of movement you can do that feels right for you. There's yoga, Qigong, Zumba, stretching, Tai-Chi, dancing and so many other ways you can move! Research and try something new. Exploring your interests is how you keep your brain young, moving is how you keep your body young. You are gaining both by indulging in this exercise.
- ❖ Did you maintain your gratitude practice throughout the duration of this course, or just for the week we mentioned it? Hm… I intentionally didn't bring it up again to give you the freedom to decide if that was something important to you. I am listing it here as a reminder of how powerful this practice is when it's done weekly. Daily is better… and you can create a micro-ritual out of it that you do either when you wake up or go to bed each day (or both). Since it's all happening in your own head anyway, it doesn't interfere with anything or anyone going on around you. You can do it in a crowded room, or as a meditation all by yourself.

- **Journal Practice:** We are going to revisit our compassionate hearts Buuuut… with a twist this time. Last time, I had you print out three images of yourself and surround yourself with loving comments. THIS time… I want you to get images of PLANTS, create a garden on two opposing pages (if you're feeling that ambitious, one is fine too). Paste your images all around with lots of colorful flowers and trees and shrubs, anything pretty, it's just a representation. Label all of them with one word each. The word is what you will HARVEST from these plants in your garden. It's a reminder page that your garden is there for your USE, not just to look pretty. You can go back and look at this page any time you forget what your plants mean and why you have them in your Mind Garden. A visual representation can be helpful during times when you feel weak, overwhelmed, and too stressed out to remember how to respond well.

- **Journal Practice: Art it!** Vision board style on two opposing pages. Make a work of art out of some of the things you might want to do in the future with your newfound ideas and momentum. Put pictures of places you want to go, label your images and DREAM BIG! The world is your oyster, and you will need to practice your definiteness of purpose somehow. It can be messy, unrealistic, and dramatic! The bigger the better. Start thinking big and you will begin living bigger.

- Write your future self a letter about everything you've learned with a message you want that person to know. Put today's date on it and put it in an envelope taped to the back of your book with an OPEN DATE on it. Pick any date you want, but don't peek until then! This inspirational message will be delivered right on time. It is a practice that Brene Brown introduced to me in the Gifts of Imperfection, and it brought such value to my life that I want to add it here as something you can do for yourself that will have a powerful impact on your extended journey.

- Shame can rear its ugly head when we are getting out of our comfort zones and trying new things. It has a way of shoving us back into dark places and keeping us quiet, so we don't get "too big for our britches" or "get a big head" with all the exciting developmental and personal growth we've been doing. So, if shame shows up in an unexpected moment, I encourage you to write down the experience. You can even share it with someone close to you, perhaps one of your cultivation team members, if you did this course in a group. By speaking about shame, you drain its power. Let it out so you can grow past the lies your brain tells you to keep you in a familiar state of being.

- Are you more present and "in the now"? What are you doing differently that has extended your sense of awareness for the present moment? Is it a micro-ritual, exercise, journal practices, meditation, or something else? Write them out, however many there are and even write how you feel about it, how it has leveled-up your human experience, how it has impacted your personal relationships. Presence can be a gift to others, and everyone benefits when we are more present, in the moment.

- If you could write a letter to your child self, what would you say? Write that letter and save it. Your inner child is deep within the trunk of the tree you have grown into, still there, still flowing through your veins, and worthy of your special message to them. Maybe there was something that the child needed to hear that would have advanced their development in an empowering way. Be the adult voice for your precious child self and tell them everything you know is true now!

- There is a list of **29 core values** on our website www.plantpeopleheal.com on the resources page. Are there any there that you might like to focus on? Add them to your journal and keep the momentum up! You are going to be alive every day you are here, and learning is an ongoing process. You can even google the word, get the definition, watch videos, and read articles about the value(s) you chose. Dedicate half a page to each. Art it up!

- ❖ **In chapter 11** you wrote your personal mission statement. Were you able to condense it down to one line? If not yet, take some time and see what you can come up with. Now that you have been getting clear on what you do and don't want in your life, what meaning and value do you want to bring into the world? I bet you're ready to get that narrowed down to a one liner that reflects who you are at your core and how you will live that mission for your and the world's benefit. What form of service brings out the very best in you?

- ❖ You practiced writing some dreams and goals down during our journey here together. How about writing out how you want to spend the next year. Get specific for the things you want to manifest in a time frame with quick results (even if they are months in advance). Go general if you don't have enough information to get all the details right and it needs some time to marinate in the Universal waters of creation. Write out all the things you feel confident about bringing into the world by your hand. Be sure to include the people who will be involved, what resources you will need, what skillsets you must learn, and how much money is required to do it. Also make sure you write out what value it will bring to others (if you include your work in this practice) so you can attach dollar signs to the services you have chosen to embark on. When you add that dollar amount, you are telling the universe that you will ensure that amount of value will be distributed to people through your meaningful work.

- ❖ You are whole, right now. Worthy with no prerequisites. Capable and willing to show up for your purpose. Read your DREAMS to yourself AT LEAST once a week, daily might be better… but do what is realistic to fit into your time management strategy. You may find that there are items you can scratch off your list as you achieve them one by one or add to them as you become more skilled at identifying your dreams and desires.

- ❖ There are over 100 questions sprinkled throughout this book like little seeds waiting for the rain to sprout them into flourishing plants. If you want to… take some time to go back through the book and find the ones that spark your imagination and curiosity. There are so many opportunities to discover wondrous insights about us. We are a planet of unimaginable possibilities. Ask better questions, get better answers! Answer the ones that intrigue or inspire you. See which ones bring up resistance for you and figure out why. Are you still getting in your own way?

- Definitions and words are a powerful way we communicate with ourselves and the world. Are there any words that you use often that you might not fully understand? Have they become part of your automations, relegated to the subconscious? Are you using them intentionally? Get them on paper and write out the definitions. Are they empowering you or limiting your manifesting? Sky's the limit… Use all the resources available to you. Words are one of our greatest tools, so use them well my friends. Take some time to write them out and flesh out what they mean to you. They call it "spelling" for a reason. The spells you cast with your words can have powerful effects in the world, make them intentional by paying attention to them.

- Create one (or several) micro-meditation rituals that you can use in moments that presence is required. Make a ritual that you can practice. Like washing the dishes. Use that time to focus ONLY on washing the dishes. OR, while you are sitting down after work, take 5 minutes (and that can feel like forever when your mind is racing!) to practice gratitude for anything that will bring you into the moment; your heart, your legs, your (aching) back… Do you drink tea? What do you think about when you do? Even this can be turned into a micro-meditation ritual. You can focus on your breathing and the aroma of the tea, the steam from the cup… all these small awareness cues will help you remain in your body and connect your mind to your physical reality.

- I have mentioned many influential people during this course. They have all been added to the reference section of this book. To further your study in any area of interest, you can learn more about the people who helped shape the ideas, philosophy, and practices I have presented here. They are a wealth of information on the topics they specialize in. Seek them out and deepen your understanding of a particular subject that stood out for you. You can even dedicate a page or section of one of your journals to the insights you gain by following the rabbit hole of your desire to learn. Curiosity is one of the ways we remain open and allow the plasticity part of our brain to continue evolving and keeping us young. The more you learn about things that interest you, the more you will discover what you didn't know you didn't know. When you do know, a new idea will present itself and you can go from there, forever, and ever.

❖ How has your **"Cultivation Team"** bonded through this experience? (If you did this as a group). Are they a part of your gratitude practice? Do you do any of these practices together as a group, weekly perhaps. If it is something that sounds beneficial, perhaps you could create a weekly ritual/meeting that honors the journey you took together by choosing to pay attention to aspects of your healing path that you can continue to do as a group. Something that is fun, engaging, and meaningful to all of you. A way to maintain the connection you all experienced while walking this journey together. It is important to maintain our relationships, and your "Cultivation Team" might just become your "Mastermind Group" (Read Think and Grow Rich for more details) as you intentionally begin manifesting things together. There is great power in numbers, the more minds, the more interesting the results.

❖ Remember how I talked about honing your intuition by playing mental games in one of my personal stories? It's really a fun thing to do with others, especially playful children! You can find more research on this topic online, and even the simple way I laid it out here for you is a good start. When you can visualize the thoughts of another, you can begin to anticipate what will be said, or thought next. I will reserve the term "becoming psychic" because

I am not sure that is what is happening when we engage in this practice. Becoming highly intuitional though! Yes. Honing our intuition is a practice filled with many rewards. Getting some like-minded people together who want to develop their intuitive skills can be a rewarding endeavor. Curiosity and cooperation are the new "cool" in our modern era. Once you ask who wants to be involved, you may just discover that more people are interested than you initially thought.

❖ **In chapter 8**, I mentioned the meditation of becoming a plant. This visualization takes you out of a chaotic mental state and offers you a chance to step outside of your humanness, which can be useful. Sit quietly on a soft cushion, pick a plant you would like to "become" and then explore all the details of each part by feeling the sensations of the petals in the wind, your leaves unfurling, your roots reaching for water. What does it feel like to experience photosynthesis? As a plant, you get nutrition from the sun and air and soil. What bugs are crawling across your body? (As weird or cringy as that may sound) What do you hear? Are you in a forest, desert, oasis, under the ocean? This meditation is my way of dropping the illusion of separation that sometimes locks my thinking into identifying with (being a mother, a worker, stressed, in pain, etc.) which can become limiting concepts. I have even envisaged myself as a rock on occasions. The results are always interesting. Play with it if it speaks to you do so. I don't expect everyone to get on board with this one.

Final thoughts

This course has been designed to ask vital questions and offer exercises you can incorporate into your life every single day. After a while you may reduce the need for some of them, like medicines that you can cut back on as your health improves. Keep your journal near you, and revisit pages when the journey brings you into encounters that are difficult to navigate. You've created a roadmap to peace of mind. You have illustrated the novel of your journey through all the practices you saved in your journals. It's a pirate's treasure! Issues will keep surfacing until you have dealt with them, and they may manifest in new and unexpected ways. New people and new situations will test your progress. That's a wonderful opportunity for you even though it may still feel frightening or anxiety ridden.

You will get many opportunities to practice! You can always go back, do the steps again, and recenter yourself in any of these exercises that will be most useful for moving through the next challenges you face. Get creative and discover new practices that can accelerate your journey by engaging with the list of suggested studies. Life is exciting, fantastic, magical, and mystical! It's yours to play with, so play! Dance through your day with grace. Grace is the neutral observer that allows you to experience anything without judgment.

I want to leave you now with a poem that my co-worker wrote while I was working on this book. Just the day before she shared it with me, my sister inquired about how I would end this book and I told her my ideas. She shared with me a parting message that was at the end of a course she was taking at the time, and it touched my heart deeply. As soon as Danessa shared her poem, I knew instantly that it would be my parting message to you if she allowed me to include it. It condenses everything I have compiled within these pages and shared with you, in a way that perfectly expresses my hope for your life journey. It is a powerful piece of writing that illustrates the divinity we all carry around within us and touches so tragically on our humanness that gets in our own way. I leave you with her words now, reader. You will interpret them in your own personal way, as I did, which was completely different from what she experienced emotionally when writing it. Universal truths are like that. They are personal and broad spectrum at the same time.

Breathe in.

Breathe out.

You have arrived home,

and we are all here with you.

Forever and always my beloved.

With my sincerest gratitude,

I say goodbye for now.

-Dannielle Nelson

The Light Through The Broken Pieces

By Danessa Wilson

I wake up in the morning thinking about your Face
Every line in your Smile came from a Time and Place
A history of Heart Ache all gone but not Erased
A Map of every moment Etched into your Face
I see the Sorrow hiding when looking in your Eyes
The grappling Responsibility you seem to feel Inside
And for a Moment in my presence it seems to Lift away
Your Eyes Began To Sparkle
And Your Sorrow Slips Away
In your Laughter I feel Happy and my own Dreams began to Grow
To start another life I thought I'd never know
And I WONDER in this moment are you really Seeing ME?
A girl who's been Broken glued together and Determined to be FREE
I think about the STRUGGLES it took me to get Here
How Hard I Worked To Live In TRUTH
And No Longer Live In FEAR
But when the Devil fights me he reminds me that I'm Weak
He tells me I'm not Worthy of the kind of Love I seek
He robs me of my Voice that tells me I am Strong
He Lies and says the feelings I know I should Trust are wrong
He brings me little false Hopes to try to make me Weak
He Whispers in my ear the Truth I want to Speak
Will isolate me further from the ones I'm holding dear
That if those words are Spoken they will all run in Fear

And sometimes in that moment the Devil seems to Win
The Voice I want to SHOUT OUT sinks further deep within
One Battle may be lost but this is but a WAR
To hold the BROKEN PIECES together once more
So I reach for My STRENGTH which is only found in HIM
The LORD of my creation who Heals me from Within
And Living in HIS Presence the Fear it melts away
My Strength is found in HIS Truth that HE will never Run away!
That picking up the Pieces is a JOURNEY I Must Take
To once again find the Voice that will No longer Shake
To find Beauty in the BROKEN PIECES that I once hid in Fear
To Speak the words that set me FREE and no longer Live In Fear
For GOD has made a Promise I know that HE will keep
If you're not the One for me my Words may fall on your Deaf Ears
And you may not Understand the Meanings of the Words you Hear
If this is Our Story and it all comes to an End
I will be Sad for I Feel I've Lost a Friend
But part of My RECOVERY is to no longer Lose Sleep
But to Value My own Worth
and the Promise that I keep
That FEAR no longer Holds
Me in the Clutches of its Keep
For I am LOVED
UNCONDITIONALLY by the
LORD GOD of whom I Seek!

References

Bickel, N. B. (2021, February 25). *Anxiety, depression reached record levels among college students last fall*. Retrieved from Michigan News, University of Michigan: https://news.umich.edu/anxiety-depression-reached-record-levels-among-college-students-last-fall/

Brewton, V. (n.d.). *Internet Encyclopedia of Philosophy*. Retrieved from IEP, A Peer-Reviewed Academic Resource: https://iep.utm.edu/ralph-waldo-emerson/

Brown, B. (2010). *The Gifts of Imperfection.* Hazelden.

Byrne, R. (2006). *The Secret.* Simon & Schuster.

CDC. (2022, June). *Centers for Disease Control and Prevention*. Retrieved from Children's Mental Health: https://www.cdc.gov/childrensmentalhealth/data.html

Cloud, H. (2003). *The Secret Things Of God.* AuthorHouse.

Cole, D. (2022). Woman In Total Control of Herself [Recorded by D. Cole]. M. Ren. Retrieved from https://www.youtube.com/watch?v=GjNY5HGcopA&ab_channel=DevonColeVEVO

Crow, D. C. (2019). *Cal Crow, Resiliency,* . Retrieved from Mind Tools (requires you to join the site to view): https://www.mindtools.com/an9dm8b/resiliency

Dictionary, C. (n.d.). *Meaning of gratitude in English*. Retrieved from Cambridge Dictionary: https://dictionary.cambridge.org/us/dictionary/english/gratitude

Dispenza, D. J. (2017). *Becoming Supernatural. How Common People Are Doing The Uncommon.* October: 21.

Dispenza, D. J. (2018, June 12). How To BRAINWASH Yourself For Success & Destroy NEGATIVE THOUGHTS! | Dr. Joe Dispenza. (T. Bilyeu, Interviewer)

Dispenza, J. (2008). *Evolve Your Brain.* Health Communications Inc; Reprint edition (October 22, 2008).

Farrell, W. (1993). *The Myth of Male Power.* (ISBN) 978-0-425-18144-7.

Foundation, T. S. (2004). *The Way of Mastery: The Way of the Heart.* The Shanti Christo Foundation.

Freud, S. (May 6, 1856 - September 23, 1939). Father of Psychology.

Gallaty, D. K. (2013, December 14). *The 7 C's of Resilience.* Retrieved from Psychologist Gold Coast - CBT Professionals: https://cbtprofessionals.com.au/the-7-cs-of-resilience/

Grouport. (n.d.). *DBT Skills for Developing Self-Compassion.* Retrieved from Grouport: https://www.grouporttherapy.com/blog/dbt-skills-for-developing-self-compassion

Hay, L. L. (1976). *Heal Your Body.* Hay House Inc.

Hicks, A. (2022, November 20). *Abraham Hicks - Should I Go General Or Specific?* Retrieved from Youtube: https://www.youtube.com/watch?v=F7TgSNACBaQ&ab_channel=FeelGood

Hill, N. (1937). *Think and Grow Rich.* The Ralston Society, ISBN 978-1-78844-102-5.

Hill, N. (1937). *Think and Grow Rich.*

Hill, N. (2017, June 14). *Napolean Hill, Law of Sucess, Lesson 1: Definiteness of Purpose.* Retrieved from YouTube: https://www.youtube.com/watch?v=YlcgCO5eFP4&ab_channel=InevitableSuccesses

Huberman, A. (2022). *Huberman Lab.* Retrieved from Hubermanlab.com: https://hubermanlab.com/

Jandial, R. (2022, April 20). Brain Surgeon REVEALS How To Heal Trauma & DESTROY NEGATIVE THOUGHTS! | Dr. Rahul Jandial. (L. Howes, Interviewer)

Jill Haupts, O. C. (2020, October 21). *The Power of Resilience.* Retrieved from The Kim Foundation: https://thekimfoundation.org/the-power-of-resilience/#:~:text=Leading%20psychologist%2C%20Susan%20Kobasa%20acknowledges,learned%20and%20personal%20growth%20opportunities.

Kader, H. (2015, November 23). *The Science of Gratitude and How Kids Learn to Express it.* Retrieved from Seattle Children's Hospital, Reasearch, Foundation: https://pulse.seattlechildrens.org/the-science-of-gratitude-and-how-kids-learn-to-express-it/#:~:text=Susan%20Ferguson%20says%20when%20humans,is%20found%20in%20breast%20milk.

Kolk, B. V. (2015). *The Body Keeps the Score.* Penguin.

Law, N. B. (2020, December 8). *3 Stages of Gratitude.* Retrieved from New Beginnings Family Law: https://newbeginningsfamilylaw.com/3-stages-of-gratitude/

LePera, N. (2021, March 9). Psychologist's Tools For Reprogramming Your Subconscious Mind | Nicole LePera on Impact Theory. (T. Bilieu, Interviewer)

Lipton, B. (n.d.). *Bruce H. Lipton, PhD.* Retrieved from brucelipton.com: https://www.brucelipton.com/

MacDougall, D. (1907). Hypothesis Concerning Soul Substance Together With Experimental Evidence of the Existence of Such a Substance. *Journal of the American Society for Physical Research*, 237, ISBN 9785874496289.

Maria A. Villarroel, P. a. (2020, September). *National Center for Health Statistics.* Retrieved from Centers for Disease Control and Prevention, NCHS Data Brief No. 379: https://www.cdc.gov/nchs/products/databriefs/db379.htm

Mary Temple Grandin, P. (Current). *Temple Grandin Ph.D.* Retrieved from Temple Grandin: https://www.templegrandin.com/

Masaki Kobayashi, D. K. (2009, July 16). *Imaging of Ultraweak Spontaneous Photon Emission from Human Body Displaying Diurnal Rhythm*. Retrieved from PLOS ONE: https://journals.plos.org/plosone/article?id=10.1371/journal.pone.0006256

Miller, K. (2021, November 11). *14 Benefits Of Crying When You Need To Just Let It All Out, According To Experts*. Retrieved from Women's Health: https://www.womenshealthmag.com/health/a38150358/benefits-of-crying/

NHS. (2019, December 10). *NHS*. Retrieved from Causes - Clinical depression: https://www.nhs.uk/mental-health/conditions/clinical-depression/causes/

Peer, M. (n.d.). *Train Live with Marissa Peer*. Retrieved from Marissa Peer: https://marisapeer.com/

Peterson, J. (2018). *12 Rules for Life, an Antidote to Chaos.*

Peterson, J. (n.d.). *Jordan Peterson Homepage*. Retrieved from Jordan Peterson: https://www.jordanbpeterson.com/

Ruiz, D. M. (1997). *The Four Agreements.* San Rafael, California: Amber-Allen Publishing. Retrieved from https://www.youtube.com/watch?v=LPzEeIapUnc&ab_channel=Self-HelpMotivation

S., S. (2020, December 10). *Reading Separates the Billionaires from Everyone Else*. Retrieved from Medium: https://medium.com/illumination/reading-separates-the-billionaires-from-everyone-else-e4411d79f8c#:~:text=Tim%20Corley%2C%20who%20is%20the,compared%20to%2015%25%20of%20poor

Samara Quintero, L. C. (2019-2022). *Toxic Positivity: The Dark Side of Positive Vibes*. Retrieved from The Psychology Group, Fort Lauderdale: https://thepsychologygroup.com/toxic-positivity/

Sandoiu, A. (2018, May 31). *How much should seniors exercise to improve brain function?* Retrieved from Medicine News Today: https://www.medicalnewstoday.com/articles/321981#:~:text=How%20much%20should%20seniors%20exercise%20to%20improve%20brain%20function%3F

Schwartz, S. H. (2012, December 12). *An Overview of the Schwartz Theory of Basic*. Retrieved from PDF: https://scholarworks.gvsu.edu/cgi/viewcontent.cgi?article=1116&context=orpc

Scotland, F. P. (n.d.). *self-compassion-booklet.* Retrieved from first psychology.co.uk: https://www.firstpsychology.co.uk/files/self-compassion-booklet.pdf

Seligman, D. M. (1990). *Learned Optimism: How to Change Your Mind and Your Life.* Knopf Doubleday Publishing Group.

TEDxBermuda (Director). (2020). *Improving our neuroplasticity | Dr. Kelly Lambert* [Motion Picture].

Webster. (2022). *Google*. Retrieved from Definitions: https://www.google.com/search?q=witch+definition&rlz=1C1GCEA_enUS994US994&oq=Witch+Defin&aqs=chrome.0.0i433i512j0i512j69i57j0i512l4j0i390l2.3578j1j7&sourceid=chrome&ie=UTF-8

WHO. (2021, September 13). *World Health Organization*. Retrieved from Depression: https://www.who.int/news-room/fact-sheets/detail/depression

You and Your Hormones, a. e. (2021, March). *Adrenaline*. Retrieved from You and Your Hormones, an education rescourse from the Society of Endocrinology: https://www.yourhormones.info/hormones/adrenaline/

Made in the USA
Columbia, SC
03 February 2025

52445159R00139